THE WORLD'S GREATEST
GOLF COURSES ON GOOGLE EARTH

THE WORLD'S GREATEST GOLF COURSES ON GOOGLE EARTH

BY ALEX NAREY WITH A FOREWORD BY ERNIE ELS

SEVENOAKS

Designed with
Google™earth

Previous page: Augusta National is America's most cherished and celebrated plot of golfing land, which hosts the US Masters every April to herald the start of the golfing season.

Published in 2013 by SevenOaks
an imprint of Carlton Books Ltd
Carlton Publishing Group
20 Mortimer Street
London W1T 3JW

Text and design copyright © Carlton Books Limited 2013

A CIP catalogue for this book is available from the British Library.
ISBN 978-1-78177-051-1
Printed and bound in China

CONTENTS

FOREWORD by ERNIE ELS

Golf has taken me all over the world and I have been fortunate enough to play in all of the great tournaments and on some of the finest golf courses, many of them featured in the pages of this handsome book. The breathtaking satellite images from Google Earth really offer a new perspective on these courses and reveal some fascinating new insights. It's a great addition to any golfer's library.

For me, looking through these pages brought back some happy memories. It's great to see Oakmont, a magnificent golf course and scene of my first US Open win in 1994. It's my favourite golf course in America and will always have a special place in my heart. So too does Muirfield, where I won my first Open Championship in 2002. That's my all-time favourite course in the world and to win there was definitely one of the proudest moments of my career.

The beauty of the game of golf is that with so many fine tracks around the world anyone compiling such a list is spoilt for choice. Some of the featured golf courses – Augusta, for example – are sadly out-of-bounds for the majority of golfers, but there's no harm in dreaming is there!

Happily, the vast majority of the courses do welcome visitors and these are the dreams you can turn into reality. I would urge any player to make the effort to play them at least once in their lifetime. Each makes a great day out with your golfing buddies and whatever scores you shoot, the special memories will never fade.

Ernie Els, a four-time Major winner, has also made his name in golf course architecture with a number of designs across the world. One of the true greats of the modern game, the South African was inducted into the World Golf Hall of Fame in 2011.

INTRODUCTION

As a golf writer and journalist, the characters I encounter in the game often intrigue people. Those complicated geniuses who dedicate so much of their lives in pursuit of perfection. They want to know if Darren Clarke is as humble as he seems in victory as he is in defeat, whether Ian Poulter is quite the Flash Harry that is portrayed through their television sets, or if Tiger Woods has a release valve that allows him to be more human than the programmed machine that we see pouting through high-pressure golf tournaments. However, the question I am asked the most relates not to the players who play the shots, but the stretch of land they play the shots on. Believe me, for all the personalities in the game, the biggest remains the golf course.

After all, it is not a case of a player going head to head with another; it is a case of a player going head to head with the 18 holes that lie in front of him. Even when players get the better of it, a great course keeps dragging them back for more. Ultimately there is only ever one winner.

Visiting, playing and reviewing many of the world's finest designs comes with the territory of writing about the game, and people always seek to pick your brain. "So what's the best," they chirp, expecting a straightforward answer

as I wax lyrical about this course and the next one. As far as difficult questions go, it's an absolute beauty because golf courses have, and always will be, the most subjective creatures. You can attempt to rank them in order of reverence, test and beauty but what suits one man is unlikely to suit another. How can you possibly compare St Andrews' Old Course with another seaside classic some 4,000 miles away at Kiawah Island on the coast of South Carolina? How can you compare a parkland gem like Wentworth West to a heathland classic such as Morfontaine in France? The answer is, you can't. Each one is different; the only thing that is consistent is their quality.

Besides, playing a golf course creates a personal intensity; playing well is a prerequisite for appreciation and it's always the little touches that make a layout so special. Even my own favourites fluctuate from each and every visit, the state of the scorecard dictating my mood when evaluating the merits of a round and course it was played on.

The easiest way to assess a golf course is to play it, but accessibility to many of the world's best is restricted. Many can only dream of teeing it up at the esteemed country clubs of America, while handicap requirements and many old-school traditions continue to keep

the pay-and-play golfers at bay across the links lands of the UK & Ireland. In many ways, this exclusivity maintains the ambience and special aura. But this does little to sate the appetite of those who are constantly fascinated by the charms of such courses.

In this book, we have profiled 30 of the finest courses in the world, with exclusive Google Earth imagery taking you to the heart of the layout and delivering a bird's eye view of how to tackle the challenge. With detailed annotations, you can instantly identify a course's preferred shot shape. How Augusta favours a draw from the tee rather than a fade; how Oakmont settles for nothing other than straight hitting; how Muirfield places a premium on shot placement rather than all-out power; how Harry Colt's Falkenstein course is demanding of the ability to move the ball both ways through the air as trees congest its single-lane fairways; and how there is simply no margin for error with your approach play on the water-ridden target-style courses across the continent, most notably at the imposing and intimidating Terre Blanche and Les Bordes in France, as well as Germany's monstrous Gut Lärchenhof.

Brought to life with stunning photography, each course's history is detailed. And our hole-by-hole guides offer an in-depth alternative

to the aerial graphics, giving a strategic plan of how to play each layout, with the essential skills needed to build a score. Where to hit, what to hit, and where, most definitely, you don't want to hit.

Despite the many grand designs featured in this book, it will be highly likely that your own favourite will be missing. Who knows, that could well be your local members' course where you share those special moments with close golfing friends. There can never be a definitive answer. Rather, this book seeks to illustrate the beauty and hidden personalities many courses carry.

Enjoy your round…

***Please note** – All course yardages are marked from the championship or men's tees, unless otherwise stated. Baltusrol, Oakmont and Winged Foot have all been marked as per their US Open yardage and par, while Pebble Beach has been marked from its back tees and par, not used for the US Open. Royal Birkdale has been marked from the back men's tees, not used for the Open Championship. Wentworth has been marked from its championship tees, as used for the BMW PGA Championship.*

The outstanding beauty and unique
challenge of its 27 holes make Augusta one
of the world's most revered golfing venues

AUGUSTA NATIONAL

Two contrasting nines make up America's most celebrated golf course, and while today it is tough for the professionals, its playability and open fairways are inviting to its members. The living legacy of the golfing genius that was Bobby Jones, Augusta National has been home to the US Masters since 1934.

As work commenced on the early building process at Augusta National in 1931, few could have envisaged the design of what has become one of the world's most famous golfing landscapes. Its co-creator and founder, Bobby Jones, had retired from playing a year earlier. Despite his achievements as a player, Jones wanted to make a further lasting contribution to the game he had dominated for the previous decade, and so it was his dream to create one of the world's great golf courses. To do so he would enlist the services of British course architect Dr Alister MacKenzie.

Jones and MacKenzie had similar views as to how a course should be set up. They wanted to use the integral contours of the land, and they wanted a natural creek to act as the course's water hazard. First, Jones had to find a plot of land that would allow MacKenzie to carry out their design philosophy. So when a friend recommended a 365-acre plot called Fruitland Nurseries, a one-time indigo plantation in the quiet town of Augusta, the legendary American, with help from an investment banker named Clifford Roberts, bought the land and went to work. By December 1932 the course was completed and in January 1933 it was opened formally to its members. A little over a year later, the inaugural Masters tournament was played here. The rest, as they say, is history.

St Andrews' Old Course aside, there is surely no golf course that delivers in tradition like Augusta National, from the indigenous azaleas that spring to life as every Masters tournament looms, to the echoes that reverberate from all corners of the layout. Every golf course has its landmarks, but Augusta is drowning in them – the 330-yard drive up Magnolia Lane; the white clubhouse that stands behind the 18th green; and the devilish trio of holes that make up "Amen Corner" – the par-4 11th, par-3 12th and par-5 13th.

Augusta is famed for its lightning-fast putting surfaces, but it is a golf course that tests every facet of a player's game. Course developments have seen the original layout lengthened substantially, while the two nines were reversed back in 1935. Over the next 60 years there would be a host of subtle changes in the form of bunkering, relocation of tees, and extensions of several putting surfaces.

Like most courses at the turn of the millennium, Augusta underwent considerable renovation as the progression in golf club technology and the advancements of the modern player left many once fearsome defences redundant. In 2002 nine tees were relocated as the yardage increased to 7,270. Four years later a further six holes were lengthened. Today, the course weighs in at a full 7,440 yards compared to its original 6,800.

Arguably, few courses have such contrasting halves as Augusta. While the front nine serves as a test of patience as players plot their way through the early stages of their rounds, the back nine is where major fluctuations in a score can take place. Risk-reward is very much the order of the day, and those who take their opportunities can often be rewarded, as birdie and eagle chances abound, while others flounder under the intense pressure needed to execute the momentum-swinging shots. Indeed, the inward stretch, as Jones claimed, "can provide excruciating torture for those front-runners trying to hang on. Yet it could yield a very low score for those looking to make a closing rush."

And that is the nature of Augusta National; a thinking man's course in every way, where the layout created by Jones and MacKenzie is absorbed into a player's subconscious.

> "First time and the next time, and every time it is absolutely the most sensational drive onto a golf course. I get goose bumps every time."
>
> *Jack Nicklaus*

COURSE GUIDE 1–9

Course yardage – Championship 7,440 yards
Course GPS – 33°30'10.97" N 82°1'10.52"W

Sweeping fairways and elevated greens are prominent features on the front nine, where patience is the key to success. Players need to pick their spots with care and attention and more club is often better than less.

Opposite: Augusta National's 9th hole has frustrated the world's greatest players. Known as Carolina Cherry, it has a green which slopes from the back, and anything that lands on the front is likely to spin back 50–60 yards.

Hole 1
Tea Olive
Par 4 – 445 yards

Do not be fooled; Augusta's opening par 4 is far from the pushover it may at first seem. The fairway sweeps uphill with a slight dogleg right. Drives to the right side of the fairway will leave an easier approach to the green, but players must be wary of a huge sand trap that lurks at the 300-yard mark. The green is undulating with another trap to its left.

Hole 2
Pink Dogwood
Par 5 – 575 yards

Here is an early birdie opportunity for longer hitters. This hole has one of Augusta's widest fairways and a single sand trap lurking on its right side. With two more traps guarding the front of the green, players are forced into hitting the target rather than having the luxury of running the ball in. The green slopes from left to right, so distance control is crucial to avoid three-putting.

Hole 3
Flowering Peach
Par 4 – 350 yards

The shortest of Augusta's par 4s; this is a classic hole where players can be easily caught out by misjudging the distance. Position, rather than length, is the priority from the tee, and a cluster of bunkers lie to the left of the fairway from where the ideal approach shot should be played. A large trap sits to the left of the green, which slopes down from the right side.

Hole 4
Flowering Crab Apple
Par 3 – 240 yards

A monster of a par 3 when played from the backs; a long iron is required by the pros who drive from an elevated tee. Two bunkers protect the green, one to the front and the other to the left side. The wind can also play a factor in club selection here, and three-putting remains a threat as the green slopes viciously from its front.

Hole 5
Magnolia
Par 4 – 455 yards

A hole that is somewhat out of keeping with the rest of the course, with its tight, tree-lined fairway demanding both accuracy and distance. Two bunkers sit on the fairway's left side at 315 yards, and firing right of these is the safe line. The green again slopes to the front and players are faced with another bunker to the rear of the putting surface to swallow those errant long hits.

Hole 6
Juniper
Par 3 – 180 yards

Another par 3 with an elevated tee box, this hole is ranked as the easiest of Augusta's one-shotters. A deep cavernous bunker protects the left entrance to a large, sprawling green, which drops severely in elevation. The wind can have an impact on club selection, which can range from an 8- to a 5-iron. It may look simple, but your position on the green is vital.

Hole 7
Pampas
Par 4 – 450 yards

Players will aim for the left-centre of the fairway around the 270/300-yard mark where they can play an approach from a flat lie. From the fairway, you will see little of the green, which is perched at the top of a hill. The hole is remarkable for the level of bunker protection around the green – three traps at the front and two at the rear.

Hole 8
Yellow Jasmine
Par 5 – 570 yards

Another par 5 that is reachable in two for the longer hitters. However, the drive is crucial as the fairway narrows in the landing zone with a huge bunker positioned here. Playing uphill, the green is tucked away to the left, so a power draw is the shot shape for success. It is one of only two greens on the course not to feature a bunker.

Hole 9 – *Carolina Cherry* Par 4 – 460 yards

The front nine ends with this sweeping dogleg left that drops and then rises. The safest route from the tee is to aim for the right side of the fairway. The hole's most notable feature is the steep-banked approach to the green, which puts a premium on distance control because anything short will roll back down the fairway. Two bunkers sit to the left of the putting surface.

460yds

290yds

9

COURSE GUIDE 10–18

The back nine is challenging but this is where a score can be made, with two reachable par 5s serving up birdie chances. But beware: players can come undone with risk-reward adding to the excitement of the test.

Hole 10
Camellia
Par 4 – 495 yards

Officially the course's toughest hole, and until 1935 Augusta's opening hole. The fairway widens and drops almost 100 feet in elevation from tee to green, and players will aim left of centre to allow for an easier approach. The course's biggest bunker lies 100 yards short of the green, which is heavily contoured, sloping right to left, and a single bunker sits to its right side.

Hole 11
White Dogwood
Par 4 – 505 yards

The opening hole of Augusta's infamous trio known as Amen Corner. The drive is tight but the approach shot is the real test. The green is raised with a trap to the back rear, while the pond that sits to its left has often been a watery grave. Many players aim right of the green, favouring caution. However, they are then faced with a delicate chip down the slope.

Hole 12
Golden Bell
Par 3 – 155 yards

Small in stature but big in bite, this is one of golf's most famous short holes. Rae's Creek guards the front of the green and there are three greenside traps. The putting surface is shaped as a footprint, leaving players little to aim at. Of the hole's many defences, perhaps its biggest is the wind, which swirls high above the pines, meaning club selection can range from a mid- to short iron.

Hole 13
Azalea
Par 5 – 510 yards

This dogleg left par 5, its greenside banks covered in azaleas, is Augusta's most photographed hole. Players will look to draw the ball off the tee, cutting the corner to open the fairway up for the second shot. A tributary to Rae's Creek runs in front of the green, so those who choose to attack in two must hit a high-flying long iron to a green protected by four bunkers.

Hole 14
Chinese Fir
Par 4 – 440 yards

The bunkerless 14th hole plays relatively straight from tee to green, requiring a well-placed drive followed by a mid- or short iron in. However, the fun begins on that green, as players are faced with perhaps the most testing of all Augusta's putting surfaces. Sloping from the front, the green has two levels; Masters champion Ben Crenshaw claimed there has never been another green built like it.

Hole 15
Firethorn
Par 5 – 530 yards

A fantastic risk-reward par 5 where longer hitters will be rewarded with extra run if their drives are on target at the 270-yard mark. The second shot is the make-or-break one, with a pond protecting the front of the green. The test doesn't end there, though, as the putting surface drops at the rear, giving those who go long a testing chip back towards the water.

Hole 16
Redbud
Par 3 – 170 yards

A hole that has witnessed some of the finest Masters moments, notably Tiger Woods' holed chip in the 2005 tournament. Played entirely over water, it makes you hit to a green that slopes severely from right to left. Three bunkers guard the putting surface, front-left and right, and to the rear. It's a classic hole that can be a real momentum swinger and always throws up excitement.

Hole 17
Nandina
Par 4 – 440 yards

Similar to the 14th in that it plays straight up and down; however, the drive is tighter. The Eisenhower Tree, which is just over 200 yards from the tee, was given the name after the former President had campaigned for the loblolly pine to be removed because he had hit it so often. Two bunkers are positioned at the front of the green, which slopes from back to front.

465yds

275yds

18

Hole 18 – *Holly* Par 4 – 465 yards

A thrilling finishing hole made to look daunting from the tee with its narrow escape route to the fairway. However, the hole opens up as it turns round to the right. With its green on top of the hill and Augusta's iconic white clubhouse in the background, longer hitters will need no more than a short iron for their approach should they get their drives away safely. Two bunkers are positioned left of the fairway; it was from the first of these that Sandy Lyle played one of the finest shots in Masters history to set up a winning birdie at the 1988 tournament. The putting surface is two-tiered from back to front, and there are two further greenside bunkers, one at the front and the other to the right side. Few holes deliver such a stirring finale to a tournament.

Andres Romero plays a delicate splash shot to escape the sand on Augusta's beautiful par-5 13th, aptly named 'Azalea'.

BALTUSROL

It may have been named after the victim of an infamous murder, but Baltusrol has a rich and celebrated golfing history, and it has thrown up some of the great moments in major championship golf. The course has seen many changes over the years, and the original layout is no longer discernible following a total rebuild in the 1920s.

Opened in 1895 in Springfield, New Jersey, Baltusrol was originally a nine-hole course. It was designed by English architect David Hunter, who had been commissioned by a New York publisher named Louis Keller. Keen to cash in as the upper classes flocked to the game, Keller purchased over 600 acres of land and named the course after a local farmer, Baltus Roll, who had been attacked and killed on the land where the course would be built in what had been one of the century's most notorious crimes some 64 years earlier.

The original nine-hole course, known today as the Old Course, had a total yardage of 2,372 yards, but within three years Keller had expanded the layout to a full 18, measuring 6,189 yards. It would host the US Opens of 1903 and 1915, before the land was ripped up in 1920 and 36 new holes were designed. Both courses, the Upper and Lower, were ready for play in 1922.

Contrasting greatly in style, the Upper and Lower have both hosted major championships; the Upper the 1936 US Open, and the Lower the US Opens of 1954, 1967, 1980 and 1993, as well as the PGA Championship of 2005. In 2016, the Lower will once again host the PGA.

While the Upper can claim to be the more beautiful, it is not considered a modern-day test for professionals, and so the Lower has come to be known as the premier design at Baltusrol. Albert W. Tillinghast designed both courses, but his blueprint for the Lower was

Opposite: Baltusrol's Lower course has hosted four US Opens, as well as the PGA Championship of 2005.

Below: Jack Nicklaus was at his imperious best during the 1980 US Open at Baltusrol, winning his 16th major with a record aggregate of 272.

length. In major championships, it plays to a par of 70 with a yardage of 7,400, and its difficulty is enhanced with many strategically placed bunkers, which means that players must complement their power with much patience and precision.

Following Tillinghast's work, Robert Trent Jones redesigned much of the layout in preparation for the 1954 US Open and that

year the professionals faced a test of 7,060 yards – a staggering length for that era. Among the holes to receive a makeover, Jones added more than 50 yards to the par-3 4th, which now tips the scales at 199 yards. Jones' work, especially on the 4th, was criticized by many who deemed the hole to be too tough and out of keeping with the rest of the course. However, when playing the hole for the first time during a

round with club pro Johnny Farrell – a winner of the 1928 US Open – Jones made a hole-in-one here, and in doing so declared that the hole was "eminently fair" for all who played it.

The 4th aside – where water features predominantly – there isn't much that is quirky about the Lower. It is relatively flat with many testing, long par 4s. But there is something of a strange finish, where players

Google™earth

must first negotiate the par-3 16th and then play back-to-back par 5s at 17 and 18.

Naturally, Baltusrol has witnessed some of major championship golf's great moments. But perhaps its most famous came in the 1967 US Open, won by Jack Nicklaus. The Golden Bear shot a final-round 65 to win the tournament by four shots from Arnold Palmer. However, standing on the 18th tee, Nicklaus needed a birdie to beat Ben Hogan's record aggregate US Open score. After hitting his drive into the right-side rough, he laid up before flushing a 1-iron to 20 feet. From there he duly sank the putt for a four-round total of 275. Thirteen years later in the 1980 US Open, again at Baltusrol, Nicklaus would beat his own record by a further three shots, winning his 16th major with a score of 272.

> "Baltusrol does have disaster holes, but it can nibble at you with bogeys that you don't really understand how you got."
>
> *Jack Nicklaus*

COURSE GUIDE 1–9

Course yardage – Championship 7,400 yards
Course GPS – 40° 42'25.12" N 74°19'43.81" W

Opposite: Phil Mickelson, the master of the short game, splashes from the sand on the 6th during the third round of the 2005 PGA Championship, which he won to claim his second major.

The front nine at Baltusrol features a number of dogleg rights that demand the ultimate respect in ball placement to avoid well-placed bunkers, and the many tight drives force players to think twice about club selection from the tee.

Hole 1
Par 4
478 yards

The fairway rises on approach to the green, out-of-bounds and a posse of bunkers hug the left side, and a ditch to the right makes the drive even more demanding. More bunkers surround the putting surface while trees and deep, heavy rough lurk at the back. A members' par 5, it was converted into a two-shot hole by Robert Trent Jones prior to the 1954 US Open.

Hole 2
Par 4
378 yards

The hole's modest yardage means the professionals will play for position and lay up with a long-iron short of the cross bunkers at 250 yards. Out-of-bounds lurks left, as do towering pines, but if in position off the tee, it is merely a wedge or short iron to a small green that slopes from right to left. If you can find the fairway from the tee, a rare birdie chance awaits.

Hole 3
Par 4
503 yards

A power draw is needed if you hope to get the better of this long par 4. The fairway drops in elevation but that only adds to the difficulty of the second shot, as finding a flat lie will come via good fortune more than anything else. A stream runs short of the green, so players must flight a high, soft-landing approach. Sand protects the green on both sides.

Hole 4
Par 3
199 yards

A hole that is out of keeping with the rest of the course, as water is the dominant feature here in front of a flat green. A trio of bunkers sit at the back, meaning those who err on the long side face the horrible prospect of playing back towards the water. A strong mid-iron is needed, and if you have to miss the green, miss it right.

Hole 5
Par 4
424 yards

There are many defences to overcome on this medium-length par 4, but perhaps the most challenging is the green, which slopes from right to left, and back to front – so distance control is critical. The landing zone is narrow with large fairway bunkers either side, and the approach is then played uphill to a contoured and well-defended putting surface.

Hole 7
Par 4
503 yards

Another two-shot hole at over 500 yards, this dogleg right tempts you to cut the corner but you do so at your peril as two deep traps sit on that line, and the right side of the fairway is lined with trees. This is another par 5 for Baltusrol's members. Bunkers sit at the front of the green, preventing players from running their approach shots in.

Hole 8
Par 4
374 yards

One of the tightest holes on the course, where a cluster of sand traps lurk on the left as the fairway sweeps uphill, while the approach is nothing more than a short iron to a kidney-shaped green. Sand is the big threat here, with the green guarded right, left and back. The 8th may offer some respite in terms of its length, but little in forgiveness for those who stray off line.

Hole 9
Par 3
211 yards

The front nine draws to a close with a long par 3. A ditch runs in front of you from the tee and then round to the right, but it shouldn't come into play. Deep bunkers protect the green – which has several vicious run-off areas. The putting surface does have a narrow entrance, but you need to take the contours out of play and aim for its centre.

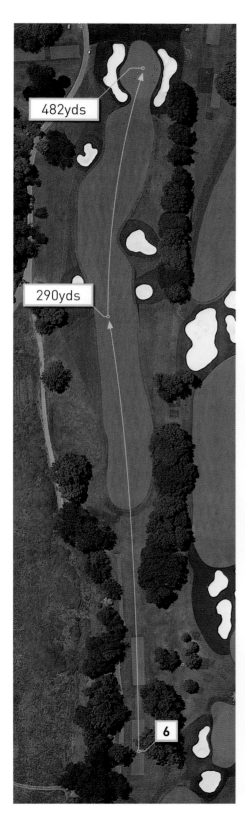

482yds

290yds

6

Hole 6 – *Par 4* – **482 yards**

Historically this is one of the toughest holes at
Baltusrol, and one that has been a card-wrecker in
previous US Opens; power and precision are needed
in equal measure from the tee, because sprawling sand
traps and a blind tee shot make this a very difficult
driving hole. The green is one of the larger ones on the
course, but once again sand defends it on both sides,
and with this fairway being very undulating, players are
more often than not playing from a downhill, uphill
or sidehill lie. Despite its length, finding position from
the tee – even if you have to hit a long iron in – is the
best route for success here. Play it with patience, take
your par, and be grateful for that.

Course Guide 10–18

After a long run of par 4s, the course serves up a thrilling finish to favour the longer hitters with back-to-back par 5s at 17 and 18 – but again it's not all about power, and placement from the tee is critical for success.

Hole 10
Par 4
464 yards

This is another brute of a driving hole, as the rolling and undulating fairway is made even tighter with bunkers and towering trees hugging its boundaries at around 280 yards. As ever, the rough is penal, but if you can hit a good drive you will be rewarded with a clear route to a green with a mass of sand both sides, and another smaller trap at the rear.

Hole 11
Par 4
444 yards

This dogleg left requires a soft draw but two huge Sassafras trees lurk on the corner. Fairway traps line the right side and, as the hole sweeps left, they come into play for those who have gone too straight off the tee. The fairway rises on approach, and then descends, and the green is difficult to hold as it drops off at the back towards the sand.

Hole 12
Par 3
219 yards

The 12th is a very tricky par 3, because it demands an accurate mid- or long iron from a slightly elevated tee that must carry a huge trap, with a grassy mound hiding the front-right of the green. The green itself slopes severely from the front to the back, so club selection can be a big dilemma. This is a great one-shot hole that asks many questions.

Hole 13
Par 4
432 yards

A dogleg left with a relatively wide landing area, although the fairway is undulating with five small, deep bunkers sitting on the right-hand side. A ditch also comes into play on the right side of the fairway, although many will simply play for position off the tee, leaving a mid-iron approach into a green that slopes from right to left, and rises at its entrance.

Hole 14
Par 4
430 yards

Players can take some of the corner off on this dogleg left by firing a driver, but for best results it's better to shape the ball from right to left, so a 3-wood could be the best option. Bunkers lie at the 280-yard mark on the right, which must be avoided to take advantage for the approach. The green, its boundary dominated by sand, slopes from back to front.

Hole 15
Par 4
429 yards

The drive needs to be threaded through the heart of the fairway with sprawling sand traps right and left. A ditch 70 yards short of the green will make players think twice about hitting a driver when the wind is in their favour, but if on the fairway, it's a mid-iron to a green that rises sharply at the front. Three traps sit front-right, with more sand to the left.

Hole 16
Par 3
230 yards

The longest of the par 3s; a long iron needs to be hit sweetly and high to a green that is encircled with sand. Many will hit a hybrid, and with more loft on the club that is not a bad policy considering the amount of sand you have to get over. A thrilling par 3 that in the US Open has yielded positive rewards for those making a final push for glory.

Hole 17
Par 5
647 yards

They called it the "unreachable green" and at 650 yards it was the longest three-shot hole in major championship history. However, that didn't stop John Daly from becoming the first to reach it in two at the 1993 US Open. For mere mortals, however, forget it; three shots are needed to hit a green that is well bunkered from an uphill approach. This is a monster of a par 5.

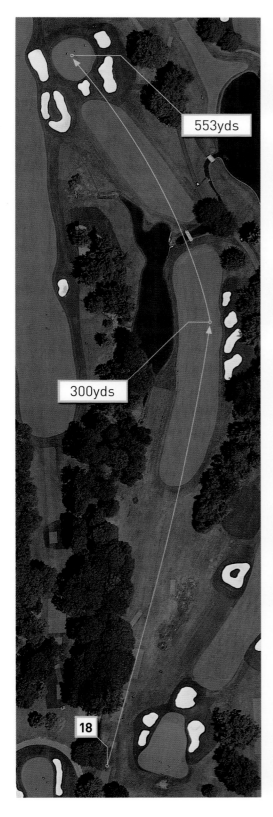

553yds

300yds

18

Hole 18 – *Par 5* – **553 yards**

This second consecutive par 5 is very different from the 17th; however, players must still fire a big, accurate drive if they are to reach this green in two to set up a closing birdie. A row of fairway bunkers hugs the right side, and if you want to take on the green, a sweet strike with a long iron is needed as sand guards every corner of the slightly elevated putting surface, which drops from the right side. Water comes into play for the second shot and poses another test for those who choose to lay up short. Perhaps the hole's most memorable moment came in the 1967 US Open, when Jack Nicklaus set the US Open championship record with a birdie four here.

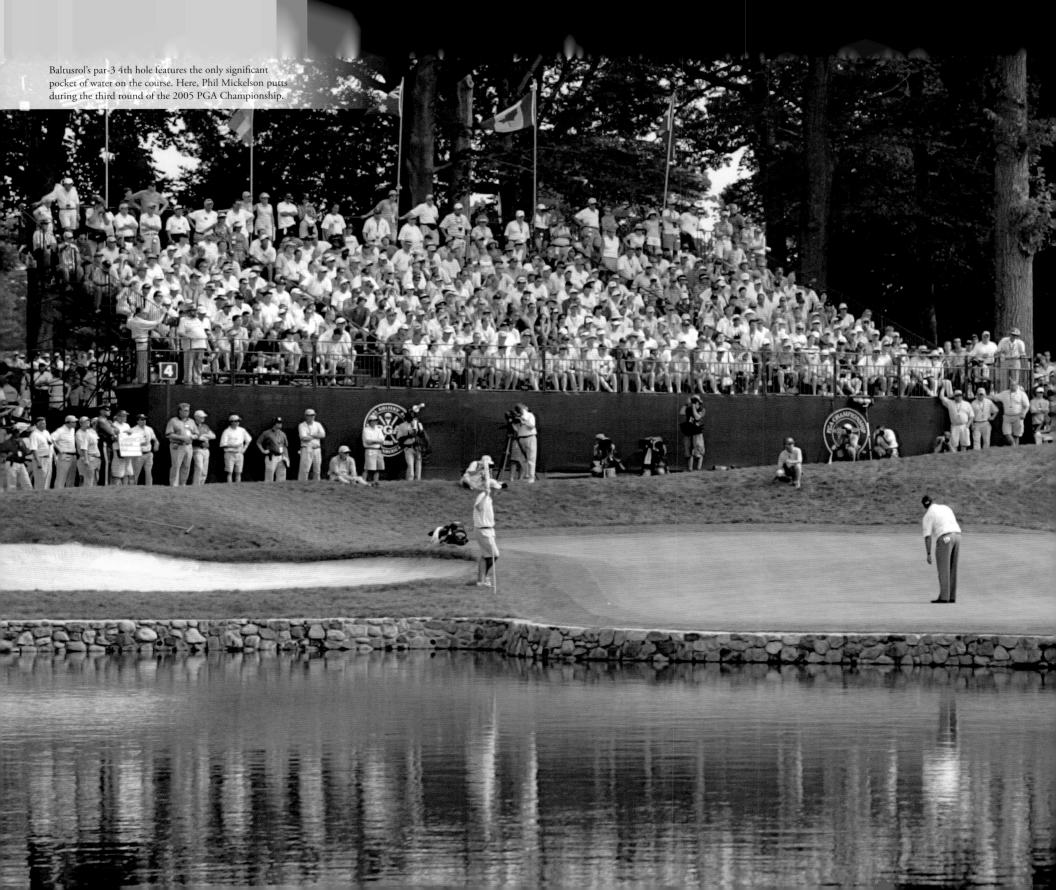

Baltusrol's par-3 4th hole features the only significant pocket of water on the course. Here, Phil Mickelson putts during the third round of the 2005 PGA Championship.

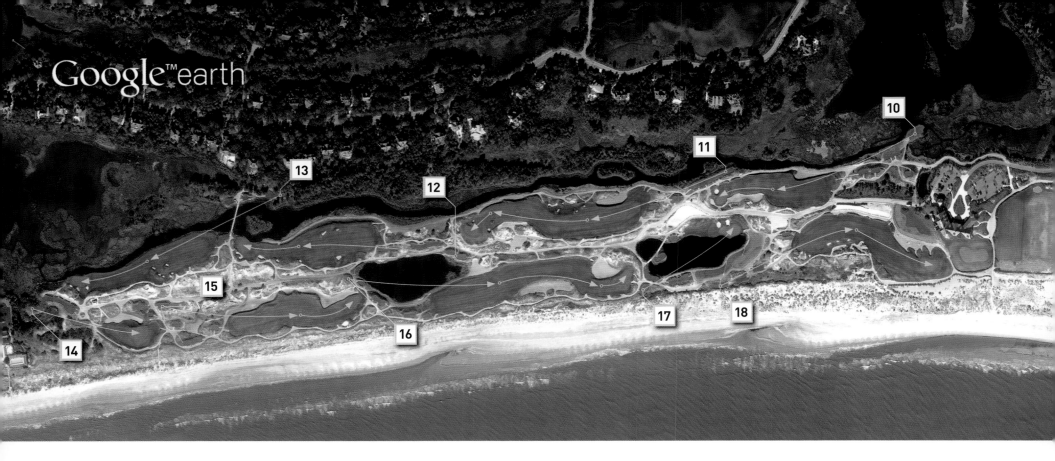

KIAWAH ISLAND

South Carolina is home to some of America's best courses, but there is none better than Kiawah Island's Ocean course, set on the Atlantic coast. The host venue for the 1991 Ryder Cup, Pete Dye's layout calls for a solid all-round game to overcome a number of testing defences.

Above: The wind is frequently a major factor during a round at Kiawah Island, due to the course's proximity to the Atlantic Ocean.

Opposite: Rory McIlroy wraps up an eight-shot victory at the 2012 PGA Championship at Kiawah's Ocean course, winning his second major title.

You head out east, you head back west; you head out west; you head back east. At Kiawah Island's Ocean course, it pays to expect the unexpected. Designed and modified to counter the blows of the modern game, its sprawling sand traps, salt marsh lagoons, fierce undulations and a stiff Atlantic breeze will all test a player's resolve from the first hole to the last.

The Ocean course is the work of renowned American course architect Pete Dye. It opened in 1991 and lies on the most eastern tip of

Kiawah Island; a golfing heartland some 45 minutes south of the city of Charleston in South Carolina. There are four other courses – the Points – all within the Kiawah boundary; Jack Nicklaus' Turtle Point, Tom Fazio's Osprey Point, Gary Player's Cougar Point and Clyde Johnson's Oak Point. But it is Dye's Ocean design that is the signature layout – simply a wonderful golf course with a procession of fantastic holes.

Essentially, the course is two layouts in one. The front nine plays east before cutting

back at the par-3 5th, with the next four holes hugging the coast back towards the clubhouse. The back nine takes you west to the par-3 14th, before again turning in the opposite direction as the waves of the Atlantic lap against the shore to your right. The two nines are symmetrical in that their holes' pars match one another's. That said, owing to the course's routing, the prevailing wind is never a consistent factor and no two rounds are ever the same.

The Ocean course has been the venue for

a number of top-level events. Shortly after opening, it welcomed the 1991 Ryder Cup, an explosive and emotional contest that witnessed a series of incidents where players became embroiled in a tempestuous battle over three days. With a partisan crowd behind them, Dave Stockton's US team – who had not won the Ryder Cup since 1983 – were desperate to stamp their mark on a tournament that was later dubbed "The War on the Shore". In the end, Bernhard Langer faced a six-foot putt for Europe to retain the cup on the final hole.

He missed, and the home team claimed victory by 14.5 points to 13.5.

Numerous other tournaments have been played here, including the World Cup of Golf in 1997 and 2003, and the Senior PGA Championship in 2007. Most recently, in 2012, it was the venue of the USPGA Championship, which Northern Ireland's Rory McIlroy won by eight strokes. Shooting an almost faultless final-round 66, McIlroy wrote the blueprint on how to play Kiawah's Ocean course, hitting fairway after fairway as he surged clear of the field on a layout that was set up as the longest in major championship history at a mammoth 7,676 yards. From the standard tournament tees, the course stretches to a slightly more accommodating 7,356 yards. But the same rules apply: hit it straight, and hit it long, as a number of carries are needed over hazards to put you in a position from which to attack the green.

Originally, Dye intended to create a duneland effect to the course, with towering sandhills lining the fairways to protect players from those Atlantic winds. However, his wife and co-designer Alice, who is recognized as "The First Lady" of golf course architecture in the United States, persuaded her husband to raise the course so players could be blessed with clear views out to the Atlantic. The result is a truly stunning visual masterpiece, albeit one that is open to the elements to make scoring just that little bit tougher.

"The green complexes are very severe and there are some extreme penalties for a miss."

Adam Scott

COURSE GUIDE 1–9

Course yardage – Championship 7,356 yards
Course GPS – 32°36'50.98" N 80°1'8.79" W

There may be a number of wide-open fairways, but positioning is key and the second shot continues to ask questions to raised greens where players can suddenly find themselves scrambling just to make par.

Opposite: On the par-5 2nd, players must pay attention to the demanding sloping green that features run-offs and deep bunkers.

Hole 1
Par 4
395 yards

In view of what is to come, this par 4 is a reasonably modest opener with the green tucked away to the right. From the tee, deep rough and dunes sit to the left, with woodland and a large waste bunker positioned right. With a good drive that finds the left side of the fairway, it's a short iron in to an undulating green with a pond positioned short right.

Hole 3
Par 4
390 yards

The toughest decision a player has to make on this hole is what club to pull from their bag for the drive. It's the shortest par 4 on the course, and your tee shot from an island-style tee takes you over marshland to a fairway that is wide, but very undulating. The less club you hit in, the better, because the green is perched up high with a number of run-off areas.

Hole 4
Par 4
453 yards

This par 4 is a real test, with the second shot one of the toughest you will face on the course. The fairway is wide open around the landing zone with more room right than left. But another strip of marsh that cuts across at 280 yards forces players to lay up short, with the prospect of hitting a long iron for the approach. Two deep traps lurk to the putting surface's right.

Hole 5
Par 3
207 yards

The first of the Ocean course's short holes plays directly out to the sea as you begin to turn back west to the clubhouse for the second half of the outward nine. It's pretty much all carry to the green over marshland, but the real challenge comes on that putting surface with a severe change in elevation, so pin placement is vital when determining club selection.

Hole 6
Par 4
455 yards

Another tough par 4 where position off the tee is crucial, with sand hugging the left side and thick, lush rough to the right. The fairway is narrow, so the drive is tough. The green is protected left and right by bunkers, but if you are in position on the fairway you can run your approach into the green. A great hole that rewards straight hitting.

Hole 7
Par 5
527 yards

With the wind behind, it's a birdie opportunity. With the wind against, it's a scrap just to make par. Sand and dunes pinch the fairway around the 230-yard mark, but the landing zone is relatively wide. Longer hitters should aim left-centre if they want to shorten the hole and go for the green in two. The entrance to the green is open, so players can run in a long iron.

Hole 8
Par 3
197 yards

At first it may look straightforward, but the hole can be extremely fiddly, depending on pin placement, as the green is large and undulating. Sand lies to the right, while woodland and trees come into play when approaching from the left as the winds buffet in off the Atlantic. The putting surface drops off at the front and sides. If you miss your target here, a big number awaits.

Hole 9
Par 4
464 yards

The closing hole of the front nine and a testing two-shotter at that; waste bunkers line the left side of the fairway, although left-centre is the ideal line from the tee to shorten your approach. The green, which is elevated, drops off at the front so you may need more club going in. Sand lurks on both sides, with dense patches of rough adding to the challenge.

2

400yds

240yds

543yds

Hole 2 – *Par 5* – **543 yards**

When Pete Dye designed this hole, he took every shot into consideration and it is one of the cleverest par 5s in world golf. The drive is tough; players have to fire over a salt marsh, and as the hole doglegs to the left, the gamble comes with how much of the corner you shave off, with water and dense rough lurking here. The safety option is right, with a wide-open fairway. But the hole then becomes longer, and hopes of reaching the green in two become ever more distant. Most will play it as a three-shot hole, but there is more to consider with a strip of marshland running across the fairway 120 yards short of the putting surface. The green slopes off to the front-left side, and is narrow with a number of contours.

COURSE GUIDE 10–18

The back nine is a test of your shot-making skills, as a number of long carries are needed to overcome the Ocean course's demonic defences. Good driving is again vital to take the pressure off your approach play.

Opposite: The 17th is one of the most daunting par 3s the pros will play. Here, Vijay Singh faces up to the challenge at the 2012 PGA Championship.

Hole 10
Par 4
439 yards

The inward stretch – which is arguably the tougher of the two nines – begins with this daunting par 4 where any shot sent to the right off the tee is almost certainly going to be costly. It pays to be arrow straight or just left of centre with your drive. The undulating green has sand at the front and back, and two good blows are needed to find it in regulation.

Hole 11
Par 5
562 yards

A great par 5 that is reachable when the wind is in your favour, and then presents a good birdie chance. Although relatively straight from tee to green, the fairway snakes subtly right and then left to a green that is elevated. The drive needs to be left-centre to avoid the sand to the right. From here it's a simple lay-up or a long iron over the left corner.

Hole 12
Par 4
466 yards

Long and straight, the 12th requires two meaty blows to find the green. Dunes and dense rough will deter you from going left, while water and marshland lurk close on the right. The undulating green does not make putt-reading easy, and it runs off to the left side. Don't get clever on this hole and chase the flag; play to the heart of the green for the best results.

Hole 13
Par 4
404 yards

The tee is over a footbridge, and a strong fade is favoured with players having to drive over marshland and water to find the fairway. Anything that goes long and straight is liable to run into the dunes and rough, or one of the two deep pot bunkers set here. The entrance to the green is open, but water to the right and bunkers on the left add pressure to the approach shot.

Hole 14
Par 3
194 yards

The 14th begins the Ocean course's final run of holes – all along the coast – that takes you back to the clubhouse. A raised green forces players to float in a high, soft-landing long iron. Sand lurks down the left, and if you are going to miss the target, it's best to do so on the right, as there is plenty of space from which to recover.

Hole 15
Par 4
421 yards

A clever hole where a short-iron approach is the reward for a drive that finds a generous landing zone on an undulating fairway. Dense, thick rough and waste areas defend the left side, and low dunes protect the right. The putting surface is narrow, meaning there is no margin for error with positioning, and it is elevated slightly in the duneland.

Hole 16
Par 5
579 yards

A par 5 that is reachable for the longer hitters, but position from the tee is key. The best side to play down is the right, despite a large waste bunker sitting here. If you are playing the hole in three, the lay-up area is to the right entrance of the green. Anything left will be drawn to a deep bunker, and an up-and-down from here is very tough.

Hole 18
Par 4
439 yards

A finishing hole that demands two well-executed shots to find the green. The hole doglegs to the right, and with the tee set in high sand dunes on the boundary of the beach, many players will fire at the elbow, looking to draw the ball back away from a cluster of bunkers and waste areas that lie here. The green is elevated with run-off areas to the left.

Hole 17 – *Par 3* – **197 yards**

A number of teeing options – six in total – create a very different test on this classic par 3 that has served up some thrilling moments in tournament golf. From the championship pegs, it is an imposing sight with a full carry to a green that runs almost parallel to the tee-shot line. That green is kidney-shaped – widening towards the back – with bunkers lurking to the left side on the front half. During the 1991 Ryder Cup, Mark Calcavecchia was two-up on Colin Montgomerie by the time they got to this hole in their Sunday singles match. After shanking into the water – and with Montgomerie in trouble also – the American still had a three-foot putt to secure the match with a double bogey. He missed, and then lost the final hole to hand Europe a most unlikely half point.

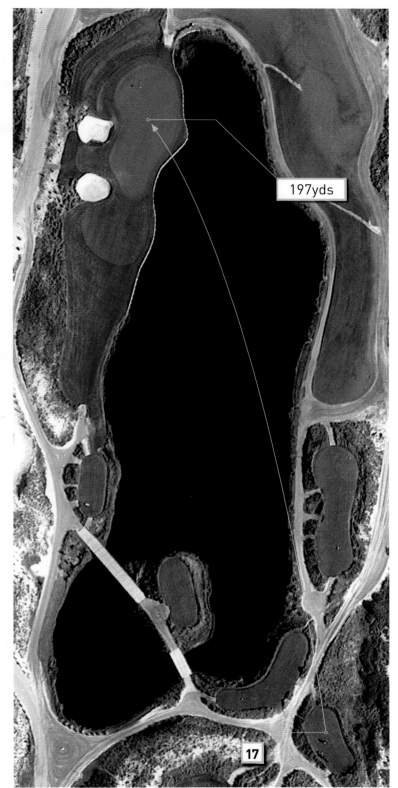

197yds

17

MEDINAH

Medinah is one of the classic country clubs of America. Course Number 3, host to the 2012 Ryder Cup, is big and bold. Its length is the immediate defence, but with many doglegs and overhanging trees, accuracy is needed in almost equal measure.

Set in the western suburbs of Chicago, Medinah Country Club has long been institutionalized with major championship golf. Instantly recognizable with the imposing Byzantine clubhouse that towers above its fairways, it is revered for its beauty and the landscape is a classic example of an American target-style golf course.

The club was founded in the early 1920s by the Medinah Shriners, who sought to build their dream country retreat. They wanted Medinah to be the finest country club in America, with 54 holes to satisfy its 1,500-strong membership. As a result, three layouts were designed and opened in quick succession through the mid-to-late 1920s. Courses nos. 1 & 2 opened in 1925 and '26 respectively. However, it is Tom Bendelow's "Course Number 3" with its rolling fairways that defines this most iconic of golfing homelands. It opened for play in 1928 and has since played host to five major championships – the US Opens of 1949, 1975 and 1990, and the PGA Championships of 1999 and 2006 – as well as the 2012 Ryder Cup, where Europe staged one of the great comebacks to overcome an American team who had dominated the contest for two days.

Bendelow's design was always intended to excite, and while it may be easy on the eye, it is far from that for those who attempt to bring down its defences. Crafted through a dense oak forest, it has fairways lined by towering trees, while the threat of the gentle Lake Kadajih adds to the test on some of the most stunning par 3s anywhere in the world at the 2nd, 13th and 17th. Indeed, the amphitheatre settings of the latter two create stirring atmospheres as players are forced to navigate their way to two of the course's smallest putting surfaces while the galleries watch from the banks behind the green.

Many of the course's par 4s feature testing doglegs, so shot placement off the tee is crucial. The fairways are firm and heavily contoured, and the greens are slick with gentle run-off areas to punish wayward approach play. Tee to green, it is a thorough examination and everything has been tailored to make scoring difficult, although players are encouraged to open their shoulders with a driver on many holes because, above everything else, the course's bite comes with its length. When Medinah hosted the 2006 PGA Championship, won by Tiger Woods with a then record score of 18 under par, it did so with the longest recorded yardage in major championship history at 7,561 yards, a number since surpassed by Torrey Pines (7,643 yards – 2008 US Open), Hazeltine (7,674 yards – 2009 PGA), and Kiawah Island (7,676 yards – 2012 PGA).

Ironically, considering its length, Bendelow had originally designed the course with Medinah's lady members in mind. But it was a failure; too hard for the girls; too easy for the boys. With the club struggling financially, the lure of championship golf proved too much to ignore and the course was rejigged and tricked up throughout the 1930s by Albert W. Tillinghast. Roger Packard and Roger Rulewich were called on to make further improvements in the mid-eighties in the build-up to the 1988 US Senior Open, before Rees Jones added to the already stern test in 2002. Jones was also brought in to help advise on course changes in the build-up to the 2012 Ryder Cup; many of the greens were renovated, while the 15th was made into a driveable par 4 with a lake positioned to the right of the fairway to catch those errant attempts to hit the green in one.

> "Someone told me the large tree that guards the left of the green at 12 has been hit 100,000 times by the members – I can see why."
>
> *Lee Westwood*

COURSE GUIDE 1–9

The typical shot shape on the front nine is a soft draw, as holes sweep mostly to the left, but accurate ball-striking is called for as early as the second hole, the first of Medinah's three par 3s that require a full carry over water.

Opposite: Ernie Els pitches to the green on the monstrous par-5 7th, which has a steep raised putting surface and bunkers guarding its front.

Hole 1
Par 4
433 yards

This opening hole favours a right-to-left shape off the tee, although a single fairway bunker comes into play on the left side, so caution is needed. If you're in position, it's little more than a wedge in, but a subtle ridge in the fairway means your approach may have to be hit from a downhill lie. The green slopes from back to front, with bunkers front-left and right.

Hole 2
Par 3
192 yards

The first of three one-shot holes that require full carries over Lake Kadijah. Here the task is made all the harder as the green is narrow with a huge trap lurking back-right and water all the way down on the left. The prevailing wind from the right makes this an even tougher assignment, but there are several more examinations of one's ball-striking ability to follow.

Hole 3
Par 4
412 yards

Again this hole sweeps gently to the left, but trees dominate the left side, so the approach may be blocked off. Going right off the tee is the ideal line, though a posse of fairway traps waits here. As this is one of the shorter par 4s, there is no need to be greedy and hit a driver. A fairway wood sets up a short iron into another green that slopes from back to front.

Hole 4
Par 4
463 yards

There are no fairway bunkers to contend with here, but the fairway is narrow and the rough is penal. The land slopes – a common feature at Medinah – from the left side so sidehill lies are an issue. There is sand either side of the green, which is elevated. The hole's length means players can find themselves hitting long irons in.

Hole 5
Par 5
536 yards

The fairway drops down and then rises towards the green on this straight-looking par 5, but you will need a good tee shot to allow you to go for the green in two. Most professionals will aim right-centre of the fairway, and then it's a long iron in to a green whose neck is narrowed with sand either side. Two good shots should set up a decent birdie chance.

Hole 6
Par 4
509 yards

This long par 4 doglegs left to right, with bunkers on the corner of the left side of the fairway in case players go too straight. Trees on the right-hand side make positional play from the tee crucial, but yardage dictates that you open up your shoulders to leave a shorter, and clearer, second shot. More sand guards the green, which features many contours.

Hole 8
Par 3
201 yards

The green is the big test on this par 3, which is the only one of the four one-shot holes not to require a carry over water. Two large bunkers guard the putting surface's entrance, and another trap awaits back-right. With a number of breaks and a notable slope from the left side, this green increases the threat of three-putting, so it's crucial to pick your spot.

Hole 9
Par 4
432 yards

The front nine ends with this tight, tree-lined dogleg, and while there are no bunkers in the fairway's landing area, distance control is required to set up a clear shot into another well-guarded green. The ideal tee shot will leave a mid-iron for the approach, but once again the putting surface has many breaks and is lightning-quick, sloping predominantly from right to left.

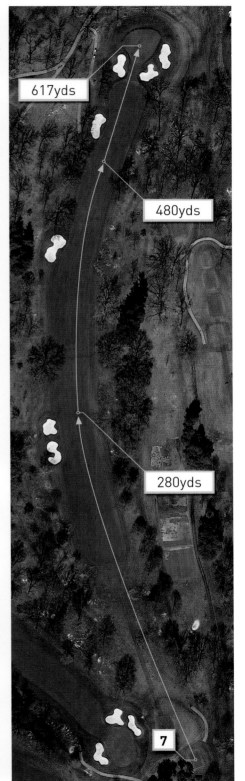

617yds

480yds

280yds

7

Hole 7 – *Par 5* – **617 yards**

A monster of a hole and the longest
on the course, this par 5 sweeps to the
right with towering oak trees calling for
precision as well as power. Although it
is over 600 yards, the pros can get there
with a wood or a long iron if they have
found the fairway from the tee, but the
approach is fraught with danger as the
green is perched up high with bunkers
guarding its entrance.

Course Guide 10–18

A lot more can go wrong on the back nine at Medinah, as, much like at Augusta National, the course serves up many make-or-break shots, most notably at the two classic par 3s at 13 and 17, and the new, redesigned par-4 15th.

Hole 10
Par 5
578 yards

This is a great par 5 that really makes players think about their strategy. If you want to attack in two, the fairway bunkers come into play at the 270-yard mark. If you play it as a three-shot hole, a lay-up short of them is the best strategy. Another trap hugs the right side for those who choose to then lay up short of the green, which slopes from back to front.

Hole 11
Par 4
440 yards

Another hole that sweeps dramatically from right to left. A bunker sits on the corner of the dogleg waiting to gobble up tee shots to the right side. The green, the smallest on the course, is undulating, with one bunker to the right and another two to the left. Again, it's all about placement off the tee, and then a short iron for the approach.

Hole 12
Par 4
479 yards

Players have to find the right side of the fairway on this par 4, but many aim left-centre as balls feed down off a bank; if they go too far right their route will be blocked. A large oak tree stands on the left of the green, making approaches from that side a challenge. The green is raised, but the real test is holding it because it drops off to the right towards water.

Hole 13
Par 3
240 yards

Take a deep breath and swing hard; Medinah's signature hole plays over Lake Kadijah in the opposite direction to the 2nd. From the back tees it is a monster, and a full-blooded long iron, or hybrid, is needed for the pros. The green is encircled by sand traps, with two either side and one short, and the surface is slick, with a testing break from right to left.

Hole 14
Par 5
609 yards

Playing in the opposite direction to the 13th, you drive back over the lake as the fairway climbs uphill. The hole plays relatively straight but if you veer off line you have no chance of reaching the green in two. Many players will attack with a fairway wood but it takes a great shot to hold this green, as deep bunkers protect its boundary.

Hole 15
Par 4
391 yards

For the 2012 Ryder Cup, this hole was redesigned to tempt the longer hitters into going for the green from the tee. Not many did, with the slope and the threat of water on the right posing too many problems. The professionals will lay up with an iron, and it's best to go to the left side of the fairway to leave yourself a bump-and-run into the green.

Hole 16
Par 4
482 yards

Another brute of a dogleg left, this one is more demanding on the second shot than it is off the tee. If feeling ambitious, players may attempt to shorten the approach by cutting the left corner, but dense trees await. The green is raised high on a steep bank; anything short runs back down the fairway, and anything right runs down into the rough.

Hole 18
Par 4
449 yards

Two bunkers guard the right side as the hole doglegs gently to the left. If the fairway has been found with your drive, it can be anything from a 7-iron to a wedge in to the green, but again the surface has many humps and hollows. That didn't stop Hale Irwin from rolling home a 40-footer here to force a play-off (which he would later win) at the 1990 US Open.

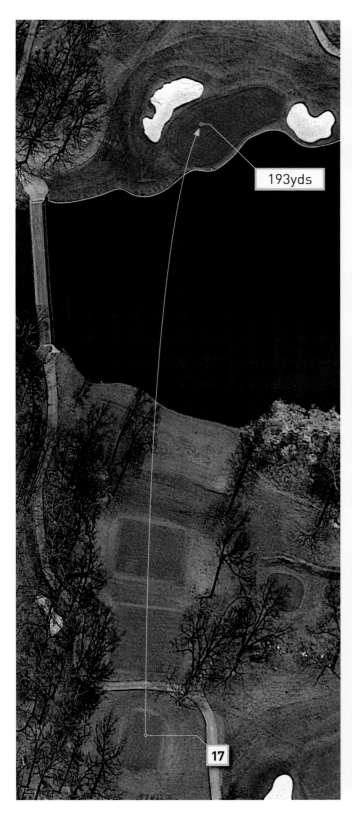

193yds

17

Hole 17 – *Par 3* – **193 yards**

This is something of a little brother to the longer 13th, but with its amphitheatre setting as grassy banks envelop the green, it is equally stunning. A full mid- or long iron is required from the tee, and many players will take an extra club to get over the water. However, the green has a steep bank to the left and back as well as bunkers, making any attempt at an up-and-down that much harder as you play back towards the water. The surface is one of the most undulating on the course, with a big change in elevation on the left side of the green. During the 2012 Ryder Cup, it was the 17th hole that saw the momentum swings as Europe fought back on the final day.

Medinah's long par-4 12th has a notable slope from the left side of the fairway, as well as a huge oak tree that guards the green's entrance.

OAKMONT

When championship golf comes to Oakmont, its members joke that the greens are slowed down for the professionals. Perhaps the toughest course in America, Oakmont doesn't need to be tricked-up in anticipation of tournament golf, because it remains at its uncompromising best whatever the occasion.

Oakmont Country Club in Pennsylvania has hosted the US Open a record eight times. Its three PGA Championships, five US Amateur Championships and two US Women's Opens make it the most celebrated championship course in the United States. Any venue with such pedigree is always going to be recognized as a challenge, and while a golf course's rank in difficulty can never be definitive, few would dispute that Oakmont stands alone as its country's most brutal and testing layout.

Oakmont was actually designed by its creator, Henry Fownes – a local steel magnate – before he had settled on the plot where it would be built. But once he had identified Oakmont Borough, a plateau of land above the Allegheny River, he brought in 150 workers to help him realize his dream. His remit was simple: to build the toughest golf course in the world. Fownes didn't care much for beauty, and with an opening par of 80, his statement was clear.

At first glance, a player's chief tormentor at Oakmont is the cruel bunkering. In total, more than 200 traps guard the course's fairways and greens, with the notorious and intimidating Church Pews – a mass of sand some 100 yards long and 40 yards wide with 12 raised grass mounds – lying between the 4th and 3rd fairways.

But even the bunkering at Oakmont was something of an afterthought following the

course's opening in 1903. Fownes' belief was that poor shots should be suitably punished, and so the myriad of cavernous traps that are now so prevalent on the course began to grow. And, to ensure the bunkers continued to be a challenge, Fownes would have them furrowed with a rake that was weighed down with a 100lb slab.

That said, Oakmont is the prototype US Open venue where those who miss the fairways are left with the prospect of playing from the

Left: Ernie Els holds the US Open trophy after his play-off victory against Colin Montgomerie and Loren Roberts in 1994.

Opposite: The Pennsylvania Turnpike – a toll highway – runs through the middle of the course.

penal rough. Many modern-day courses allow for forgiveness in that a golfer can find numerous routes to the green despite wayward play. Not so at Oakmont; it is totally unforgiving in its directness and relies on the old-fashioned straight-and-narrow approach.

Belying the course's fierce nature, Oakmont was the venue for one of the finest rounds ever seen in major championships. In 1973, en route to victory in the US Open, a young Johnny Miller fired a closing-round 63. Miller's score was not only a course record; it was a major championship record at the time. Today, it still remains the joint-lowest round shot in a US Open. Another of Oakmont's most celebrated moments came in 1962, when a 22-year-old Jack Nicklaus won the first of his 18 majors, going head to head with the great Arnold Palmer. Palmer, at the time, was the most decorated player of the era, while the young Nicklaus was merely a pretender to the throne.

Since opening in 1903, and despite constant tinkering with the bunkers, Oakmont has remained relatively unchanged. In the early 1960s a number of trees were planted, but less than 30 years later the course was brought back to its original condition with the removal of some 5,000 trees. A smaller Church Pews bunker now comes into play on the par-4 15th, which was renovated during upgrades made by Tom Fazio in 2006.

> "You can hit 72 greens [in regulation] in the Open at Oakmont and not come close to winning."
>
> *Arnold Palmer*

COURSE GUIDE 1–9

Course yardage – Championship 7,255 yards
Course GPS – 40º 31'31.22" N 79º 49'39.95" W

From the opening tee shot, questions are asked at Oakmont, with penal rough complementing those deep fairway bunkers. The key is to keep it straight and if you do stray, it's best to take your medicine and get the ball back in play.

Opposite: The huge Church Pews sits between the 3rd and 4th fairways, a sandy grave for the many who fall foul of Oakmont's most demonic defence.

Hole 1
Par 4
482 yards

Make no mistake, Oakmont's opener lets you know straightaway of the task that lies ahead. The fairway is narrow with punishing rough to its sides, and three large bunkers lie on the right, with five smaller ones to the left. Even with a powerful drive, players need a solid mid-iron to reach the green, which slopes from the right with two bunkers to its left.

Hole 2
Par 4
340 yards

A short par 4 that is the ultimate test in accuracy from the tee; a cluster of bunkers sits to the right of the fairway and there is no option to play on the other side, as a ditch meanders here. If you have found your target with a long iron or wood, the approach will be made easier, as a wedge will take you to a green surrounded by deep, cavernous traps.

Hole 4
Par 5
609 yards

Playing adjacent to the 3rd hole, the Church Pews bunker comes into play again on the left side of the fairway. Long hitters can attempt to cut the corner on this hole that doglegs round to the right, but beware of the rough. The bunkers on the approach to the green are cleverly positioned, meaning even those laying up must think clearly about shot placement.

Hole 5
Par 4
382 yards

It may look straightforward, but with bunkers lining either side of the fairway, there is a premium on accuracy. However, in position, you can play to a large green with a short iron, which will help your ball control. The putting surface is lined with sand to the right, and there are a further four traps – two at the back of the green, and two to the left.

Hole 6
Par 3
194 yards

The first of Oakmont's one-shotters at just less than 200 yards, it requires a long iron to take you to the heart of the green. It's heavily contoured, so distance control is critical on this short hole because the green slopes from right to left, and if you fire into the large right-hand trap, you'll have your work cut out holding your escape on the lightning-quick putting green.

Hole 7
Par 4
479 yards

Another long par 4 that is made even sterner with a narrow landing zone for your drive, with three bunkers right and two to the left. Even if you have got a good drive away, the chances are you will have to fire a long iron into the green, which is a task made even harder with four deep and treacherous traps guarding it. A par here feels like a birdie.

Hole 8
Par 3
288 yards

When the US Open visited Oakmont in 2007, this became the longest par 3 in major championship history, and at 288 yards, some players will need their driver just to reach it. The only respite comes with the fact that you can run your ball into the green. That said, the tee shot is all the more daunting with the sight of the Sahara bunker, some 100 yards long, that sits to the green's left.

Hole 9
Par 4
477 yards

After you've crossed back over the Pennsylvania Turnpike, the 9th, which is a par 5 for the members, plays back towards the clubhouse. There are 15 bunkers on this hole, with five down the right-hand side while a ditch lies to the left. The green's boundary is relatively bunker-free, although two sit just short to the right. The huge putting surface drops in elevation significantly.

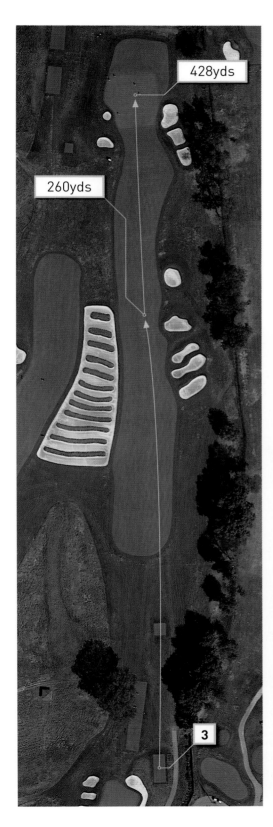

428yds

260yds

3

Hole 3 – *Par 4* – **428 yards**

Standing on the tee box, you will catch sight of the infamous Church Pews bunker that sits to the left of the fairway. Measuring 100 yards long and 40 yards wide, it is defined by 12 grass mounds – the pews – that mean once you are in there, it can be tough work just to get out. So, avoid this at all costs, but don't go right either; five deep traps lurk here, making this the ultimate test in straight and powerful driving. The fairway is heavily contoured, and the green is slightly elevated with five more bunkers guarding its entrance. Officially, this is the hardest hole at Oakmont, so pick your spot and don't get greedy; otherwise a high number awaits.

Course Guide 10–18

The test continues as players must negotiate their line to the green, but for many the fun begins once you have the putter out, with Oakmont's slick surfaces wrecking the hopes of many championship hopefuls over the years.

Opposite: The 15th is a favourite for many players, with a second Church Pews bunker on the left side – this was added to the course following redesign work by Tom Fazio.

Hole 10
Par 4
462 yards

Length and accuracy are both needed at the par-4 10th, as you have to drive past a cluster of fairway bunkers on to one of the course's narrowest fairways. If you can avoid the rough, and the sand, then you can approach the green with a short iron, but more sand awaits those wayward hitters who miss the putting surface, which itself drops from front to back.

Hole 11
Par 4
379 yards

One of the shorter par 4s on the course, with a ditch across the fairway forcing players to lay up short. Many of the pros will play nothing more than a long iron for position, leaving a short iron or wedge into the green. There are three bunkers to the left of the fairway, and another three surrounding the putting surface, which again slopes from front to back.

Hole 12
Par 5
667 yards

The longest of the course's par 5s, and a three-shotter if ever there was one at 667 yards from the backs. It means you can look for accuracy out of the blocks with something less than a driver, and fire in a long iron for your second and third shots. Bunkers are peppered everywhere, with eight guarding the green. The hole is very tree-lined, which adds to the visual test.

Hole 13
Par 3
183 yards

This is a fantastic par 3 and the shortest on the course at 183 yards. Four bunkers surround the kidney-shaped green, which is narrow and undulating. If you are going to miss the putting surface, be sure not to go right into the deepest trap, which will leave a treacherously difficult escape from the sand on to the sloping green. It may be short, but this is no pushover.

Hole 14
Par 4
358 yards

Position off the tee is crucial, so the pros will usually play nothing more than a long iron. Deep, cavernous bunkers line either side of the fairway, waiting to gobble up wayward drives. Once in position, it's a short iron into the green with a huge trap to the left and two smaller ones at the front and back. The green slopes quite significantly from right to left.

Hole 16
Par 3
231 yards

Another long par 3, where players can run a long iron in, or blast a high-flying shot straight on to the putting surface with a 5- or 3-wood. Three bunkers line the left of the green, with another to its right entrance. This was the hole where Larry Nelson sank a 60-foot putt which effectively won him the 1983 US Open while locked in a battle with Tom Watson.

Hole 17
Par 4
313 yards

This hole is pure risk-and-reward, because players can fire at the green, hoping to get there in one to set up a rare eagle opportunity. However, "Big Mouth", a cluster of savage bunkers, lies just short of the green on the line you will take to reach the putting surface. If you're not feeling brave, it's best to stick to a long iron and wedge approach.

Hole 18
Par 4
484 yards

The final test in power and accuracy, as you have to find a sliver of fairway with bunkers left and right. A mid-iron second shot takes you to another undulating putting surface, and the approach plays slightly uphill, meaning more club may be needed to maximize your distance control. This is a thrilling finale to one of the toughest tests in the game.

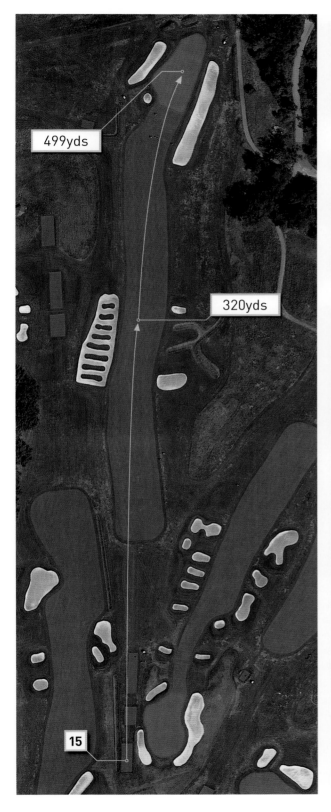

499yds

320yds

15

Hole 15 – *Par 4* – **499 yards**

A beast of a par 4 that turns gently round to the right past sand and trees, with the drive requiring pinpoint accuracy. The 15th is many people's favourite on the course because it delivers on every level. A second, newer Church Pews bunker – which was added by Tom Fazio in 2006 – lies to the left of the fairway, while a deep ditch sits to the right. You need two good blows to find the putting surface, which is huge and undulating – it once measured some 100 yards deep. Three-putting this green has been a card-wrecker for many major championship hopefuls and such is the speed of the surface that players are desperate to run the ball in close to the flag. Somewhat strangely, and despite its difficulty, the hole has a stroke index of eight.

LEADERS	TODAY
BADDELEY	8
WOODS	2
AMES	4
WATSON	3
TOMS	4
STRICKER	2
CABRERA	1
FASTH	1
FURYK	1
VERPLANK	2

USGA

PEBBLE BEACH

In many ways, Pebble Beach has become to the United States Golf Association what St Andrews is to the Royal & Ancient, the natural home of its national championship. And when you come here, it's easy to see why the US Open keeps coming back to the shores of Carmel, California.

On the Monterey Peninsula with views out to Carmel Bay and the Pacific Ocean, Pebble Beach Golf Links was rated by acclaimed golf journal *Golf Digest* as America's number-one course in 2001, despite its standing as a public venue. It's a masterpiece in every way and visually there are few designs that can rival Jack Neville and Douglas Grant's creation, which has been a regular venue for the US Open since 1972, as well as hosting the 1977 PGA Championship. Every January on the PGA Tour, it is also home to the much-acclaimed AT&T Pebble Beach Pro-Am.

When Neville and Grant commenced work on Pebble in 1918, they wanted to take full advantage of its coastal setting, and so the design features two loops in a figure of eight with no fewer than nine holes hugging the rugged Californian coastline. Opening inland, the layout heads for the shore before twisting back after the turn, with the peninsula coming into play once again on the closing two holes to set up one of the most stirring finishes in championship golf.

Unlike many modern-day courses, Pebble is not blessed with just a solitary signature hole, but

the run from the 4th through to the 10th serves up a procession of vistas that cannot be matched. Naturally, conditions can dictate how the course plays, and when the wind is up it can prove unplayable for the mere mortals who choose to pay anything up to $500 to play its 18 holes.

With narrow fairways, punishing rough and greens that jut out with deep ocean chasms below, Pebble offers little forgiveness. Its status as one of the world's toughest tests is affirmed with a look at the standing of the players who have been successful here. Out of the five US Opens played at Pebble, three were won by the greatest

players of their generation, with Jack Nicklaus prevailing in 1972, Tom Watson doing likewise ten years later, and Tiger Woods romping home by a record 15-stroke winning margin in 2000. Tom Kite (1992) and Graeme McDowell (2010) were also victorious here in America's national championship, while the talented Lanny Wadkins claimed the 1977 PGA. But, even if your game is off key, the sense of fulfilment one gets from playing here overshadows the perils you will face. To play it is something of a rite of passage and a chance to find your golfing soul as the waves of the Pacific lap below you.

Google™earth

Despite numerous changes, Pebble has maintained Neville and Grant's overall design philosophy, and the figure-of-eight routing remains. In 1922, William Herbert Fowler made the 379-yard par-4 18th into the 500-plus-yard par 5 we see today, which many argue is the finest home hole in the game. Further extensions to several of the holes were made by H. Chandler Egan in preparation for the 1929 Amateur Championship; greens were reshaped and rebunkered, while length was added to the 2nd, 9th, 14th and 16th holes.

"This is one of the most special golf courses on the planet."

Graeme McDowell

But Pebble's biggest change came with the rebuilding of the par-3 5th hole in the mid 1990s. Originally, this hole had been routed inland because the course did not own the oceanfront land where Neville and Grant wanted it to be positioned. However, by 1995 the land had been acquired, and Jack Nicklaus was brought in to design a new hole overlooking the majestic Still Water Cove.

In preparation for the 2010 US Open,

Opposite: Tom Watson chips in for a birdie two at Pebble's par-3 17th to all but guarantee victory in the 1982 US Open.

Above: It is one of the finest designs in the game. Pebble Beach's figure-of-eight routing features nine holes played by the shore.

Arnold Palmer spearheaded the development and restoration of four of the course's greens. Eleven tees were enhanced and Pebble's total length was stretched to 7,040 yards from the championship tees.

Course Guide 1–9

Course yardage – Back tees 6,830 yards
Course GPS – 36º 34'7. 23" N 121º57'1.40" W

With Pebble's figure-of-eight routing taking you out to the peninsula at the 7th hole, you will be blessed with some of the finest views anywhere in the game of golf. But don't let them distract you from the ultimate test in front of you.

Opposite: It may be little, but Pebble's par-3 7th has left many a player frustrated over the years. The hole affords you magnificent views out to the Pacific.

Hole 1
Par 4
377 yards

A relatively gentle opener with a dogleg right, where players can be lured into attempting to cut the corner with a driver. Most will opt for a 3-wood and the safety of the fairway, leaving a mid-iron approach to a green well guarded by bunkers on either side. Patience is the key to playing this short par 4 successfully and getting off to a solid start.

Hole 2
Par 4
511 yards

Normally a par 5, but a long par 4 during the US Open; the drive is tight with bunkers peppering the fairway for those landing the ball around the 250-yard mark, so accuracy is at a premium. The green is tough to hit due to its entrance being narrowed by two sprawling sand traps. If the fairway is missed it will likely be played as a three-shotter.

Hole 3
Par 4
390 yards

Players will look to draw the ball around the corner of this dogleg left, but if too straight from the tee they will run out of fairway and find sand. If in position from the tee, it is nothing more than a wedge to a large green with bunkers either side. The putting surface is steeply contoured; so position is important if you are to avoid three-putting.

Hole 4
Par 4
326 yards

This may be a short par 4, but it is highly demanding in accuracy with the right side of the fairway hugging the coast. A driver is not the best option from the tee as that brings the bunkering into play on the approach. Most will favour a 3-wood or even a long iron to leave them with a pitch to the green, which slopes significantly from back to front.

Hole 5
Par 3
192 yards

A testing par 3 with the waves of the Pacific crashing against the shore and views out to Stillwater Cove; four deep bunkers guard the green, three on the right side and one to the left-rear. With the wind buffeting in off the ocean, this will add to the test and club selection is vital. It's best to opt for safety first and aim for the left-centre of the green.

Hole 6
Par 5
506 yards

This is a classic par 5 that many players will go for in two. However, a powerful tee shot is needed as the second plays up a steep slope, where you need as much loft on your club as possible. Bunkers are in play all up the left side of the fairway and the green is protected with three traps, two to the right and one to the left.

Hole 8
Par 4
427 yards

This remains one of Pebble's most testing par 4s, where players face a demanding tee shot to set up an approach over a deep chasm with the ocean below. Long hitters need nothing more than a long iron or a 5-wood to find the perfect spot from which to attack the green. But the less the club you are hitting in with, the better, as the green is surrounded by sand.

Hole 9
Par 4
481 yards

The 9th plays long and requires two decent blows to find the green, so par here is a good return. Players will fire left of the fairway, opting for safety first. However, this makes the approach even tougher as there is a deep gully to the left of the putting surface, forcing you to hit over it. The fairway slopes from left to right, so flat lies are hard to find.

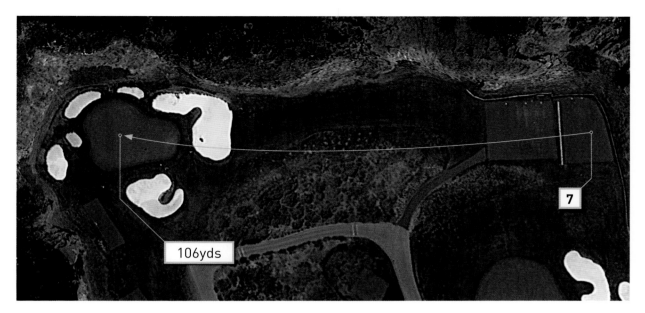

106yds

Hole 7 – *Par 3* – 106 yards

This is perhaps Pebble's most photographed hole, a short par 3 that can be a real test of nerve as the wind howls in off the Pacific. Though it only plays just over 100 yards, players will not always choose their most lofted wedge and will sometimes choke down on an iron, as they have to contend with the elevation from the tee and a contoured green. Bunkers surround the putting surface, and those who overclub and go long will face deep traps which are difficult to escape from. Many players will play safe and fire at the centre of the green, because those who get greedy and attack the pin can fall foul of the green's vicious slopes. A par here is never bad – however short the hole may be.

COURSE GUIDE 10–18

The layout heads back inland after the 10th hole, but the test doesn't ease up, as there are many well-placed bunkers and sloping greens. It all leads up to one of the grandest finishes in the game at the par-3 17th and par-5 18th.

Opposite: Pebble Beach's 18th serves up one of the game's finest finishes, its fairway sweeping to the left as the ocean waves crash against the rocks below.

Hole 10
Par 4
446 yards

With the ocean winds still forcing you to think about shot placement from the tee, you will need to aim to the left side of the fairway, avoiding a cluster of traps that lie in wait here. If you can find your target with an accurate drive, you will have a relatively straightforward mid-iron approach to a green that slopes quite dramatically from left to right.

Hole 11
Par 4
373 yards

An inviting fairway allows you to open your shoulders from the tee on this shortish par 4; however, the approach is the testing shot as the green is once again guarded by sand traps. The best route in is from the left side, with two bunkers to the right. This green slopes from back to front, so you don't want to leave it short.

Hole 12
Par 3
201 yards

This is a long par 3 that requires more force than Pebble's three other short holes, as well as plenty of precision. The task is made even tougher by the narrow approach to the green with bunkers lurking either side, which forces players to land high-flying shots on the putting surface. Two other traps sit behind the green, waiting to catch errant long shots.

Hole 13
Par 4
403 yards

A testing par 4 that plays slightly uphill, which means you will have to take more club than normal. There is a huge bunker on the left side of the fairway, with another three on the right side. Although the green is not as nearly protected with sand as many on this course, there are notable changes in elevation and it is one of the quickest.

Hole 14
Par 5
572 yards

The dogleg right means this par 5 should be played as a three-shotter. Players will attempt to cut off the corner on the right side, but beware: deep, thick rough will leave your ball buried, while two narrow bunkers also lurk here. Even the longest will struggle to get to the green in two, so a lay-up, followed by a well-placed pitch to another sloping green, is the best way forward.

Hole 15
Par 4
396 yards

This is another tee shot that calls for accuracy, rather than power. Deep bunkers come into play around the 230-yard mark, but even if you take a long iron off the tee, a mid-iron will suffice for your approach. That said, the putting surface is protected either side and at the rear with deep bunkers. Play it safe and aim for the centre of the green.

Hole 16
Par 4
401 yards

One of Pebble's more fiddly holes; you will need to aim your drive over a bunker placed in the centre of the fairway. Taking a driver here could mean you run out of fairway, or leave yourself blocked out for your second shot, while going right is a no-no with deep rough and trees. The green is relatively bunker-free, and it feeds down from the right-hand side.

Hole 17
Par 3
177 yards

Like the 7th, the 17th is one of the world's most iconic par 3s and it has witnessed some classic moments, like Tom Watson's chip-in for a birdie two to all but seal the 1982 US Open. The hole is made difficult by its narrow green and the monster sand trap that guards its front. With the course now back on the peninsula, the wind will also play havoc with club selection.

Hole 18 – *Par 5* – 545 yards

One of the great finishing holes in major championships; this classic par 5 is best played as a three-shot hole with its myriad of defences testing players from tee to green. However, those chasing a closing birdie will let fly with a 5- or 3-wood with their second shot to a green that slopes towards the ocean on the left. The ideal landing zone for a drive is left of the trees that are positioned in the centre of the fairway. Sand then hugs the left side of the approach from 150 yards in, but this can actually help players, saving hooked shots from finding a watery grave as the waves crash against the rocks below. Three other bunkers lie around the green's boundary, and there is another tree blocking out pitched approaches from the right side.

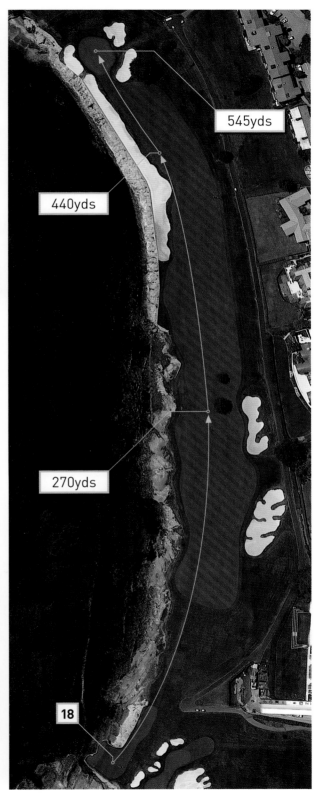

WINGED FOOT WEST

Winged Foot's West Course has been a host venue for the US Open since 1929, with its length and many daunting carries into undulating greens making it a perfect venue for arguably golf's toughest major. But there is much more to Albert W. Tillinghast's design than the fabled difficulty of the test.

Winged Foot's West Course, which was designed and opened for play in 1923, has a reputation that belies its true nature. Many view the course as a brute; a layout that serves only to wreck the hopes of tournament challengers rather than to excite and enthral. That said, there are few courses that have stirred the emotions to the same extent as Albert W. Tillinghast's creation that was built on rolling farmland in the town of Mamaroneck, New York.

There are many references to Tillinghast's course that go down in major championship folklore, but perhaps the most cutting was the title bestowed on the 1974 US Open, following Hale Irwin's victory there. Irwin, one of the great grinders of his day and a player who would go on to win the tournament three times, needed a seven-over-par total of 287 shots to prosper in what was dubbed "The Massacre at Winged Foot" owing to the course's unrelenting set-up. It was the third time the US Open had visited here. At the time, the world's best players would have been hoping it must be the last.

This was the year following Johnny Miller's runaway final round to win the US Open at Oakmont in 1973. The USGA, whose remit for their national championship has always been to exhaust golfers' playing capabilities in order to find the best, were not keen on making matters easy. They wanted to stamp their authority back on the game, and the West Course's fairways were narrowed, its greens made slicker, and the rough grown to preposterous proportions. If the idea was to leave Irwin and his pursuers bereft of ideas, the United States Golf Association succeeded with aplomb.

In truth, the course should not be judged on how it is tricked up for a major championship, but rather by its natural and invigorating feel. Yes, it is a test; its long carries and sloping putting surfaces ensure it will never be a pushover. But to suggest it is a savage underplays what the golf course is all about.

Tillinghast, just as he did at Baltusrol, designed two courses at Winged Foot – the East and the West, with the latter his signature layout, which today measures a total of 7,264 yards. As well as that 1974 US Open, the West has hosted the championship on another

"The last 18 holes are pretty tough."

Jack Nicklaus

© 2013 Google
Data SIO, NOAA, U.S Navy, NGA, GEBCO

12

11

10

1

four occasions (1929, 1959, 1984 and 2006) and it was also the venue for the 1997 PGA Championship, won by Davis Love III.

To contradict its reputation, the course has no out-of-bounds, water hardly features anywhere and it rarely looks daunting from the tees. But many of the course's greens sit on steep banks, as Tillinghast used the rocky Westchester terrain to full effect. These surfaces are also relatively small, but big in bite, with devilish contours adding to the test of a player's approach skills.

Two highlights stand out at Winged Foot; after holing a clutch putt to force a play-off, Bobby Jones saw off Al Espinosa in perhaps the most one-sided shootout in history at the 1929 US Open, winning by 23 strokes. And Greg Norman holed the most snaking of long-range putts to force another play-off, this time with Fuzzy Zoeller in the 1984 event.

Like Jones, Zoeller made short work of the ensuing Monday play-off, beating Norman by eight strokes. But he and Norman remain the only players to have finished a US Open at Winged Foot with an under-par aggregate. Admittedly, 13 years later in the PGA Championship, Davis Love III carded an 11-under-par winning score on the same course, but this was on a layout that was missing the tricks and treats of America's national championship – proof, if ever, that the West is far from the bully we are often led to believe.

"It's just the toughest US Open venue, and the scores reflect that."

Phil Mickelson

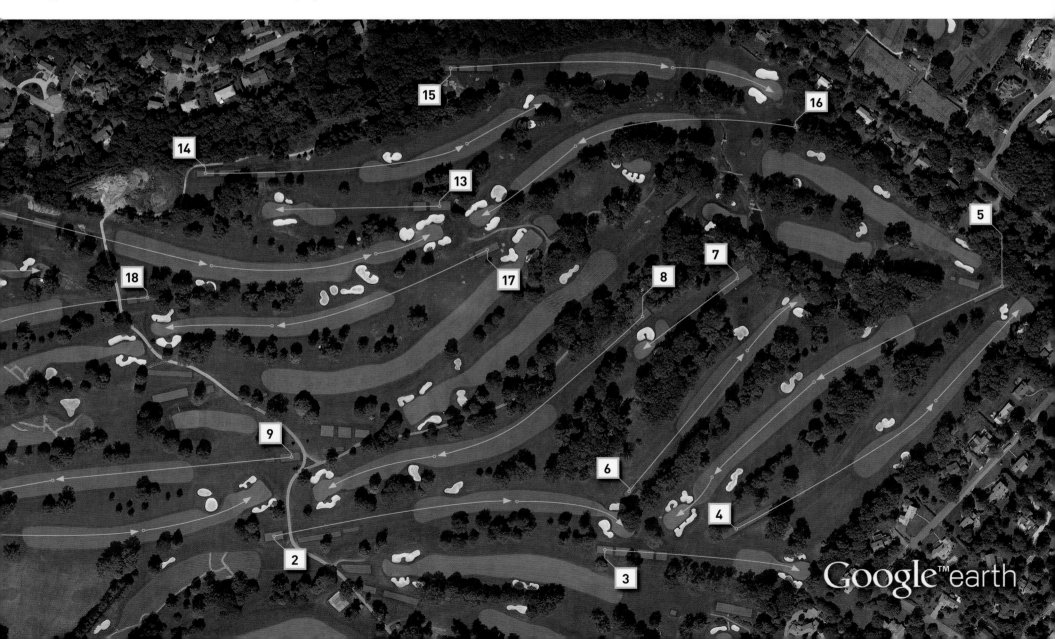

COURSE GUIDE 1–9

Course yardage – Championship 7,264 yards
Course GPS – 40º 57'25.31" N 73º 45'15.21" W

Players must find their rhythm early as Winged Foot asks questions from the off, with a series of dogleg two-shotters that feature undulating greens. Position from the tee is a must, and distance control is essential to find the right portion of the putting surface.

Opposite: Winged Foot's 2nd hole is a fine example of how tough approach play can be, with a narrow green that is protected by sand and trees. This is an early examination of distance control.

Hole 1
Par 4
450 yards

There are no immediate defences to overcome with the drive, although trees lurk to the right. As the fairway sweeps to the left, a mid-iron should be played to the heart of the green but beware, it is very undulating and if players go long they will have a difficult chip back towards a surface that slopes from back to front. Par here is a more than solid start.

Hole 3
Par 3
216 yards

The green on this long par 3 is heavily contoured, but you'll need a good shot to get there. Two bunkers sit either side and as with many holes at Winged Foot, you don't want to go long. In all four rounds of the 1959 US Open, Billy Casper played intentionally short of the green, then pitched on and putted successfully for par.

Hole 4
Par 4
469 yards

A testing par 4 that turns to the left, favouring a soft draw. Traps sit either side of the fairway waiting to catch those errant strokes from the tee. Mature trees hug the right-hand side tightly; meaning approaches are best played from the left. However, one of two deep greenside bunkers lurks here, so hitting the green is vital if you are to make par.

Hole 5
Par 5
515 yards

A three-shot hole that is reachable in two for those who find the fairway from the tee. Two bunkers guard the right of the fairway, the second of which, at around 300 yards, can catch out those looking for extra distance. A narrow green is heavily protected by two bunkers, and its uncompromising slopes can guide your ball to the sand on either side.

Hole 6
Par 4
321 yards

The longest hitters will be tempted to fire for the green in one, but don't underestimate Winged Foot's shortest par 4. The entrance to another pear-shaped putting surface is narrow, and traps either side make the approach, or tee shot, even more demanding. A stream also meanders to the back of the green. In the 1929 US Open, Bill Mehlhorn took a ten here.

Hole 7
Par 3
162 yards

The shortest par 4 is followed by the shortest par 3, and little more than a 7- or 8-iron is needed to reach another green that is perched on a plateau. Trees line the left, so players will opt to draw the ball in high, looking for a soft landing. That said, a single greenside bunker sits to the right, waiting to catch out those who fail to get enough on the ball.

Hole 8
Par 4
475 yards

The course bites back at the 8th with this testing dogleg right, and it begins a tough trio of holes where your score can take a hit, with tee shots and approaches demanding in both accuracy and power. Those who go straight or left off the tee will run out of fairway, and position is crucial for your approach to the green, which is protected on either side by deep sand traps.

Hole 9
Par 4
514 yards

A members' par 5 that in 2006 became the first par 4 over 500 yards in US Open history. Long and straight, it has no fairway bunkers to contend with, but the threat of penal rough remains. Because of the hole's length, players will need to hit long irons or utility clubs into the green, which is surrounded by sand. This is a beast of a hole, and par is a solid return.

453yds

300yds

2

Hole 2 – *Par 4* – 453 yards

Trees feature on both the drive and the approach on this punishing par 4. The hole doglegs gently to the right, and there is a bunker at the 250-yard mark left of the fairway. Trees guard the entire right side, so those who hit too straight from the tee could face their route being obstructed, and playing from here makes it very difficult to hold the green. Two large bunkers protect either side of the putting surface, and another huge tree, which overhangs back-left, makes positional play even trickier. Fortunes can fluctuate, depending on how you approach the task. In the 1984 US Open, Fuzzy Zoeller took control of his Monday play-off with Greg Norman on this hole by rolling in a 65ft birdie putt as Norman carded a double-bogey six after finding tree trouble from the tee.

COURSE GUIDE 10–18

Opening with a tough par 3 – one of the great one-shot holes in the game – the back nine also features the course's longest hole at the par-5 12th. Five consecutive par 4s, all doglegs, then make up the finish, and players must plot their way home with patience.

Hole 10
Par 3
188 yards

A par 3 that requires you to hit the green if you're to have any realistic hope of making par. Bunkers sit either side of the green, with another short left. The putting surface is one of the most undulating on the course, set on a hill with its front dropping towards a deep swale. Position, therefore, is key. If you go long it's a treacherous chip back down the slope.

Hole 11
Par 4
396 yards

A rare opportunity to put the driver away, so players can look for position short of the left-side fairway bunker at 250 yards. From here, it's nothing more than a short iron to a green with another narrow entrance. A large bunker sits front-left, with another back-right. By Winged Foot standards, the green is relatively flat. A possible birdie chance – if you hit your targets.

Hole 12
Par 5
640 yards

A long par 5 that was set up as a genuine three-shotter for the 2006 US Open. From the forward tees you can take on the green in two, but you need to be in position and the fairway rises on approach. Trees on the left-hand side also make positioning difficult for lay-ups. Questions are asked of the player on every shot, with five bunkers around the green.

Hole 13
Par 3
214 yards

A green sitting on top of a hill makes positioning vitally important on what is another long one-shot hole, albeit with limited defences around the putting surface. The green is once again pear-shaped and if you are short, your ball can easily roll back down the hill. With that in mind, players will often take an extra club if unsure, as it's safer to go long.

Hole 14
Par 4
458 yards

The 14th begins a finishing stretch of five testing, long par 4s. From the back tees, the drive is daunting as it is semi-blind, and you have to hit a soft draw with a fairway bunker lurking at the 260-yard mark. The approach is then played to another elevated green, which slopes from the back-left. Bunkers lie either side, with overhanging trees a factor on the right.

Hole 16
Par 4
478 yards

Trees dominate the left side of this hole, with overhanging branches making the tee shot one of the most difficult on the course. If you can find the right side of the fairway you will have an easier shot in, although the path is made narrower with a deep bunker front-right and a huge maple tree front-left of the green, which again, is very undulating.

Hole 17
Par 4
449 yards

Another tough examination in ball striking, the penultimate hole plays round to the right with a cluster of sand traps lurking on the corner. If you are in position, you will have the benefit of being able to run your ball into the kidney-shaped green. That said, its contours will test the very best putters and its length can make two-putting even more of a challenge.

Hole 18
Par 4
450 yards

A fine finishing hole that sweeps from right to left and demands an accurate drive. The pros may opt for a 3-wood off the tee to lay up short of the right-hand fairway bunker at 280 yards. But the second shot can be deceptive, as the green rises with a steep bank to the right side where the rough is brutal. As a parting gesture, the green is one of the most contoured you will play.

416yds

270yds

15

Hole 15 – *Par 4* – **416 yards**

At first glance it can look innocuous, but there is much to think about on this mid-length par 4. The fairway, which features many undulations, sweeps gently to the right, and then rolls down to the left. Distance control, therefore, is at a premium and players can find themselves playing their second shot from penal rough even when the right line has been found from the tee. A stream comes into play around the 300-yard mark, so long hitters will often choose to lay up short and play from an uphill lie with a mid-iron. You can go longer off the tee and leave yourself with less club; but you risk playing from a downhill lie into yet another pear-shaped green that is elevated and difficult to hold on account of its many humps and hollows.

One of the most iconic sights in golf. The view from the 17th green of the Old Course at St Andrews, with the Road bunker in the immediate foreground and the 1st and 18th fairways beyond.

GREAT BRITAIN & IRELAND

MUIRFIELD

Every serious golfer should want to play a round at Muirfield, one of the grandest links courses in the world. A 15-time host to the Open Championship, its bottlenecked fairways, cavernous pot bunkers and undulating greens make it one of the most revered stretches of golfing land.

Opposite: Muirfield's front nine plays in a clockwise direction, the back nine predominantly anti-clockwise.

Below left: Nick Faldo claims the first of his six majors with victory in the 1987 Open at Muirfield.

Golf Monthly magazine has rated Muirfield as the UK & Ireland's top course since its 2008 Top 100 Rankings, and when you visit the East Lothian links you cannot help but be beguiled by its old-world charms. The club is home to the Honourable Company of Edinburgh Golfers (HCEG), and its history dates all the way back to 1744, when a competition was set up on the Leith Links on the Firth of Forth some two miles from the city of Edinburgh.

The competition was open to "as many noblemen or gentlemen or other golfers" as submitted their entries, and it was these men who would write the first Rules of Golf ten years before the formation of The Royal & Ancient. As the membership of the HCEG grew, the club's original home on the Leith Links was deemed too small. A move to Musselburgh Old Course followed, but with membership still swelling, a new 18-hole course was designed by Old Tom Morris on the links at Muirfield in 1891. The following year the club hosted its first Open Championship.

There is no doubt they do things a little differently at Muirfield; some critics claim it can underwhelm. It doesn't possess the rocky coastline and sweeping sea of Turnberry, or the mountainous dunes of Royal Birkdale. But its minimalist feel is all part of the package that makes the course so loved, and so respected. It is also regarded as one of the purest tests in the game. When Old Tom Morris first went to work on the layout, it was one of the first "created" links in the respect that its greens, bunkers and tees were placed strategically rather than using the natural lie of the land. The front nine traces a clockwise circle, while the back nine forms its inner ring as it heads back in an anti-clockwise route.

There are many defences; Muirfield's greens are small and heavily contoured, the rough is lush and penal, while a number of the par 4s require lusty blows to reach the putting surface in two. But its bunkers remain the most demonic force. They pepper the course to such an extent that, in conjunction with the wind, they can drastically influence club selection from one day to another. From the tee these bunkers lurk ominously on the fairways' landing zones, while the greenside traps are deep and cavernous. Muirfield is renowned for its revetted bunkers: the walls are retained with grass, meaning your ball can roll in from all angles. Today, the course has a championship yardage of 7,245 yards, although Old Tom's original design has seen several changes. The most major overhaul was by Harry Colt in the 1920s. Most notably, 50 acres of land were added to the layout.

Since Muirfield first hosted the Open, the battle for the Claret Jug has been played out there another 14 times. As at Birkdale, the calibre of winners is testament to the skills a player needs to be successful, with modern-day greats such as Jack Nicklaus, Lee Trevino, Tom Watson and Nick Faldo complementing the early dominance of Harry Vardon and James Braid. And it is course management that is the key to success; when Faldo won the first of his three Opens here in 1987 – he also won at Muirfield in 1992 – his final round was a masterful display of long-iron play. Negotiating a successful path in bleak, thick fog, the Englishman fired 18 consecutive pars to win the championship by a single stroke from a wilting Paul Azinger as the young American fell foul of the bunker-strewn back nine.

"There are no weak holes at Muirfield."

Tom Watson

COURSE GUIDE 1–9

Course yardage – Championship 7,245 yards
Course GPS – 56º 2'31.19" N 2º49' 17.36" W

The front nine sets out in a clockwise route, taking in the sights of the imposing Archerfield Wood. There are a series of testing par 4s where a player must play with patience, while at the same time picking the right spot to attack from.

Opposite: Muirfield's 6th hole features a cluster of bunkers on the corner of the dogleg, from where Justin Leonard plots his escape in the 2002 Open.

Hole 1
Par 4
450 yards

Once a 200-yard par 3, this hole now plays 450 yards into the prevailing wind and can be one of the toughest openers in major championships. A large, c-shaped bunker sits to the left of the fairway, and from the back tees you have to shape your shot to the left to avoid the punishing rough. The green is relatively flat; but it's a tough task to get here in two on a blustery day.

Hole 2
Par 4
367 yards

With the wind behind, big hitters will fancy their chances of driving this hole, but this is a risky strategy. The biggest peril is the out-of-bounds that comes within yards of the putting surface's left-hand side. Instead, it is best to take advantage of the open fairway with a long iron and play an approach with a more controlled short iron, as bunkers protect the right side of the green.

Hole 3
Par 4
397 yards

Big hitters need to think twice about taking driver here, as the fairway bottlenecks just shy of 300 yards with two bunkered mounds. A lay-up is the smart choice, but if you miss the fairway left or right, your view to the putting surface will be obstructed. The green rises at the back, and it pays to be longer here as bunkers lie in wait at the front.

Hole 4
Par 3
229 yards

Numerous teeing options alter the test from 136 to 229 yards, but from the championship tees this is a full-blooded long iron or more, requiring pinpoint accuracy. Two bunkers lurk short right of the green, with another one to the left. The putting surface slopes away towards the sand and is slightly elevated, making it difficult to hold.

Hole 5
Par 5
561 yards

Played with the prevailing wind, the green is reachable in two but you have to craft a fine drive to get into position to attack. Sand traps hug the right of the fairway and the best angle is to take these on and fire over them. Fighting against the wind in the 1972 Open, Johnny Miller needed a 3-wood for his approach, which he holed for an albatross.

Hole 7
Par 3
187 yards

This is a tricky one-shot hole where the green is missed at your peril. The prevailing wind makes the tee shot even more challenging. Three traps guard the left side, with another deep pot bunker on the right. This is another difficult green that is tough to hold, as it slopes steeply from back to front, and also to the left towards a ring of sand.

Hole 8
Par 4
445 yards

A group of fairway bunkers lies on the corner of this dogleg par 4, so it's a gamble if you want to shorten the hole by going right. Ideal position is left from the tee to set up a mid-iron approach over a series of cross-bunkers 50 yards short of the green. Out-of-bounds and Archerfield Wood hug the left side of the approach, and the putting surface drops away back-left, so don't go long.

Hole 9
Par 5
558 yards

Out-of-bounds lines the left side all the way up the hole, and the fairway's landing zone is narrow with a deep trap on the left and penal rough right. Some players will take the green on in two even from the new back tee, but with no man's land on the left, a cluster of bunkers on the right, and a prevailing west wind, it demands a pure and committed strike.

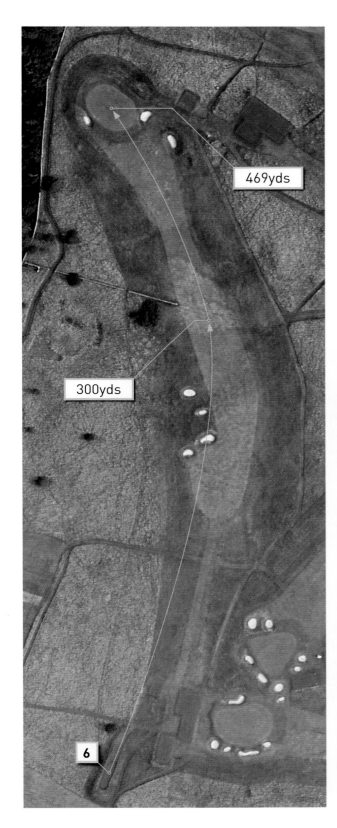

469yds

300yds

6

Hole 6 – *Par 4* – **469 yards**

A classic two-shot hole that could well be the toughest on the course. This par 4 doglegs to the left. Four bunkers lie on the elbow, but they should be taken out of play by the pros, who will aim to cut the corner here. The second shot is difficult to judge as the fairway drops and the green then rises. A 4-foot stone wall sits to the left of the approach, and Archerfield Wood dominates the backdrop, giving the hole a very un-links-like feel nearer the green. Prevailing crosswinds make it an even sterner test and two fine shots are needed to find the target in regulation. Par is always a good score here.

COURSE GUIDE 10–18

The back nine forms the inner route of the layout, with a finish that is one of the finest in the game, as players negotiate a series of challenging holes with heavily contoured greens, making distance control essential for a good score.

Hole 10
Par 4
472 yards

With holes now heading into the inner circle of the layout, players are faced with the threat of crosswinds. The drive needs to stay left, but it can easily drift right where a trio of bunkers await. Two cross-bunkers 100 yards short of the green can restrict your view of the putting surface. A triple bogey seven at this hole cost the great Arnold Palmer heavily in the 1966 Open.

Hole 11
Par 4
389 yards

This hole features the only genuine blind tee shot on the course, as players have to drive over a hilly ridge towards the Firth of Forth. Two bunkers lie at the 250- and 280-yard marks on the right of the fairway, with another at 270 yards on the left. The green features many contours and sand dominates its boundary, so the approach is fraught with danger.

Hole 12
Par 4
382 yards

A clever par 4 that may be lacking in length but has bags of character. The ideal position on the fairway is left of centre, because of which many players will take a 3-wood or long iron off the tee. This is the best route into the green as the putting surface is well guarded on the right of the approach with a cluster of sand traps.

Hole 13
Par 3
193 yards

The hole plays slightly uphill, and it is an absolute must that you hit the green if you are to have any hopes of making a score here. The green is very narrow, with deep, cavernous bunkers right and left, and the right side drops severely, while also sloping dramatically from back to front. It's a hole where you pick your spot and hold your breath. This is a thrilling par 3.

Hole 14
Par 4
478 yards

This is a very long and extremely attractive par 4 that is played from an elevated tee. Bunkers tighten the drive on the left with the fairway narrowing just after. This hole will usually play into the wind, so players will need a long iron, and sometimes more, to find the heart of an elevated green that drops off on all sides, making it hard to hold.

Hole 15
Par 4
447 yards

On the tee, the line takes you out to the right of the fairway so you need to shape the ball left to avoid the punishing rough. Bunkers sit either side, and many will opt for position over power from the tee. However, that will still leave a long iron into a green, christened Camel's Back, as it channels balls off in all directions. Another tough par 4.

Hole 16
Par 3
188 yards

Sand lurks everywhere around the green on Muirfield's final one-shotter, and the putting surface slopes down to the left side. The hole can play very differently depending on wind direction, with club selection ranging from a 7-iron to as much as a hybrid to help with a high-flying and soft-landing shot. Ignore the flag and aim for the middle of the green.

Hole 18
Par 4
473 yards

A fine finishing hole where players must contend with right-to-left prevailing crosswinds. One bunker sits at 220 yards on the right, but it is the two on the left at 240 yards that are more of a threat. Past these traps, the fairway is narrow so the rough comes into play. Sand awaits on either side of the green, the most prominent feature being a ring bunker to the right.

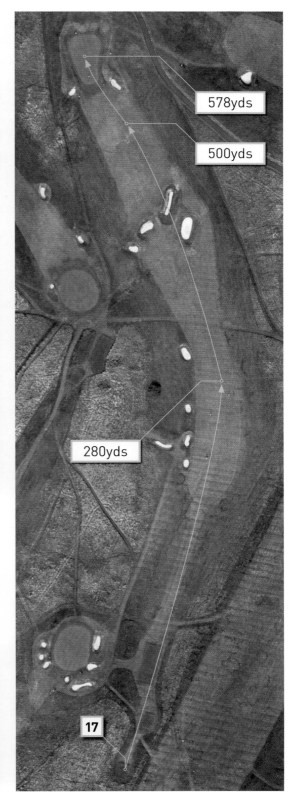

578yds

500yds

280yds

17

Hole 17 – *Par 5* – **578 yards**

In the 1966 Open Championship, Jack Nicklaus played a 3-iron off the tee on this par 5, and then reached the green with a 5-iron. Two putts later, a birdie had effectively won the Golden Bear his first Claret Jug. On that day the wind was in Jack's favour, but others haven't been afforded such comfort, and the hole can play as a testing three-shotter when the gusts are against. As the fairway doglegs to the left, a row of bunkers lining the left side come into play for those attempting to cut the corner. When laying up with an approach, the cross-bunkers 100 yards short of the green are also a factor. The green has two bunkers short right and left, and is encircled by attractive dunes.

PORTMARNOCK

Ireland is blessed with some of the most rugged landscape for links golf, and on the east coast lies Portmarnock's Championship course with stunning views out to the Irish Sea. Framed by low duneland and blooming gorse, this is perhaps the Emerald Isle's most famous stretch of golfing terrain.

A golf course that is steeped in history, Portmarnock was designed by William Pickeman, a Scottish insurance worker, and George Ross, who set about constructing it in 1893. It was developed on a two-mile stretch of peninsula some eight miles north east of Dublin, land that was owned by the Jameson family, of Jameson's whiskey fame. Portmarnock opened in 1894 as a nine-holer, before an extension took it to a full 18 holes two years later.

In 1971 another nine holes were added to Portmarnock, making a total of 27. However, it is the Red & Blue nines, the original work of Pickeman and Ross, that make up the Championship links that has welcomed a long list of top-level tournaments and players.

It was a regular – and some would say spiritual – home to the Irish Open after hosting the inaugural tournament in 1927. That was

Opposite: The Red & Blue nines make up the Championship course at Portmarnock, with the Irish Sea protecting its boundary.

Below: Few settings can rival the tranquillity of Portmarnock.

> "Pickeman and Ross were able to spot a true gem and what they left is a rare golfing challenge."
>
> *Peter Alliss*

the same year the course's only real major development took place with the building of the signature par-3 15th – rated by many players to be one of the toughest – and finest – one-shot holes in the world. With out-of-bounds all down the right side and magnificent views out to Ireland's Eye and Lambay Island, it is a visual treat in equal measure. After the 1976 Irish Open, American Ben Crenshaw called it the shortest par 5 in the world. Despite struggling with a double bogey on the hole, Crenshaw had dramatically won the tournament.

The Irish Open made its last, and 19th, visit to Portmarnock in 2003, the year New Zealander Michael Campbell won. The course also hosted the Amateur Championship of 1949, and the Canada Cup (now the World Cup) in 1960. In 1991, Portmarnock welcomed the game's best amateur players for the 34th staging of the Walker Cup, where leading non-professionals from the United States take on their UK & Ireland counterparts. That year, golf fans were treated to an early sighting of a young Phil Mickelson,

Google™earth

"I know of no greater finish than the last five holes at Portmarnock."

Bernard Darwin

who helped steer the visiting American team to a 14–10 victory.

The course wends its way through low, rolling sandhills, with a number of pot bunkers and plenty of lush, penal rough to test positional play. There are subtle contours that can take control of your ball, but by and large the land looks relatively flat, and at first sight there is an argument that Portmarnock doesn't quite deliver in the "wow" factor as other classic links do. But, like Muirfield, it has built a reputation as one of the game's fairest tests where you can see every defence laid out in front of you. Blind shots are at a minimum, and undoubtedly the biggest demon a player will have to overcome is the stubborn wind that sweeps in off the Irish Sea.

Today, Portmarnock weighs in at a meaty 7,466 yards from the back pegs, though the members and paying public will be happier to tackle the challenge from the white tees, still imposing with a total yardage of 6,926. As at Muirfield, course management is necessary for scoring well here. After a relatively gentle opening over the first three holes, the challenge comes to life on the par-4 4th, a beast that stretches to an intimidating 474 yards.

While it has been lengthened substantially over the years, much of Pickeman and Ross's routing is still relevant today. Consistently rated as one of the finest courses in the British Isles, Portmarnock's Championship links is proof that a great golf course does not need to be endlessly tricked-up to test the very best.

COURSE GUIDE 1–9

Course yardage – Championship 7,466 yards
Course GPS – 53°24'27.09" N 6° 7'26.69" W

The course heads out in an anti-clockwise direction, then cuts back inland. Players must hit the fairway to have any hope of a good score here, with a number of traps making positional play critical.

Opposite: New Zealand's Michael Campbell won the Irish Open the last time it was staged at Portmarnock in 2003.

Hole 1
Par 4
417 yards

Portmarnock's opener demands an accurate drive, with the estuary to the right. Most will look to aim to the left of the fairway, hoping to cut the ball back to the right with a fade; anything too straight is liable to run into thick rough as the hole turns gently. More sand awaits either side of the green, so aim for the centre and play for par.

Hole 2
Par 4
411 yards

If you can get a good drive away, you will be in position to play a mid- or short iron into this two-tiered green where the pin position can dictate your strategy. Two fairway traps lie in wait on the right, and there is heavy rough to the left. There is a lot of sand around the putting surface; most notably a trio of pot bunkers lie to the left side.

Hole 3
Par 4
398 yards

The hole sweeps gently to the left, but there are no fairway traps to contend with, so players can pick a line over the corner and let fly. Ideally, the best angle to approach from is the right-centre of the fairway. A large bunker lies 60 yards short of the green, so running the ball in is not an option. Three small pot bunkers guard the contoured putting surface.

Hole 5
Par 4
442 yards

Long-time club pro Harry Bradshaw, one of Ireland's greatest players, always rated the 5th hole as the club's best. The tee shot is blind, and you need a strong drive to reach the fairway. This is pinched tight with dunes, pot bunkers and penal rough, and the putting surface slopes from the back. This is a stunning hole that asks questions from tee to green.

Hole 6
Par 5
603 yards

A great par 5 that will be a three-shotter for all but the longest of hitters; one fairway trap lurks on the right and the landing zone at around 250 yards is very tight. If laying up, there is a pond to the left side of the fairway that will need your attention. Aim for the right-centre of the green, as a deep pot bunker lurks to the left.

Hole 7
Par 3
184 yards

The first of the short holes and a clever one at that; depending on the wind, it will be a solid mid-iron to a green that has bunkers on either side. There are also raised mounds protecting the entrance to the putting surface, which features a number of changes in elevation. From the tee, this hole is beautifully framed by low dunes and gorse bushes.

Hole 8
Par 4
427 yards

Gorse and lush rough lines the fairway on this pretty par 4 that sweeps to the left, so positional play from the tee is the priority here, and right-centre is the ideal target to aim for. There are no fairway traps, but the big test is the second shot to a green that is perched on a slight plateau. One solitary greenside bunker guards the left entrance.

Hole 9
Par 4
454 yards

A great finish to the front nine. The ideal shot shape is a gentle fade, so aim left of the fairway to cut the ball back. Be careful, though, as bunkers lurk on both sides. The approach is a beauty with gorse bushes making it visually stunning. Two deep pot bunkers sit to the right of the green's entrance, and two crisp shots are needed to finish the outward stretch with a par.

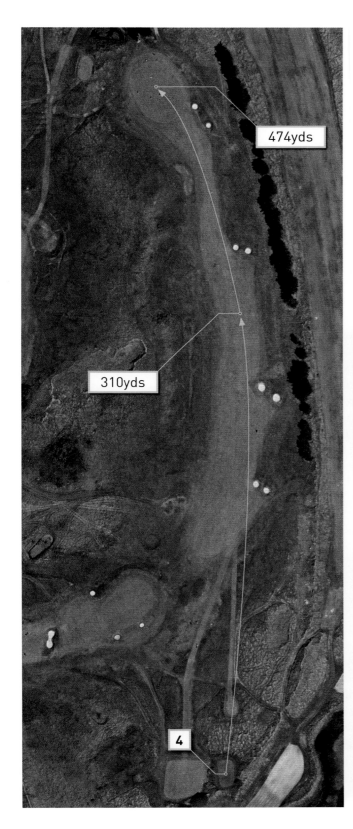

474yds

310yds

4

Hole 4 – *Par 4* – **474 yards**

This hole is ranked as the toughest at Portmarnock, and for good reason. Another two-shotter that sweeps gently to the left; again, right-centre of the fairway offers the best position for your approach shot. However, care must be taken here, as there is a series of bunkers to deal with all the way up to the hole, as well as trees and lush rough. The green has a number of contours, so ball position is crucial to make par or better. Two solid blows will be needed if you are to have any hopes of hitting the target in regulation. Even from the white tees it is still a daunting challenge at 441 yards – and for many amateurs it will be played as a par 5.

Course Guide 10–18

The inward nine has some classic holes, as well as one of the most thrilling finishes in the game. This is where the course really begins to bite, from the magnificent par-3 15th to the long home hole that plays predominantly into the prevailing wind.

Opposite: Portmarnock's par-3 15th is the course's signature hole. With a stiff breeze sweeping in off the sea to the right, and dense dunes left, it pays to hit the target here.

Hole 10
Par 4
370 yards

Players are confronted with a swathe of gorse bushes directly in front of the teeing area, but play over them to find the left side of the fairway. The green is long and narrow, with run-off areas on both sides – especially to the right. It has one bunker to the right, and some players may choose to run in their approach shots if playing from the left-hand side.

Hole 11
Par 4
428 yards

This is a stunning-looking hole where you need to aim right-centre of the fairway to find the best angle from which to approach. Three bunkers sit to the right side, with another two pinching in on the left. The green is kidney-shaped, with two bunkers to the right and one to the left. Aim for the centre of the putting surface and don't get too clever.

Hole 12
Par 3
177 yards

The wind can be a huge factor on this par 3, as you are playing directly out towards the sea. The green is heavily contoured, with a steep bank running off to the right side. Anything long will end up smothered in the deep rough on the banks that envelop the back of the putting surface. This is another wonderful short hole that looks great from the tee.

Hole 13
Par 5
565 yards

A par 5 that is dominated by sand from tee to green; the fairway is relatively generous but there are no fewer than seven bunkers cleverly positioned to catch errant tee shots. From here the hole turns gently left and then right, and for those players who choose to attack in two, another cluster of sand traps lies to the right side of the green.

Hole 14
Par 4
411 yards

From the tee, you can see everything in front of you, and it's best to fire right as a trio of pot bunkers lie on the left side of the fairway. Once in position, a high-flying approach is needed to carry two deep greenside traps front-left. Sitting on a slight bank, the green slopes from the back with a subtle tier towards the front.

Hole 16
Par 5
577 yards

A three-shotter that is full of character, and one that is reachable for the longer hitters if the wind is helping. As the hole turns to the right, players may look to cut the corner over two fairway bunkers. A trio of traps then runs across the middle of the fairway, and four more bunkers lurk by the green with the backdrop complemented by trees and gorse.

Hole 17
Par 4
472 yards

Now heading back to the clubhouse, this long par 4 demands an arrow-straight drive with two bunkers either side of the fairway. The land is fairly flat here, with an open view all the way up to the green. The approach also needs to be accurate to avoid a series of traps at the front, while anything long could run into a ring of gorse bushes at the back.

Hole 18
Par 4
452 yards

Another long par 4 to finish. The green is framed by low dunes, with the clubhouse beyond. The safest landing zone is left-centre of the fairway, as three traps are gathered around the 250-yard mark on the right. Depending on the wind, you may need something more than a mid-iron to take you to the putting surface with three bunkers protecting its entrance.

Hole 15 – *Par 3* – **204 yards**

This is one of the world's greatest par-3 holes, and one of the most daunting. Portmarnock's 15th was designed some 31 years after Pickeman and Ross had finished work on the original 18, and ever since the first Irish Open in 1927, many of the world's best players have been left frustrated but charmed by its fiendish ways. Out-of-bounds, the beach and the Irish Sea are immediately to the right, and anything left will be buried in the dense rough of the dunes. It offers one of the more imposing views on the course and many players can be spooked out by the challenge. Three bunkers lie in wait for anything short, and the hole drops down on the left side of the green – an epic one-shotter.

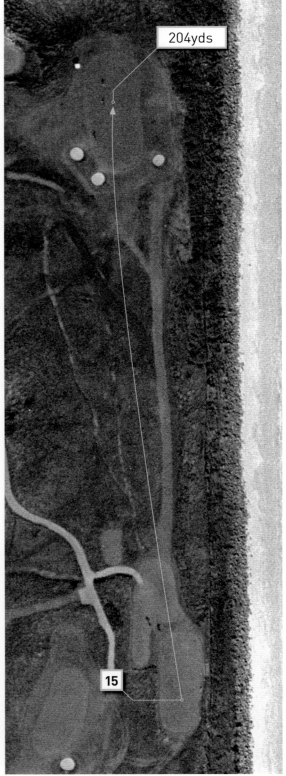

ROYAL BIRKDALE

Royal Birkdale has built a reputation as the finest golf course in England, and its imposing layout makes it one of the most exciting to play. With monstrous dunes and sandhills that line the fairways, not to mention the warm welcome you will receive, there are few courses that can match the experience of playing here.

In England's north west you will find a number of wonderful links layouts that have come to define this corner of the country simply as "England's Golf Coast". From Royal Lytham & St Annes to Formby, Hillside and Southport & Ainsdale, golfers are blessed with some of the most rugged settings in which to play the game. But Royal Birkdale is arguably the region's number-one course and, for many, the standout links in the country.

Since 1954 the course has been a firm favourite with the R&A. It hosted its first Open that year, and golf's oldest major championship has made eight subsequent visits to Birkdale. It also hosted the Ryder Cups of 1965 and 1969, and in 2013 will welcome the over 50s for the Senior Open Championship.

The original club was formed in 1889 by a group of locals for the cost of around £7. Five years later it moved to its current site, just two miles from the Irish Sea coast. George Lowe, who had created the nearby links at Royal Lytham, was credited with the early design work, but the championship layout we are familiar with today did not come about until the 1920s when Fred G. Hawtree and JH Taylor set about a major redesign.

> ## "Birkdale is one of the finest tests you will find anywhere in the world."
>
> *Padraig Harrington*

They created a masterpiece, and what you see is what you get at Birkdale; from the tee, towering dunes beautifully frame its holes and the course is simplified with a minimal number of blind shots. It means straight hitters will be rewarded and the fate of your round is almost totally dictated by your own game. That said, when the wind is up it can be a beast, despite those imposing sandhills partially protecting the golfer from the elements.

No two holes are the same as the layout cuts back and forth in direction, and while the course has been renovated over the years, much of the original routing by Hawtree and Taylor remains evident today.

The pedigree of Birkdale is enhanced by the roll call of its Open champions. Australian Peter Thomson, a five-time winner of the Claret Jug, won twice at Birkdale in 1954 and 1965.

Below left: A 17-year-old Justin Rose finishes his 1998 Open challenge by holing a 60-yard pitch for a closing birdie three. The Englishman finished in a tie for fourth place to win the coveted Silver Medal, awarded to the highest-placed amateur.

Opposite: Royal Birkdale has been a regular home of the Open Championship since 1954.

Arnold Palmer and Lee Trevino were victorious in 1961 and 1971 respectively. The enigmatic Johnny Miller held off the challenge of a swashbuckling Seve Ballesteros in 1976, and Tom Watson, arguably the finest exponent of links golf, claimed his fifth Open here in 1983. Ian Baker-Finch and Mark O'Meara, both fine players of their generation, won in 1991 and 1998 respectively.

During its most recent staging of the Open in 2008, players were met with fierce gales that for two days made the course almost unplayable.

On that occasion, reigning champion Padraig Harrington held firm to see off the challenge of Greg Norman. Most memorably, the Irishman effectively sealed victory with one of the finest shots in Open history when he struck a crisp 5-wood to 4 feet on the par-5 17th, setting up an eagle three to hand him a four-shot lead.

Arguably, no Open venue can rival Birkdale's

quartet of short holes, with the 181-yard 12th the pick as players are forced to hit to the course's smallest green, guarded to the left and front with deep bunkering, and to the rear with dense duneland. But as well as the challenge, there is so much to love about Birkdale. It is a fantastic spectator course, with its dunes creating natural grandstands from tee to green. And its ambience cannot be matched as players complete their round under the watchful eyes of those sitting in the famous Art Deco-style clubhouse behind the 18th green.

> # "There is nothing like a range of noble sandhills to set the heart of the average golfer leaping with excitement."
>
> *Bernard Darwin*

COURSE GUIDE 1–9

Course yardage – White tees 6,817 yards
Course GPS – 53°37'19.72" N 3°1'52.62" W

Starting with a tough par 4, Birkdale's famous routing is immediately evident as the course twists and turns in direction. Two fine par 3s complement a number of left-to-right doglegs during the opening nine holes.

Opposite: Colin Montgomerie plays to the green of the tough par-4 6th – a par 5 for Birkdale's members – during the 2008 Open Championship.

Hole 1
Par 4
450 yards

A very tough opening hole with a fairway that snakes left and right to a sloping green. Out-of-bounds hugs the right side, while the landing zone is narrow around the 230-yard mark, bringing the rough and a left-side bunker into play. Longer hitters may choose to shave off some of the left corner, but an accurate second is needed to hold the sloping green.

Hole 2
Par 4
418 yards

The fairway opens up slightly at the 260-yard mark, but two deep bunkers lie on the right side to thwart long hitters. The approach is the tricky shot as the hole narrows towards a small green with testing run-off areas. A bunker looms 30 yards in front of the putting surface waiting to gobble up anything short, and if you go long the rough is penal at the back.

Hole 3
Par 4
406 yards

A drive to the left side of the fairway will open up the hole for an easier approach. However, two bunkers lie here that can ruin any hopes of making par. The green is oval-shaped with bunkers at the front, while run-off areas again mean distance control is crucial. Adopt a safety-first approach and play to the centre of the putting surface.

Hole 4
Par 3
200 yards

A great par 3 featuring an elevated tee that demands a crisp, high-flying shot to hit the heart of a kidney-shaped green. A lot of players will take an extra club here as sand guards the front-left approach. Out-of-bounds is to the right, and an area of punitive rough awaits those who stray long and left. This is the longest of the par 3s on the course.

Hole 5
Par 4
343 yards

A dogleg right, this hole is framed by rugged dunes. Many players will attempt to reduce the yardage by firing their drives over the right corner of the fairway. Beware though, the rough is punishing and the length of the hole makes position more important from the tee. The green is surrounded by sand, so a soft-landing short-iron is needed to hold the putting surface.

Hole 7
Par 3
177 yards

The tee shot requires nothing more than a mid-iron, but you will need to hit your target as the putting surface is totally surrounded by bunkers. The pros will play this hole from a different line to amateurs, but the same shot is needed with a high-flying strike that must carry the rough and rugged landscape between the tee boxes and the green.

Hole 8
Par 4
413 yards

This is a narrow driving hole with towering dunes all the way up the left side of the fairway. Two bunkers sit on the right, and the hole rolls gently round to the left to another elevated green, which is protected with deep bunkers that can be treacherous to escape from. The green is quite large, but very undulating, making two-putting tough.

Hole 9
Par 4
410 yards

The tee shot is blind, so players need to pick their line from the tee and commit to the shot. A good drive should leave a mid-iron approach as the fairway sweeps gently downhill. Beware though, because the green is slightly elevated with a steep drop at the back. Gorse bushes lurk perilously close to the right side, while two bunkers narrow the entrance.

488yds

450yds

270yds

6

Hole 6 – *Par 5* – **488 yards**

The 6th is a par 5 for the amateurs, but a very tough par 4 for the pros during the Open Championship. However you play it, you need to plot your way to the green as the hole sweeps round to the right. In position from the tee, a lay-up approach isn't made easy as the narrow fairway features many humps and hollows. The kidney-shaped green is protected at the front with three sand traps, and the putting surface is also elevated with notable contours. Birkdale's distinctive mounding envelops the right, where penal rough will swallow errant shots. This is a superb hole that can be hugely rewarding to the professionals in the Open, while also equally damaging to the Birkdale members who dare to take it on.

Course Guide 10–18

Elevated tees are a key feature on the inward stretch, and the eclectic mix of holes only adds to the playing experience. For amateurs, back-to-back par 5s mean there is an opportunity to make a score late on. But accuracy is essential for success.

Hole 10
Par 4
408 yards

A tough dogleg left; players often play for position from the tee, maybe with an iron, otherwise they may run out of fairway. However, if you leave your tee shot short, you could find yourself playing blind as the green is tucked away around the corner. Some will attempt to cut the corner, but they will need an element of fortune to find the fairway over the dunes.

Hole 11
Par 4
378 yards

Playing from an elevated tee, you can see everything in front of you on this superb par 4. Again, some players will take an iron or 3-wood just to find position as the fairway traps come into play around the 260-yard mark. The second shot is key because the putting surface is again heavily contoured. Get yourself in position and aim for the centre of the green.

Hole 13
Par 4
433 yards

Three deep, well-positioned sand traps lurk on the right side of the fairway. When the course is playing firm in the summer, they are reachable for those hitting driver. Keeping to the left side of the fairway will open up the approach, but you will still need a decent strike to find the target in two. Sandhills and gorse bushes dominate the backdrop of this green.

Hole 14
Par 3
199 yards

Another great one-shot hole; players will need to hit the heart of the putting surface as there are many run-off areas that feed down into the cavernous traps which encircle it. The elevated tee makes club selection tricky, and the green slopes at the front so another full carry is needed. This is the last of the par 3s, with three par 5s (for amateurs) still to come.

Hole 15
Par 5
544 yards

Fifteen bunkers feature on this hole, where power and precision are needed if you want to attack the green in two. Firstly, the drive needs to avoid the deep sand traps on the right side of the fairway. Those choosing to lay up will have to contend with a cluster of menacing bunkers that lurk ominously 100 yards short of the heavily contoured green.

Hole 16
Par 4
370 yards

This hole is a subtle dogleg right. Longer hitters will fire to the right corner of the fairway, though it requires a big carry over dense rough. Pot bunkers then come into play for the approach shot; the green sits on top of a hill where balls not holding the surface will feed back down into trouble. It's best to be cautious from the tee and then play a short iron to the green.

Hole 17
Par 5
527 yards

The drive needs to be aimed between two dunes, as the fairway turns round to the left with out-of-bounds on the right. Three deep pot bunkers guard the green, which was rebuilt in preparation for the 2008 Open Championship, and now features many dramatic changes in elevation. Keeping your ball on the short grass is key because the rough on the dunes is simply punishing.

Hole 18
Par 5
472 yards

The pros play this as a par 4 from an elevated tee, while for amateurs, it offers a closing birdie opportunity as a par 5. From the amateur tees, you have to play through the middle of two sand dunes. Fairway bunkers come into play from 230 yards and it's out-of-bounds again on the right. More deep bunkers ensure the approach is even trickier, while run-offs make the green challenging.

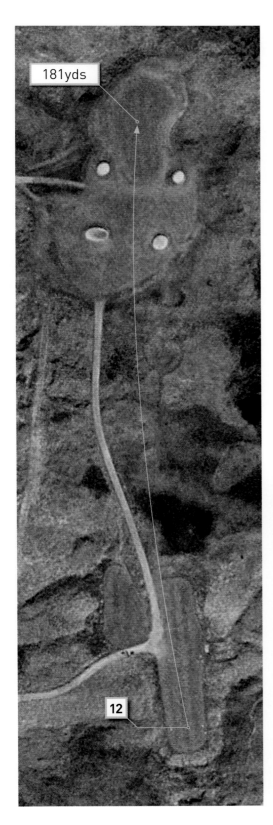

181yds

12

Hole 12 – *Par 3* – **181 yards**

This stunning par 3, set in the dunes, was only designed and built in 1963 by Fred W. Hawtree, although his father, Fred G. Hawtree, had originally planned it for the course back in 1932. It was discarded then due to a lack of funds. Playing to a narrow green that is framed with dense mounds and heavy rough, players must make sure they take enough club to avoid coming up short, as their balls will drift back down the steep slope at the front. Two deep pot bunkers sit either side of the green, and several run-off areas add to the challenge. A natural amphitheatre, the hole is one of the course's best viewing spots for spectators at the Open Championship.

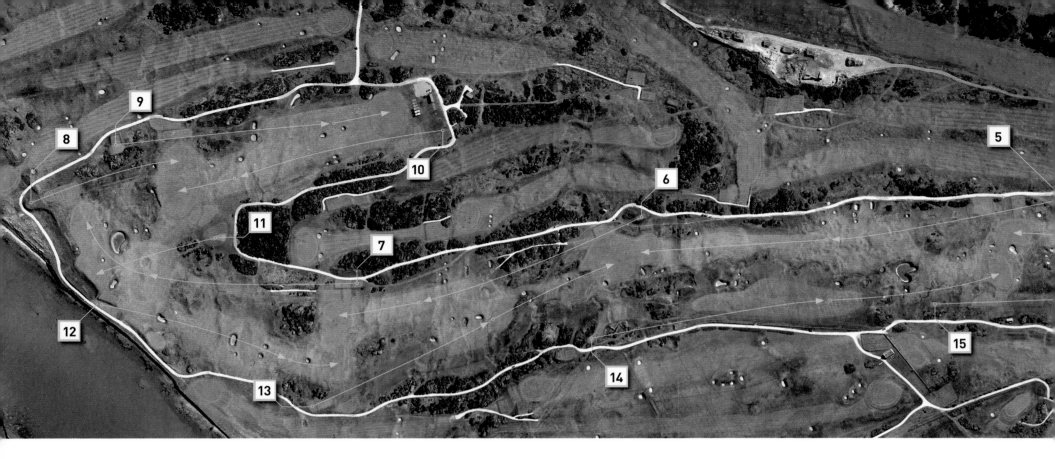

Above: The most famous stretch of holes in the world makes up St Andrews' Old Course.

Opposite: It's there! One of the game's most defining images as Seve Ballesteros punches the air in delight after making a final-hole birdie to seal victory in the 1984 Open.

ST ANDREWS OLD COURSE

No course in the world serves up such an emotional experience as St Andrews' Old Course – with a history that is unmatched in the game. With its huge double greens, undulating fairways and the myriad of bunkers, it is a layout where all your shot-making skills are needed for success.

It is the most famous and sacred golfing land in the world, and to play here remains one of the most awe-inspiring experiences. St Andrews' Old Course is the Home of Golf, and when you tee off at the 1st, with the imposing R&A clubhouse just yards away, you cannot help but feel the emotions, knowing you are following in the footsteps of every golfing great who has played here.

There is a received wisdom that all golfers must play a round on the Old Course before they die. It sounds extreme, yes, but it is the

one golf course that stands above all others in reverence and history, and its appeal as a public links makes it even more alluring.

Golf was first played here in the 1400s. Its original designer is unknown, and the course's early layout was really a process of evolution. Old Tom Morris made notable changes in the late 1800s and the renowned Dr Alister MacKenzie also lent his hand to renovation work here. In the modern age, there have been, and continue to be, minor changes to counter the progression of the game as the Old Course prepares to stage

the Open Championship. That even the smallest of tweaks is met with disbelief and controversy speaks of the course's reputation and standing.

The Old Course has hosted the Open on 28 occasions since 1873, more than any other course. Today it is the only venue on the R&A's rota to welcome the game's oldest major championship on a regular basis, with the tournament returning every five years. South African Louis Oosthuizen won the last time the Claret Jug was contested on the famous links and it remains the dream of every top player

to win the Open at St Andrews. All the greats have played and won here, among them Bobby Jones, Jack Nicklaus and Tiger Woods. Indeed it was Woods who set an Open scoring record (to par) at the Old Course, winning in 2000 with a four-round total of 19 under par.

Though you wouldn't immediately say the course was a tough test, it can catch you out, especially if you are a first-timer, unaware of its subtle defences and 112 bunkers. But this only adds to its appeal, and once you have played it you will be itching to return. What you will

Google™ earth

notice above all are the huge double greens and the daunting, cavernous bunkers that are beautifully revetted.

The layout plays as a classic out-and-back links; after teeing off on the 1st and pitching over the Swilcan Burn, you head out north west of the town, then face a looping quartet on the 8th, 9th, 10th and 11th before the layout takes you back home from the 12th. Because of this, depending on wind direction, players can have two contrasting nines.

Once you approach the closing stretch, you'll find yourself playing to the galleries of the St Andrews public as townsfolk go about their everyday business. And the finish is as

grand as anywhere; the Road Hole 17th is one of the most imposing challenges in major championships, while the 18th, which runs adjacent to the opening hole, serves up one of the most spine-tingling feelings as you cross the Swilcan Bridge and play over the Valley of Sin which lurks at the front of the green.

The Old Course has been known to get the better of some who play here. Such is the privilege to tee it up that visitors can be overcome with emotion, their nerves shredded, knowing that this is such a historic moment in their golfing careers. That said, they would always want to come back. How could you not want to come back to the Old Course?

"This is the origin of the game, golf in its purest form. And it's still played that way on a course seemingly untouched by time."

Arnold Palmer

COURSE GUIDE 1–9

Opposite: The Swilcan Burn protects the front of the 1st green. Players face a tricky early test of ball control as they pitch over the hazard to the putting surface.

A run of par 4s gets your round started, and course strategy is paramount. If you can find position off the tee, you will be able to attack the greens on the front nine. But if you stray off line with the driver, your score will suffer as a result.

Hole 2
Dyke
Par 4 – 453 yards

Gorse bushes line the right side of the fairway on this tricky par 4 that sweeps gently to the right off the tee. Cheape's bunker sits at the 300-yard mark from the championship tees, but on dry days when the fairways are fiery, even the mid-length amateur can fall foul of it. The big test is the second shot to a green that is narrow and hard to hold with a deep bunker front-left.

Hole 3
Cartgate-out
Par 4 – 397 yards

The landing zone of this short par 4 is relatively wide, but there is a line of deep pot bunkers hugging the right side. If players find the fairway, it is a wedge or a short iron into a large double green – shared with the 15th. Cartgate bunker is short left of the approach and the putting surface runs down into this trap, while also sloping off to the right-hand side.

Hole 4
Ginger Beer
Par 4 – 480 yards

A par 4 that really tests your course management, with small pot bunkers either side of the fairway. Gorse bushes line the right side, so you need to keep it straight. The approach then narrows over mounds and humps, and the green is peppered with deep bunkers that you cannot see from ground level. Chasing a tricky pin position can lead to a bogey or worse.

Hole 5
O'Cross-out
Par 5 – 568 yards

Small pot bunkers abound here, with seven guarding the right side of the fairway. Players should keep the ball left if possible, to give themselves a better opening to the hole if they choose to take on this par 5 in two. Bunkers narrow the neck of the approach 60 yards short of the green, which is protected with more sand traps to the left.

Hole 6
Heathery-out
Par 4 – 412 yards

Deep bunkers again guard the landing zone for the drive; but the longer hitters may choose to thread their tee shots through the middle, taking them out of play. The fairway then hits a slope 70 yards short of the boot-shaped green, which mercifully has no bunkers. The biggest danger here is going right, where dense gorse is waiting to swallow your ball.

Hole 7
High-out
Par 4 – 371 yards

Short hitters need to be aware of the gorse on the right, although the fairway is relatively bunker-free on this short par 4 that makes you think about position rather than power. The green, which is shared with the par-3 11th, is angled to the right, and the Strath bunker lurks at its front. Go long with your approach to find the flatter section of the putting surface.

Hole 8
Short
Par 3 – 175 yards

It may look easy, and with a huge double green that is shared with the 10th, you have a fair target to aim at. However, dense rough and mounds guard the front of the green, and you have to hit a high, soft-landing shot to hold it and ensure you don't have too much to do with the putter. Players can be lured into taking too little club here.

Hole 9
End
Par 4 – 353 yards

A driveable par 4 for the pros, and many amateurs will also take their chances here. Two small pot bunkers sit in the middle of the fairway 90 and 60 yards short of the green, so you can lay up short of them and then play a straightforward pitch to a putting surface with no sand defences. Whatever way you choose to play it, it's a birdie chance.

Hole 1 – *Burn* – **Par 4 – 376 yards**

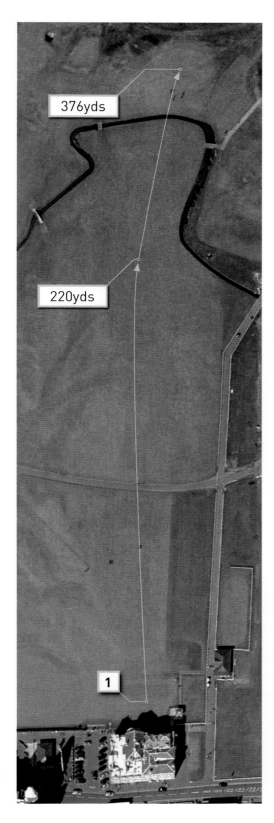

It features no bunkers, with a fairway so wide you could land a jumbo jet on it, and yet so many players succumb to the pressure of playing the most famous opening hole in the game. From the tee, with the R&A clubhouse towering behind, players must suck it all in. Out-of-bounds is right, but the comfort of the adjacent 18th fairway means there is plenty of room to the left. The pros will lay up well short of the Swilcan Burn with either a long iron or a 3-wood, while most amateurs will fire their drives over Grannie Clark's Wynd – the public pathway that crosses the fairway – and then pitch on to the green, which slopes from back to front. Don't pitch short of a forward flag, as your ball can easily roll back into the burn.

COURSE GUIDE 10–18

The run for home gets more interesting as townsfolk watch your every move, with anything right finding the out-of-bounds. Again position is key, although a good deal of brute force is also needed, especially on the testing par-4 17th.

Hole 10
Bobby Jones
Par 4 – 386 yards

This par 4 runs alongside the 9th, and the pros are unlikely to take on the green as the entrance narrows with two bunkers on the right side. Position, therefore, is key, and a 3-wood leaves merely a wedge in, with the pin of the par-3 8th to the right. Be wary of going long with your approach as the back of the green has testing run-offs and rough.

Hole 11
High-in
Par 3 – 174 yards

This is a very tricky par 3 because the green is narrow and you once again have to carry Strath bunker, but from an altogether different angle than when playing the par-4 7th. Therefore, another high-flying 7- or 6-iron is required depending on the wind. The big danger is going long, as the green runs down a steep bank at the rear, leaving a tough chip back up.

Hole 12
Heathery-in
Par 4 – 348 yards

Depending on the wind direction during the front nine, the back nine may represent a different test as you head back towards the town. Here an accurate drive is needed, with four deep traps lurking in the middle of the fairway. The green, shared with the 6th, features only one bunker but it runs down to the right side – so place your approach wisely.

Hole 13
O'Cross-in
Par 4 – 465 yards

A very demanding par 4 that tests both the drive and approach shot. Players must aim to the left side of the fairway to avoid a trio of traps that sit at its right-centre. Then a blind approach is played over sweeping mounds, with the neck of the green narrowed and with a ragged grassy area threatening to kick the ball into the Lion's Mouth bunker short-left.

Hole 14
Long
Par 5 – 618 yards

Out-of-bounds lines the right side of the fairway and The Beardies bunkers sit to the left. Once in position in the fairway, you will catch sight of the looming threat of Hell bunker – a deep, cavernous sand trap that sits 90 yards short of the green, making a lay-up more testing than it should be. The putting surface slopes at the front and back, and can be difficult to hold.

Hole 15
Cartgate-in
Par 4 – 455 yards

With the right side out-of-bounds, a lot of players tend to bail out left although caution must be taken, as a bunker lies centre-left of the fairway. It can be tricky to find the right position on the green, because it is protected with a gentle hump at the front as well as a small pot bunker, so the ball may need to be played through the air on approach.

Hole 16
Corner of the Dyke
Par 4 – 423 yards

There is out-of-bounds once again on the right side of the fairway, and it's all about your position off the tee. The drive is made extremely difficult as the Principal's Nose and Deacon's Sime bunkers lurk left. If players choose to lay up they will need more club to fire into a green that slopes down to the right, making ball control tougher.

Hole 18
Tom Morris
Par 4 – 357 yards

As on the opening hole, there are no bunkers and the length is modest. However, as the crowds mingle up the right side on the Links Road, you need to fire left-centre of the fairway, back over Grannie Clark's Wynd. Some pros will take it on and get there, but for mere mortals it's a drive and then a short iron over the Valley of Sin and on to the green.

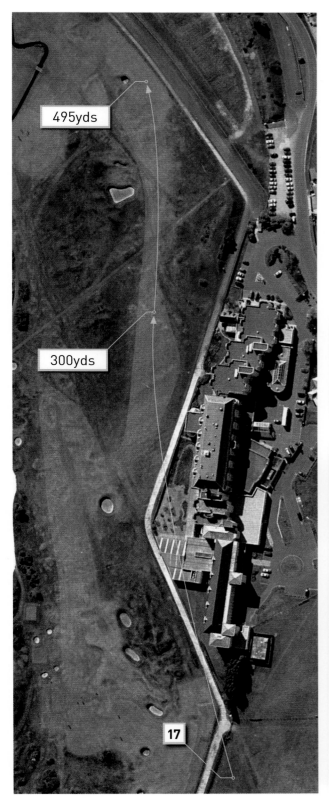

495yds

300yds

17

Hole 17 – *Road* – **Par 4 – 495 yards**

One of the most famous holes in major championship golf; from the back tees, the drive forces players to cut the corner of the Old Course Hotel – which is out-of-bounds – in order to hit a sliver of a fairway. It is one of the most demanding tee shots, with heavy rough left for those who are too straight, or draw the ball. Even in position, many players will be hitting long irons into a green that rises and then slopes off towards the road at the back. However, the 17th's most demonic feature is the Road bunker, a formidable sand trap that is treacherously deep. It has been the downfall of many Open hopefuls over the years. Tommy Nakajima took a quintuple bogey here in the 1978 Open, needing four shots to get out.

The notorious and punishing Hell bunker on the 14th, which makes lay-ups on this par 5 difficult. During the 2000 Open Championship, Jack Nicklaus found sand here and ended up signing for a ten.

WENTWORTH WEST

In the post-war years, Wentworth's West course was christened Burma Road owing to its hills and the length of the journey. A long-time regular host to some of the biggest tournaments in the UK, the course has undergone a modern-day redesign to bring it back to the big beast it was always intended to be.

There are few courses that can boast the championship pedigree, and indeed the history, of Wentworth's West course. For many, it has long been the standout inland course in the UK, and being the home of the European Tour, there is certainly something of a sacred feel to it. With its magnificent clubhouse, not to mention the impressive neighbouring East course, Wentworth has become one of the most high-profile venues in the world of golf.

Designed by the great Harry Colt, the West has a wonderful mixture of holes that cut through oak, pine and silver birch trees. There is something of everything; length is needed if you are taking the course on from the backs at just shy of 7,300 yards, but the canny placing

of defences forces players to think about position as well. Fairways sweep up and down, and the changes in elevation make the layout look even more attractive when you stand on the tee and see it all in front of you.

Opened for play in 1926, the West had its reputation enhanced in 1953 when it hosted that year's Ryder Cup, and three years later the World Cup – named the Canada Cup at the time. Today, it is home to the European Tour's flagship event, the BMW PGA Championship, held as the late spring sunshine breaks through every May. The tournament always attracts the continent's top players, with England's Luke Donald winning back-to-back titles in 2011 and 2012.

However, the tournament with which most would associate the course is the World Match Play, which ran at the Surrey venue from 1964 through to 2007. Regularly welcoming the world's best players from both sides of the Atlantic, it was seen as something of an end-of-season duel between the top performers of the year, more often than not featuring a host of major winners and serving up some of the most thrilling golf for worldwide television audiences. For proof you only need look at the names of the Match Play's regular winners, such as Jack Nicklaus, Arnold Palmer and Gary Player in the early days, followed by Severiano Ballesteros and Nick Faldo, and later Ernie Els, the South African a record seven-time winner of the event.

Below left: Englishman Luke Donald won back-to-back BMW PGA Championships at Wentworth in 2011 and 2012.

Opposite: Wentworth's West course forges a path through oaks, pines and silver birches, and its championship length of 7,281 yards makes it one of the toughest inland tests in the UK.

© 2013 Inforterra Ltd and Bluesky
© 2013 Google

1

18

It was Els who was first asked to oversee redesign work on the course in 2005. The general consensus was that the West had lost some of its bite and needed refining to bring it back to play as Colt had originally intended. Els, a resident of the Wentworth Estate since 1998, worked on rebunkering and renovation of the course's greens, while length was added to a number of holes. But Els' biggest change to the layout came in 2009, with a heavy and slightly controversial rejig on the 18th. Once a relatively straightforward par 5, water was added to the front of the green, forcing players to flight long irons in if attempting to reach the putting surface in two.

Despite the changes, Wentworth's West course has, happily, retained much of that classic Colt feel. For shorter hitters, it can undoubtedly become a bit of a slog if their games are off-colour. Its tight, tree-lined fairways mean you must find the straight and narrow from tee to green, and a number of doglegs make positioning all the more important. Sand peppers the landscape, and those changes in elevation, with many greens perched above the fairway, force you to think carefully about club selection. Once more a fitting test, the West is a modern classic in every way.

> "I love it here. Wentworth is a special place."
>
> *Ernie Els*

Google™earth

Course Guide 1–9

If you are looking to make a score, there are more opportunities on the front nine, but you will still need to be on your game. Fairway bunkers make you think about position, but from tee to green there are many defences to overcome.

Course yardage – Championship 7,281 yards
Course GPS – 51° 23'56.68" N 0°35'22.83" W

Opposite: Luke Donald fires to the 8th green during the final round of the BMW PGA Championship in 2012. This testing two-shotter was heavily redesigned by South African Ernie Els in 2009.

Hole 1
Par 4
473 yards

For amateurs, this is a relatively straightforward three-shot hole, but for the professionals, it's a testing par 4 as the fairway sweeps down and up towards the green. There are large traps at the 250- and 280-yard marks. If you get a good drive away, you can attack the green in two, but more bunkers lurk to the left, and the surface slopes off at the front.

Hole 2
Par 3
154 yards

This is a classic short hole that can punish those who make the wrong club selection. The professionals, needing little more than an 8-iron, will be good enough to attack any pin position. However, sand covers all four corners of the green and a large oak tree towers over the right side. The putting surface is raised, so anything short will run back down the steep bank at the front.

Hole 3
Par 4
465 yards

This tough par 4 is played gently uphill and requires two great strikes to find the green in two. Out-of-bounds lines the right side, but a mass of trees makes it unlikely you will find your ball anyway should you fire that way. The best position is left side of the fairway, which should help to open up your approach to another raised green that features many undulations.

Hole 4
Par 5
552 yards

Another hole that differs greatly for the professionals when playing championship golf at Wentworth, as they have to tee off 54 yards further back. The fairway sweeps round to the left, and gently down towards a well-bunkered green. This is a definite birdie chance for the longer hitters, but care must be taken on the putting surface, which slopes from right to left.

Hole 5
Par 3
203 yards

Both power and accuracy are needed here as players will need to fly a long shot into the heart of the green. Bunkers surround the boundary of the putting surface and woodland lurks to the left. Again, the professionals will face a sterner test, with an additional 19 yards making the club of choice a mid- or long iron, even for the best ball-strikers.

Hole 6
Par 4
418 yards

This is a shorter two-shot hole, but even shorter for the Wentworth members who face only 351 yards in total from tee to green. Players have two options; they can go longer off the tee and fly their ball over the three fairway traps from 190 to 245 yards, then play a short pitch to a well-protected green; or they can lay up further back and play a full iron in.

Hole 7
Par 4
396 yards

This hole sweeps steeply down and then up. The drive is tight as trees hug the right side of the fairway close to the tee boxes; taking a full-blooded driver here could result in your ball ending up in the ditch that runs across the fairway just short of 300 yards. Instead, play for position with a 3-wood, and the approach is easier to a two-tiered green that has sand to the right.

Hole 9
Par 4
449 yards

Officially, this is the toughest hole on the course, and there are defences all the way up to the green. Firstly, out-of-bounds hugs the left side in the form of a railway line; secondly, fairway bunkers are positioned both left and right from 240 yards out to 100 yards short of the green; thirdly, the putting surface is small and guarded at the front by more sand.

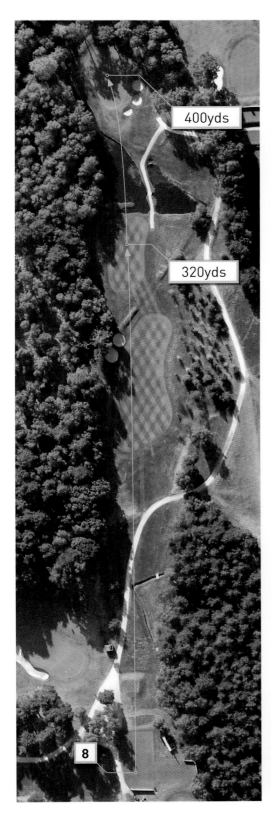

400yds

320yds

8

Hole 8 – *Par 4* – **400 yards**

This is one of the holes that was heavily redesigned by Ernie Els in 2009, and it is highly demanding from tee to green. Again, the tee shot is daunting as trees tighten up the fairway, and it's best to go right (but not too far as those trees will block you out) because the left side brings a solitary fairway bunker into play. If you are in here, going for the green presents a big risk as you have to play over a lake. That water closely guards the front of a narrow, contoured putting surface with a bunker on the right – so players face the prospect of playing back towards the wet stuff from the sand. The green also slopes from the back, and a par here is a solid return.

COURSE GUIDE 10–18

Arguably, the West's back nine delivers even more of a thrill, but patience is needed as a procession of card-wrecking holes lie in wait. From the stunning par-3 10th to the grandstand finish at 18, the West affords little margin for error from the tee.

Opposite: The par-5 17th swings sharply to the left and is a three-shot hole for all but the very best ball-strikers.

Hole 10
Par 3
184 yards

The green is raised with a bunker at the front and another further to the right. A mid-iron is needed, but depending on the wind you may have to take more club. You don't want to come up short, as your ball will drop away if it doesn't find the bunker. From the tee, heather stands between you and the green, giving the hole a very attractive look.

Hole 11
Par 4
405 yards

Another picturesque hole, it rewards those who can get themselves into position from the slightly elevated tee. You fire over a ditch that runs across the fairway, with bunkers either side from around 240 yards. From here, the hole begins to turn round to the left, rising slightly to a green guarded by three bunkers, and which plays semi-blind because of its elevation.

Hole 12
Par 4
520 yards

Like the first hole, this is a par 5 for the members, but a par 4 for the professionals. Aim your tee shot over the right side of the trees that cross the fairway to find the best angle from which to approach. The hole turns left, and if you are on this side, trees will block you out. Once again the green is perched up high, with two large bunkers to its side.

Hole 13
Par 4
470 yards

A difficult par 4 where players must aim to the right side of the fairway from the tee to avoid having their route to the green blocked out. If you go too far right, however, there is danger in the shape of a bunker at 250 yards and pines that hug the fairway, where your ball can kick down. The green is round to the left, and it slopes off at the front.

Hole 14
Par 3
179 yards

A tricky little one-shot hole where you must hit the small green if you hope to make par; anything short and your ball will scurry back down a steep bank that leads up to the putting surface; anything long will nestle in the rough on another bank, and that means you have to play back down the slope. One bunker sits to the right, with another three to the left.

Hole 15
Par 4
481 yards

Perhaps the tightest drive on the course, with dense trees and out-of-bounds squeezing the fairway on both sides. What's more, there is a ditch that snakes its way up the right side, so the best landing zone is on the left, to open up the second, long shot in. Three bunkers guard the putting surface, which slopes right to left with many testing contours.

Hole 16
Par 4
383 yards

A short par 4 by the West's standards, it's out-of-bounds again left and right, with fairway traps coming into play on both sides between 215 and 270 yards. This hole will usually be a 3-wood for the professionals, who need to be in the best position to hit this small green surrounded by many deep traps. It may look easy, but its devilish defences can easily catch you out.

Hole 18
Par 5
539 yards

During his 2009 redesign, Ernie Els raised the green, and an 8-foot-wide brook was added to the front of it. It means players can no longer simply run a long iron in to chase a closing birdie. From the tee, the hole sweeps sharply to the right and some will look to cut the corner. But it's all about that second shot to a tiny green with sand also lurking at the back.

510yds

610yds

310yds

17

Hole 17 – *Par 5* – **610 yards**

One of the most iconic holes on the West course, and a great three-shotter that poses questions at every stage. Playing from an elevated tee, there are no bunkers to contend with on the fairway or, for that matter, anywhere on the hole. Residents' gardens are very much in play on the left side; so players will often choose the safer line out to the right. However, the fairway rolls down that side, and going too far can leave you struggling among the trees. Only the longest hitters will go for this in two, but the contoured green is more welcoming to a floated wedge approach than a bludgeoned wood or long iron, as there are run-offs on both sides, especially the right, which features a steep bank.

Located 60 miles from Barcelona and famed for its tight fairways and challenging water hazards, PGA Catalunya Stadium is one of Europe's finest courses.

SPORTING CLUB BERLIN

Sir Nick Faldo, a master of links golf with three Open Championship wins, brings a touch of Scottish flair to Berlin with his first continental design. One of Germany's premier layouts, the Faldo course at Sporting Club Berlin tests every element of your game.

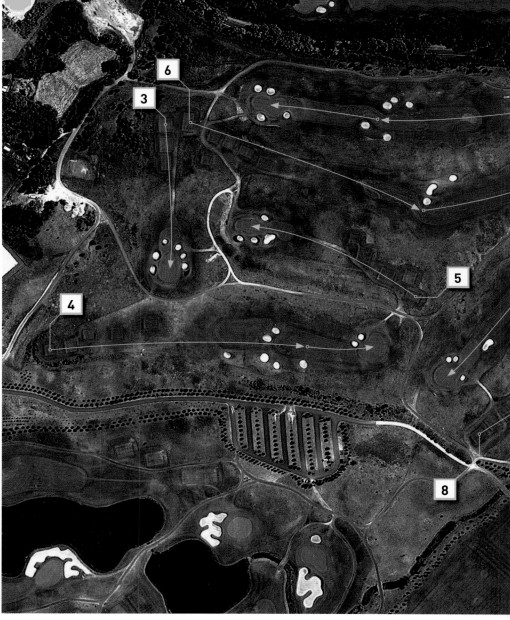

The term "inland links" is an overused one when it comes to golf course design, and even today there are those who insist that there can in fact be no such type of course. An inland links may look like a genuine links, the critics, or golfing purists, will claim, but away from the sea and its complementing coastal breeze, it lacks the true essence of its more exposed forerunner.

There is, some would say, an argument to be heard here. But it is a slightly worn-out view that overlooks the qualities of a fine inland links. And a fine inland links is exactly what can be found at Sporting Club Berlin in the Brandenburg March region of Germany – some 50km outside the capital. It was 1995 when Sir Nick Faldo was first commissioned to go to work here, and by 1997 the six-time Major winner, along with European Golf Design, was busy putting the finishing touches to one of Europe's great modern designs. The following year, it played host to the German Open, and has since become one of its country's most established tournament courses.

The Faldo course is not the only one available at Sporting Club Berlin. Another 45 holes can be played on the estate, where players of all abilities can enjoy the game in the tranquil surroundings of a five-star resort. As well as a quaint little nine-holer and the Stan Eby course, there is a second championship design from the great Arnold Palmer; a parkland test that is equally charming and also senior in years after opening for play in 1995. However, the Faldo course is the greater test and a serious challenge for even the most competent of players.

Its length is not the main factor. From the men's tees it stretches to 6,665 yards, while the pros will play from the tips at a full 7,093. But Faldo – one of the greatest exponents of utilizing course management skills to good effect – was never likely to lend his name to a course that failed to put a high value on an astute golfing brain. As a result, the course can be rewarding to those who display creativity, while others will be suitably punished for attacking without due care and attention, especially from the tee. There are the usual defences one has to consider: fairways that snake a menacing path through man-made dunes; deep, wispy rough that swells to the

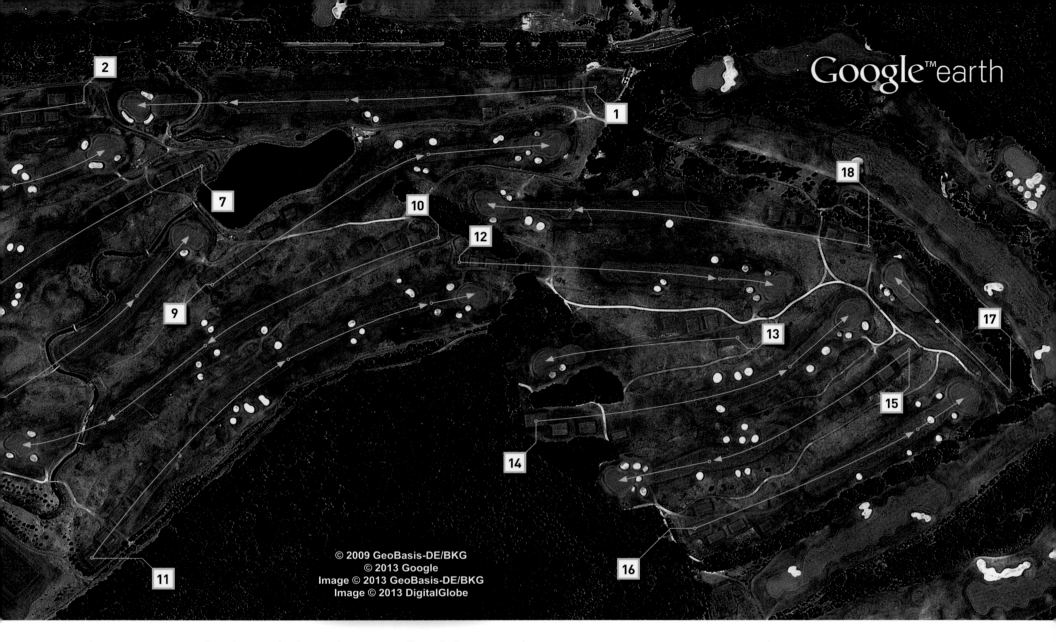

Google™earth

corners of every green; putting surfaces that are elevated, with sweeping borrows and fiendish run-off areas; and cavernous pot bunkers that are hidden from your scouting eye.

Indeed, it is the bunkering that is perhaps the most challenging aspect of the Faldo course. Well positioned throughout the layout, they are punishing in both depth and size, with thick heather sprinkled around their borders. The fairways, rolling in nature and defined by gentle humps and hollows, can easily channel any ball that strays off line. And once you are in, it's very much a case of taking your medicine and

playing safe to get yourself out; the key is to not get greedy.

There are other notable challenges, like the cross burn that runs across the entrance to the 1st green and the lay-up area of the par-5 10th. But, generally speaking, it is the sand and acute undulations that most frequently demand your close attention.

The course is all the more impressive since Faldo and the team at European Golf Design worked from bare, flat land. They have designed a special track that, inland links or not, should be appreciated simply as that.

"A golf course that inspires players to dig deep and push their golf to the very limits."

Sir Nick Faldo

Below left: Fierce pot bunkers, topped with dense heather, will pose the biggest threat for errant ball-strikers from both the tee and fairway.

Opposite: The Faldo course lies at the heart of the magnificent Sporting Club Resort, with the Stan Ebay and Arnold Palmer layouts either side.

Course Guide 1–9

Course yardage – Yellow tees 6,665 yards
Course GPS – 52°14'19.99" N 14°1'40.24" E

Opposite: Making a birdie on the par-5 6th is dependent on avoiding the myriad sand traps that pepper the fairway.

Right from the start, the course's defences stare you in the face. Those who are too aggressive and attempt to overpower the course will find themselves in trouble. The best advice is to try to build an early score through positional play.

Hole 1
Par 5
547 yards

This is a great opening hole that could reward those who take on the challenge with a birdie. Two pot bunkers lie to the left side at 280 yards, and there are a number of undulations in the fairway, so you may be playing your second from a downhill lie. In that case, attacking the green in two is risky as a water hazard snakes across its entrance some 70 yards short.

Hole 2
Par 4
390 yards

A posse of bunkers on both sides of the fairway come into play at 240 yards, and the landing zone is pinched very tight around this area, making the drive difficult. The ideal line is left-centre, but the approach to the green is tough with bunkers positioned cleverly on both sides. The putting surface is kidney-shaped, narrowing towards the back.

Hole 3
Par 3
185 yards

The first of the par 3s, where seven pot bunkers surround the putting surface. The white tees are on a slightly different angle to the left, and the best strategy is to aim at the trio of sand traps on this side of the green, with a fade bringing the ball softly back to your target. The green opens up more towards the back, and it's better to err on the long side.

Hole 4
Par 4
378 yards

This hole features a number of sand traps, with fairway undulations adding to the test, so players must counter the threat of downhill lies. The first decision to make is whether to play over the traps that cut across the fairway at 250 yards, or lay up short of them. More sand lurks further right, and the green has two small pot bunkers to its left entrance.

Hole 5
Par 3
214 yards

Again, a number of teeing options create a very different test, but from the white pegs you will have to fly a large bunker that sits at the green's left entrance. The length of the hole dictates that you will need to hit a long iron or hybrid, and while there is a landing zone short of the green, its contours can easily take your ball off on a different course.

Hole 7
Par 4
439 yards

Rated as the course's toughest hole, the 7th presents a devilishly difficult test from the tee. From 230 yards, sand dominates, with no fewer than eight fairway bunkers peppering the landing zone up to 290 yards. If a drive can be threaded through the middle, it's a mid-iron into a green, which has two small pot bunkers to the right entrance, with another lurking left.

Hole 8
Par 4
381 yards

The hole wends its way gently to the left, and a stream runs across the fairway at 170 yards and then up the left side to 270. The best line into the green is from this side, but aiming left and fading the ball right is not the worst strategy. The green is slightly raised with a number of run-off areas, and a single trap lies to the right-hand side.

Hole 9
Par 4
447 yards

The outward nine ends with a very tough two-shotter that doglegs to the right – a good carry is needed to reach the fairway at 200 yards, but the first obstacle comes with the bunkers at 260. The fairway is narrow and the entrance to the green undulating and pinched tight by sand traps either side. Par here is always a good score.

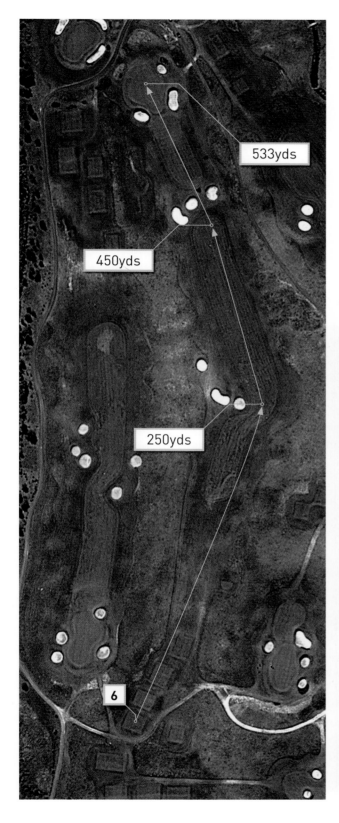

Hole 6 – *Par 5* – **533 yards**

The 6th is a sweeping dogleg left, with bunkers guarding the corner to catch out those who attempt to shorten the hole for the second shot. There isn't much room on the fairway to the right side, so attacking from the tee may be the best option. Players can run a 3-wood into the green, but bunkers narrow the entrance on both sides, with another pot bunker lurking back-right. Also, a cluster of sand traps run across the fairway 90 yards short of the putting surface, so you need to clear these. If playing the hole as a three-shotter, it's best to lay up short of the sand and then pitch over it to a green that slopes in all directions. Depending on a good drive, a birdie opportunity awaits.

COURSE GUIDE 10–18

A wonderful mix of holes form the back nine, from long par 4s to stunning par 3s. Birdie opportunities open up at back-to-back par 5s at 10 and 11. But it is the bunkering and how you tackle it that will dictate the outcome of your round.

Opposite: The tree-lined par-3 13th offers an alternative backdrop to the otherwise open feel of the Faldo course. Word of warning: don't go long or left.

Hole 10
Par 5
558 yards

The back nine starts with this attractive-looking par 5 that plays straight from tee to green, despite the drive favouring a soft draw. Course management is important and if you are chasing a birdie, you will first need to avoid the bunkers at 280 yards. A stream snakes its way across the fairway 100 yards short of the green, so it's a bold play to take it on in two.

Hole 11
Par 5
570 yards

From tee to green, 14 bunkers come into play, and a smart strategy is needed to avoid them as you plot your way to the putting surface. The sand fest starts at 235 yards on the right-hand side, with another three traps nearby. For those who choose to lay up, there is also a cluster of bunkers that juts into the fairway 150 yards short of the green.

Hole 12
Par 4
377 yards

After two tough par 5s, the 12th is a straight-up-and-down par 4 that plays over rolling dunes with two fairway traps lurking to the right at 240 yards. Beyond these, the landing zone opens up, with nothing more than a wedge needed to find the green. Whichever club you use, you don't want to leave it short as that brings a number of greenside traps into play.

Hole 14
Par 4
414 yards

Another dogleg left where it is tempting to try and cut the corner, but beware; three menacing fairway bunkers wait here. Right-centre is the safest landing area, and to have any prospect of making par, you need to be in position, as the approach is very narrow with traps all the way up the right-hand side. The putting surface has a number of changes in elevation.

Hole 15
Par 4
390 yards

Sand, sand, and more sand; the fairway is pinched very tight from 230 yards with four bunkers to the right and another two left. The approach is the toughest shot, though, with six deep traps lurking in front of the green. The ability to float in a high, soft-landing mid-iron will leave you in the best position on another green that has some subtle humps and hollows.

Hole 16
Par 4
360 yards

Straight hitting is rewarded on this short par 4. A solitary fairway bunker lies on the right at 210 yards, and then it's simply a short iron to the green. Trees line the whole of the right side from tee to green, while dense rough lies to the left. There are bunkers on both sides of the entrance to the putting surface, forcing players to float in their approach shots.

Hole 17
Par 3
170 yards

The penultimate hole is the shortest on the course, but you'll still need a solid mid-iron to find the green. Trees dominate the right-hand side, but they are not in play. Rather, players will need to avoid two fairway bunkers to the left of the putting surface. The green drops off at the back, and leaving yourself beneath the hole is the best strategy.

Hole 18
Par 4
457 yards

The closing hole is a tough examination of ball-striking as it sweeps to the left, with traps coming into play from 250 yards. The fairway is also undulating, and the approach is fraught with danger because the green is small and difficult to hold, with menacing pot bunkers on both sides. This stroke-index-four hole is a tough finish in anyone's book.

Hole 13 – *Par 3* – **200 yards**

The longest of the par 3s, where a long iron or hybrid will be needed to find the green. The entrance to the putting surface is open, so it looks tempting from the tee. However, two sand traps hover to the left side, so care and attention are needed, and the ability to play a soft draw is ideal here. Unlike most holes on the Faldo course, trees come into play as they surround the green, especially on the left-hand side of the approach. Anything long or far right will be buried in penal rough, and if you have to miss your target, it's better to be short rather than long.

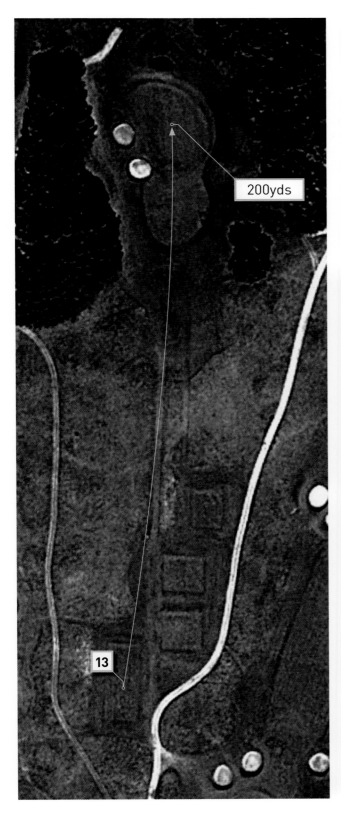

Bunkers line both sides, so the 2nd hole is a challenge from the tee. The ideal line is left-centre, but be aware of further bunkers as you near the kidney-shaped green.

BEUERBERG

With the Bavarian Alps as its stunning backdrop, Beuerberg has a beauty that few courses can rival. The layout is impressive too: a challenging par 74 that mixes five par 5s with some tempting, short par 4s.

Below left: Don't let the magnificent views of the Bavarian Alps distract you from the challenge of the course.

Opposite: An eclectic mix of holes makes up Donald Harradine's impressive layout at Beuerberg, which features a number of subtle doglegs to test your positioning.

You will feel instantly at home at Beuerberg, where a warm welcome and a wonderful ambience complement a fine golf course. In the foothills of the Bavarian Alps, the visitor is struck first by the stunning panoramic views across the south-east tip of Germany. But once you have played here, the golf course will be just as memorable.

The legendary Donald Harradine designed the layout and the course opened in 1983. Though it was one of Harradine's late designs before he passed away in 1996, it remains one of his best. Much of his work came in Switzerland and Germany, where he thrived on crafting and sculpting courses to conform to their natural landscapes. It can be argued that many of his designs have something of an understated nature. However, they always retain the essential qualities that make for a great course.

Donald's son, Peter, has continued to carry his father's architectural philosophy to other parts of the world, delivering the same quality in service, but working on a much grander scale and budget. While prominent in Europe, the company furthered its reputation as the golf boom hit the Middle East. Al Hamra, a sand-swept resort track in the thriving Emirate of Ras al-Khamaih, continues to win international plaudits; the magnificent Abu Dhabi Golf Club, host to the HSBC Abu Dhabi Championship, has become one of the European Tour's most iconic designs; and the Doha Golf Club, another tour course that is home to the Qatar Masters, features a procession of lakes combined with a daunting length of 7,400 yards, making it the perfect challenge for the world's best players.

Unlike these Middle Eastern greats, Beuerberg, despite its quality, carries little professional pedigree. It did host the 1992 European Ladies Open, but Harradine's craft is respected more for its timeless feel than for the tournament coverage it receives. Just ask the critics; Beuerberg has always been rated as one of the best courses in Germany, as well as consistently featuring in top-100 rankings on the continent.

Laid out over 120 hectares, it is both quirky and imposing. Its par of 74 is affirmed with five par 5s, all of them demanding in their nature, but individual in their defences. With so many three-shot holes, something had to give and so Harradine built only three par 3s; the longest 187 yards, the shortest 154. There are also two superb short par 4s at the 5th and 10th, reachable at 273 and 312 yards respectively, but riddled with danger as trees encroach the fairway, bringing your ball-striking into sharp focus.

The routing is also interesting; the first three holes playing straight, before the course cuts back at the par-5 4th, turning through small posses of trees and up and over the rolling terrain. A number of water hazards add to the test, and though not intimidating in their size, razor-sharp positioning is needed to avoid them, especially with your approach play. Although the course is not overly populated with trees, they do come into play on the apex of Beuerberg's subtle doglegs, while framing the greens of several holes to add to the already tranquil setting.

There are a number of strong holes, but the par-5 12th is one of the cleverest in terms of its design. From the men's yellow pegs it tempts players to throw everything into their drive to set up an easier approach to the green, which is tucked behind a pond. Play it well and a birdie chance looms; play it badly and a seriously high number is the only result. Make sure to pay a visit to Beuerberg if you can.

> "One of the most beautiful settings in which to play the game."
>
> *Golf Monthly Magazine*

COURSE GUIDE 1–9

Course yardage – Yellow tees 6,835 yards
Course GPS – 47°49'8.68" N 11°25'37.83"E

The outward nine opens with a fine par 5 over the beautiful, rolling terrain. There is no margin for anything loose from the tee, and the par-4 3rd brings the first sight of water, as players need to carry a pond in front of the green.

Opposite: The par-4 6th is one of Beuerberg's tighter holes where two solid blows are needed to find the green in regulation.

Hole 1
Par 5
531 yards

The course opens with an inviting drive. Trees congest the left side of the fairway, with more coming into play on the right at 280 yards. There are no bunkers to worry about until you get to the green, with a solitary trap lying at its front-right entrance. For those who choose to lay up, a small tree narrows the approach some 120 yards short of the putting surface.

Hole 2
Par 4
387 yards

Playing from the yellow tees, the drive is tightened on the right side with dense trees, and the ideal line on the fairway is left of centre. From here, the approach to the green is more open, and with a greenside trap to its right, coming in from this angle allows for a low-running long iron. Again, there are no fairway traps to negotiate a way past.

Hole 3
Par 4
368 yards

The tees are set back in a short channel of trees, and although the hole opens up, there is no room left so you need to hit a gentle fade to find the best position on the fairway. However, a fairway bunker sits to the right at 220 yards, so you don't want to go too far. The big test comes next with the second shot over water to the green.

Hole 4
Par 5
562 yards

A dogleg par 5 that is rated as the third toughest on the course; one fairway bunker sits to the right, so it is tempting to fire left and shorten the hole. Be wary if attacking the green in two: there is a narrow creek in front, and the apron of the putting surface drops down towards it, so a full carry is needed. One bunker sits to the right.

Hole 5
Par 4
273 yards

It may be short, and it may be rated as the second easiest hole at Beuerberg, but the drive is fiendishly tight with trees waiting to catch anything slightly off line. The temptation is obvious and many players will go for the green with their driver, but a bunker protects the right side and more trees pinch the left side tightly. A sensible lay-up leaves a pitch and a putt for birdie.

Hole 7
Par 4
379 yards

One of the wider fairways on the course, but it's a tricky drive because anything too straight, or too long, from the tee could run into the rough at around 280 yards. If players can find the fairway to the right side it will leave an easier approach to the green. A path runs short of the green, and a bunker lies to the left-hand side.

Hole 8
Par 3
162 yards

The first of the par 3s offers no option but to fly a mid-iron into the heart of the green because a large trap pinches the entrance from the right, while trees hug the left side. The putting surface is also raised slightly and the green features a number of undulations and run-off areas. This is a tricky one-shot hole that isn't as simple as it may appear.

Hole 9
Par 4
381 yards

The drive looks tight with trees either side, but the fairway does open up at 200 yards despite a bunker lurking at 230. The rolling fairway demands good ball control, and left-centre is ideal. The green is huge – and if you are out of position then two-putting is tough. To get to that green, players must play over one of the course's largest bunkers.

Hole 6 – *Par 4* – **450 yards**

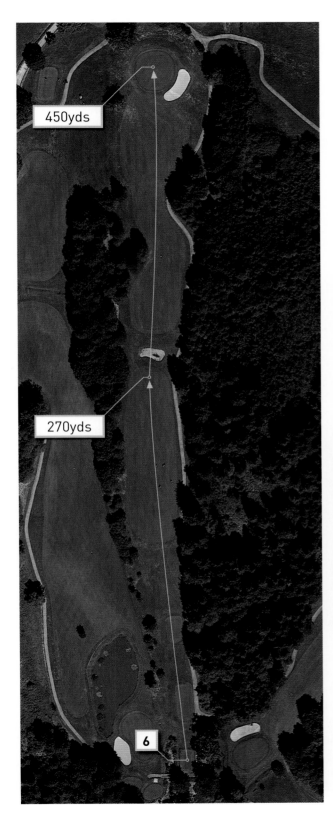

450yds

270yds

6

The 6th is the course's stroke-index-one hole, and for good reason because two well-executed shots are needed to find the green in regulation, as well as plenty of course management skills. From the tee there is no room right for the drive, and a soft draw will leave you in the best position because the fairway snakes through a narrow tunnel of trees 100 yards short of the green. There is also a creek to factor into your game plan, which will be reachable from the tee for the longest of hitters at around 280 yards. If attacking the green, there is plenty of room out to the left-hand side, but getting past the trees is the big test. One greenside bunker sits to the right.

COURSE GUIDE 10–18

The par 5s at 12 and 17 stand out for special praise, pure risk-reward holes with the threat of water waiting to catch out those who choose to attack. The 18th sweeps grandly over undulating land, and is a fine finish in anyone's book.

Hole 10
Par 4
312 yards

Another short, tight, tree-lined par 4 where an iron is the safe option; there is more danger on the left side, while a bunker sits to the right of the fairway at 220 yards. Like the 5th hole, it is tempting to go for the green, which is raised above the fairway. However, two bunkers – one at the front and one at the back – lie in wait for errant approaches.

Hole 11
Par 3
187 yards

The tee is elevated, so players may choose to take less club, but it is still a solid mid-iron even for the best ball-strikers. Bunkers – two deep, narrow traps – encircle the green, and players will need to carry a water hazard positioned short. If you are going to miss the putting surface, the right-hand side is the best place from which to recover.

Hole 12
Par 5
485 yards

A short par 5 which is a great risk-reward hole; the fairway lifts up and then drops down after a creek that runs across at 220 yards, so the first task is to get over this. Then it's a choice of a lay-up, or a full-blooded 3-wood that needs to carry a large water hazard in front of the green. One bunker is positioned right of the putting surface.

Hole 13
Par 4
398 yards

A very tough par 4 – rated as the second hardest hole on the course – that features a drive over a small water hazard, which also needs to be threaded through trees. Once past the traffic, the fairway opens up – although there is a bunker at 300 yards on the right. The entrance to the green is also open, with another bunker to the right.

Hole 14
Par 3
154 yards

This is the shortest hole on the course, but it's another tricky one-shotter with a number of defences. A stream runs up to the green and there are trees both left and right. Anything short may not hold the putting surface, in which case there is a danger of your ball running back into the water. One deep greenside trap is positioned left.

Hole 15
Par 5
510 yards

A fairway bunker on the left-hand side is the first obstacle on this dogleg par 5, but just right of this hazard is the perfect line. From here, the entrance to the green opens up, though it has sand either side. The lay-up zone is pinched tight with another trap to the right, but if you are in position this is one three-shot hole that is worth attacking.

Hole 16
Par 4
380 yards

A straightforward-looking hole that bends gently to the right as you approach the green; a solitary fairway bunker lies at 220 yards on the right, with a cluster of trees further up tightening the landing zone on the fairway. The green is protected by a long, narrow bunker on either side. The rolling contours of the fairway mean downhill lies can be an issue.

Hole 18
Par 4
396 yards

The home hole runs alongside the 9th, sharing its fairway and greenside bunkers. There is more room out to the right-hand side as the trees become less dense past 180 yards. The approach plays gently uphill, so more club is often needed to find the green. The surface is undulating, so provides one final test of a player's putt-reading skills.

Hole 17 – *Par 5* – **528 yards**

This is a great par 5 where players are encouraged to open their shoulders from the tee, especially those chasing a score on the back nine. The fairway drops off on the left-hand side and there is a menacing bunker here at 220 yards that is tough to escape from. There are some subtle undulations en route to the green, and it's a brave decision to try to reach it in two because a full carry is needed to a narrow putting surface with marshland guarding its entrance. If playing the hole with a lay-up, it's a mid-iron and a short pitch over the hazard, but just make sure the bunkers either side of the green are avoided as they can ruin any hopes of a late birdie.

528yds

430yds

240yds

17

PGA Catalunya – Stadium

Beautifully manicured and pretty it may be, but PGA Catalunya's Stadium course is one of Europe's most feared layouts. It was designed for the very best with Tour golf in mind, and players need a sharp golfing brain to work their way through its tight fairways while avoiding a number of water hazards.

The Catalonia region of Spain may not have the golfing reputation of the Costa del Sol where Valderrama lies, but at PGA Catalunya you will find two courses that deserve their place among their country's finest layouts. As its name would suggest, Catalunya's Stadium course was built with tournament golf in mind. Ten years in the making, it was originally intended to be a potential venue for the 1997 Ryder Cup.

A year after opening in 1999, it hosted the Spanish Open; ten years later the same tournament returned. The neighbouring Tour course is shorter and less challenging. Both were designed by former players Neil Coles and Angel Gallardo under the guidance of the European Tour, who wanted to offer its alternative to the US PGA's TPC Sawgrass.

PGA Catalunya is set in the town of Girona some 60 miles from Barcelona on the north east

"A magnificent spectacle."

Neil Coles

tip of the country just below the border with France. There is a wonderful ambience to this part of the country, the local Catalonian language has something of a French feel to it, and the cooler northern climate makes playing here more appealing during the hot summer months.

While both courses are rightly regarded as being among Spain's heavyweights, it is the Stadium that stands out – for the challenge it presents more than anything else. Cut through dense woodland with a series of drops in elevation from the tee, Coles and Gallardo's creation is one of the continent's great golfing adventures.

It is also a visual delight with a backdrop of the Pyrenees to the north. Always maintained in beautiful condition, the course twists and turns continually. Tight and lined with fir and pine trees, the fairways are firm and fiery, and steep banks hug their boundaries. Lush vegetation and even purple heather bring a touch of heathland Surrey to proceedings.

Right from the off, you are blessed with a procession of stunning views with the course's manicured fairways a sight all golfing aficionados would appreciate. On the first tee, the fairway drops dramatically before sweeping round to the left to a green enveloped by trees, with deep sand traps a secondary defence. Few courses begin with such a challenge.

In terms of strategy, there is really no hidden agenda; you need plenty of muscle to get round and if you dare to veer off the straight and narrow then scoring is nigh impossible. While few courses are so demanding from the tee, you are asked questions on every shot and you know that until the ball has dropped, your score is not safe.

Water is a constant menace as several natural lakes come into play on no fewer than seven holes. The greens, heavily contoured and with vicious run-off areas, are some of the fastest in Europe, and players with the ability to float high-flying shots in for their approaches will be rewarded. Despite the imposing challenge in terms of its length – the course measures over 7,200 yards from the championship tees – there are five teeing options, enabling players of all standards to take on the challenge.

But for the pros, it will always be a test of brute force and nerveless ball-striking. Every November, those professionals left scrapping for their European Tour futures head to Catalunya for the annual Q School finals, where over 120 hopefuls play three rounds on both the Tour and Stadium courses to earn playing rights for the following season. In many ways, this has always been something of a battle of endurance, where only the fittest will survive over one of Europe's most daunting layouts.

> ## "When I first saw the site I thought it would make such a natural golf course."
>
> *Angel Gallardo*

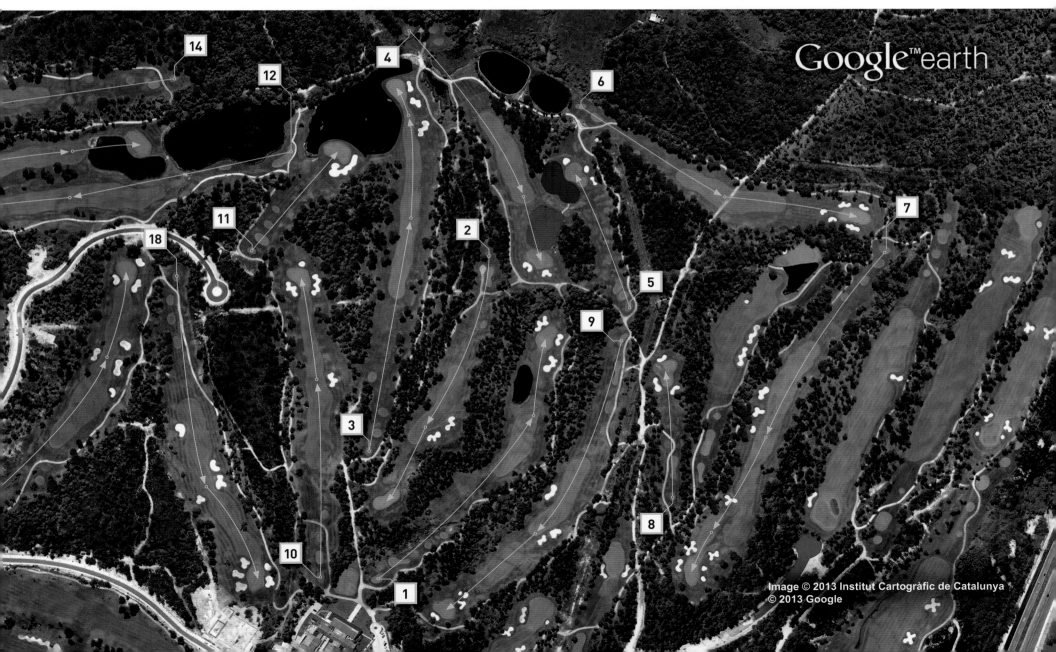

Google™earth

Image © 2013 Institut Cartogràfic de Catalunya
© 2013 Google

COURSE GUIDE 1–9

Course yardage – White tees 6,579 yards
Course GPS – 41°51'25.99" N 2°45'46.84" E

From the word go, you need to have your eye in. The opening hole sets the tone for what is to come, players must keep it straight off the tee if they hope to score well. The par-5 3rd is a stunning three-shotter where water comes into play.

Opposite: The par-5 3rd is an early test in ball-striking. With the green perched on the bank of a lake, it's a brave player who tackles the challenge in two blows.

Hole 1
Par 4
396 yards

A thrill of an opening hole, with an elevated tee where you feel you're high in the sky. A good strike is needed to find the middle of the fairway, which turns to the left. Once in position, you'll need a crisp mid- or long iron to find the heart of a small green perched up on a slight plateau. This is an intimidating start for all but the very best players.

Hole 2
Par 4
354 yards

The fairway narrows and there are two sprawling bunkers to the left at around 250 yards. The shape of the hole favours a gentle fade, which will leave you in prime position to attack the green with a short iron. The putting surface is over a shallow ravine, so it's crucial to take more club if you are unsure of your distances. This is an early birdie chance.

Hole 4
Par 4
380 yards

The tee shot is blind on this par 4 that features water to the left of the fairway and a steep bank of trees to the right. So, getting good position from the tee is important here. The green has two large bunkers at its rear, from one of which a player faces the daunting prospect of chipping back towards the water over the other side.

Hole 5
Par 3
191 yards

The first of the par 3s, and another test in ball-striking with water left and three bunkers to the right; the tee is elevated, so you may not need as much club as the yardage book suggests. The green slopes from back-right to front, so if you are faced with a forward pin position the ball will feed back down the slope. Pick your spot and swing with conviction.

Hole 6
Par 4
375 yards

The drive is semi-blind and uphill, and like many of the holes on the Stadium course, it is fiendishly tight. A road runs across the fairway at around 250 yards, and from here the hole turns left. Short of the road leaves the ideal distance for an approach to a green heavily contoured with lush, penal rough surrounding its boundary, not to mention five bunkers.

Hole 7
Par 5
478 yards

This is another great par 5 that is reachable again for the bombers. However, players must pay attention to a row of three fairway bunkers that comes into play at the 250-yard mark. The green is tucked away up to the right on a plateau, with three more sand traps protecting the left side, and with its diagonal slope demands a severe test of putting skill.

Hole 8
Par 3
170 yards

It's all about the green on this par 3, where you will need a mid-iron to reach its centre. The tee shot can look imposing with trees squeezing the approach all the way up. However, it's when you have the putter in your hand that the questions really begin. The surface has three tiers, rising from bottom-right, to middle-left and then top-right. Pin placement, therefore, is all-important.

Hole 9
Par 4
427 yards

A long, sweeping par 4 that was rated as the toughest hole on the course in the 2009 Spanish Open. Despite its standing as a two-shotter, many amateurs will play this as a par 5. Bunkers lie in wait on the left side of the fairway at 260 yards, before the hole turns to the right. Dense rough surrounds the green with three bunkers at the front and one to the rear.

489yds

420yds

300yds

3

Hole 3 – *Par 5* – **489 yards**

A wonderful par 5 that is reachable in two for the longer hitters, but with water hugging the left side of the green, it's all about risk-and-reward. The drive is tight, with trees narrowing your route from the tee box. Steep banks line the fairway on either side, with dense trees and lush vegetation waiting to gather your ball, so anything wayward will need to be wedged back into play. If you are in position and decide to take the green on in two, as well as the water, there are three traps to contend with to the right of the putting surface. That said, the sand isn't the worst place to be; better there than in the lake.

COURSE GUIDE 10–18

Big in stature and bite, the Stadium course's inward stretch continues to be a thorough examination, with the par-4 13th the course's signature hole played from an elevated tee with an approach to an island-style green. It's scary stuff.

Hole 10
Par 4
397 yards

The hole plays predominantly downhill from an elevated tee, and the fairway is one of the course's more generous offerings, opening up at the 240-yard mark. The backdrop to the hole is stunning, with mountains adding to the visual feast. Two greenside bunkers sit to the right, with another, large trap to the left. Take what you can get here. It's a rare scoring opportunity.

Hole 11
Par 3
173 yards

Players will need to hit a high, soft-landing mid-iron for the best results on this testing par 3, with water at the back of the green waiting for those who overclub or, worse, don't get enough air time on their tee shots. To make matters even tougher, the green is very shallow, and lush rough hugs its perimeter. This is a hole where a player should be grateful for a par.

Hole 12
Par 5
491 yards

The ideal line is left of the fairway, as the land rolls down to the right and trees can block out the approach. Again it is reachable for the longer hitters, but if you choose to lay up, attention needs to be given to the overhanging oak tree on the left side that could restrict your third shot to the green. Two sand traps lie to the right of the green, with another to the left.

Hole 14
Par 4
408 yards

A long, straight par 4 that offers no forgiveness for wayward hitters. Bunkers lie either side of the fairway; first left at 230 yards, then right at 260. From here the approach looks fiendishly narrow as trees pinch the neck of the green. Position on the putting surface is important: the green slopes from back to front, so it's best to leave yourself under the hole if possible.

Hole 15
Par 5
461 yards

The last of the par 5s, and perhaps the toughest to reach in two as the hole turns sharply to the right. Pine trees narrow the landing zone of the fairway, and with two bunkers positioned left at 280 yards, players may opt to lay up with a 3-wood. Once again the approach is narrowed by dense woodland, and the green is small with traps on both sides.

Hole 16
Par 3
186 yards

The final trio of holes begins with this testing par 3, which plays uphill to a green that slopes from back to front. Two large, deep bunkers sit short; the first isn't really in play, the second to the left is, while another trap lurks to the back of the green. With all this sand, distance control is critical if you are to keep your score going on the closing stretch.

Hole 17
Par 4
423 yards

This is another long and difficult par 4 that sweeps round to the left. One fairway trap lurks on the left-hand side, so those attempting to cut the corner need to be wary, while three more sit to the right to swallow anything that fades too much. If you have found position from the tee, it's a mid-iron into a green with sand either side.

Hole 18
Par 4
415 yards

In a parting gesture, this is another tight and imposing tee shot where trees envelop the fairway and bunkers pinch in at its side. Sand traps lurk left and right from 220 yards. The green is slightly raised, with five bunkers protecting it. Once on the putting surface, getting the ball in the hole is not easy because it has two tiers and a number of undulations.

365yds

280yds

13

Hole 13 – *Par 4* – **365 yards**

This stunning par 4 is the Stadium's signature hole – one that can delight and frustrate, putting a premium on ball control. From the tee, it is tempting to open the shoulders and let fly with your driver, but a cluster of trees comes into play at 200 yards on the right-hand side, so it needs to be straight if you hold any hopes of making par or better. The green is the standout feature, a lone island-style putting surface that is shallow in depth – so there is no margin for error with your approach. Another problem is that the fairway drops down after 260 yards, which means you will invariably find yourself playing from a downhill lie – as if matters were not tricky enough already.

CRANS-SUR-SIERRE

Crans-sur-Sierre has become one of the most iconic courses in Europe, and is a favourite with the tour stars thanks to an idyllic setting that offers jaw-dropping views over the Swiss Alps. Heavenly isn't the word…

Ask any professional who plies a trade on the European Tour to name their favourite course, and there's a good chance that the magnificent Crans-sur-Sierre will be the answer. At 5,000 feet above sea level, this championship layout sits on a plateau in the Swiss Alps, with striking views out to the Valais region and the snow-capped mountains that encircle its fairways.

Crans has been the host venue of the European Masters since 1939. Bar the years of the Second World War, the tournament has been back ever since, making it one of the most established tour courses on the continent. Although the club's history dates back to 1905 at Crans Montana, the layout that is recognized and played today did not come into being until the mid-1920s. It was originally laid out as a nine-holer, with a second nine coming in 1926. Shortly afterwards, the English architect Harry Nicholson was called in to oversee some refinements, leaving a design that would remain untouched for the next 60 years.

The high altitude means that you are playing with a ball that travels greater distances through the air. But Crans is not demanding of a long ball flight, and while there are opportunities to open the shoulders from the tee, a number of sharp doglegs and reachable par 4s force players to pick their way through the routing. As the fairways sweep up and down dramatically from tee to green, this is not a straightforward test

> ## "A staggering place, with a view stretching 60 miles down the Sion Valley to Geneva."
>
> *Colin Montgomerie*

where all you need to do is simply take aim and fire. What you must do, however, is embrace the challenge – take in the sights and let them inspire you, because there are very few golf courses like this anywhere in the world.

Despite its location and the impending winter freeze that closes the course for the best part of half a year, Crans is maintained in immaculate condition. The searing climate in the build-up to the European Masters sees the course baked under the sun, and it usually plays hard and fast. Its fairways, a mixture of Poa Annua and Rye grass, are beautifully manicured, while the greens, heavily contoured due to the course's mountainside location, are small but fast running. The pace of the putting surfaces adds to the difficulty of holding them with your

> ## "One of the most beautiful places to play the game."
>
> *David Howell*

approach, which is made even tougher as the altitude adds to the challenge of controlling your natural distance.

Although Crans is considered a tough test for amateurs, the professionals have always scored well here during the European Masters. At less than 7,000 yards, it is not long, and better players – with the ability to overcome the demands on ball control – will be more concerned with picking an attacking line from where to set up a birdie chance.

Over the years, there have been a number of highlights as Europe's best players have flocked to play here. In the tournament's early years, notable winners included Dai Rees, Kel Nagle and Bob Charles, while in more recent times heavyweights such as Nick Faldo, Colin Montgomerie, Luke Donald, Ernie Els and Sergio Garcia have all won here.

But of all the players to have created a lasting legacy at Crans, it is the great Severiano Ballesteros whose name rings loudest. It was Seve who was responsible for a major redesign of the course in the mid-1990s, reworking many of its bunkers and later the greens. Upon completion, the layout was renamed the "Seve Ballesteros" course. It is a fitting title for a track that always lives up to expectations. Even without those wonderful views, Crans-sur-Sierre is a fine golf course in its own right.

Course Guide 1–9

Course yardage – White tees 6,904 yards
Course GPS – 46°18'11.00" N 7°27'48.96"E

On the front nine, a mixture of great holes is complemented by those views out to the Alps. There are opportunities to open your shoulders from the tee, but a couple of short par 4s will also bring accuracy into play.

Opposite: Crans begins to bite hard at the long, snaking par-4 4th, with bunkers lurking on either side of the green's entrance.

Hole 1
Par 5
540 yards

A relatively gentle opener; this par 5 represents a birdie opportunity for those who can keep it straight enough to avoid the single fairway bunker on the right-hand side. The approach to the green is very narrow with more sand on both sides. The large putting surface is made tricky to read by some subtle breaks, so pay attention to the pin position.

Hole 2
Par 4
437 yards

This par 4 plays back in the opposite direction to the 1st, but the strategy remains the same: keep it straight. The fairway is tight with trees pinching in on either side. There is a large bunker on the right at 240 yards, and the best line to take is left of centre. Two large fir trees frame the green at the back, while two sand traps protect the entrance.

Hole 3
Par 3
192 yards

The first of the par 3s requires a solid shot with a long iron, on account of the towering trees dominating the approach. The tee shot is played over a road, and the shape of the hole will reward those who can play a soft draw as the green is tucked away slightly to the left side. There is plenty of sand around the putting surface.

Hole 5
Par 4
340 yards

A short par 4, but with the green tucked tightly away to the right behind dense woodland, it is one where players must plot their way with two well-placed shots. A fairway bunker visible on the corner at 280 yards is a good line to take from the tee. Then it's a floated pitch to an undulating green with sprawling sand traps right and left.

Hole 6
Par 4
324 yards

An even shorter par 4 than the 5th, which is driveable for those who dare to take it on; however, it is extremely tight, and overhanging trees ensure anything off line will be stopped in its tracks. It's best played with an iron down the right side, then a wedge through a channel of trees to find the green. Although short, it's a potential card-wrecker.

Hole 7
Par 4
331 yards

After a number of tight, tree-lined holes, there is some respite because this is one of Crans-Sur-Sierre's more open tests. With the green perched up on the right, there is plenty of room left from the tee, and this is a good line from which to approach with the second shot. Anything short or right will find the sand that surrounds the putting surface.

Hole 8
Par 3
174 yards

A mid-iron is needed on this friendly-looking par 3 that is open all the way to its kidney-shaped green, which features a number of undulations, plus mounding that runs from the left side round to the back. Bunkers guard the entrance both right and left, so a full carry is the only safe route to the green on what is the shortest hole on the course.

Hole 9
Par 5
628 yards

From the shortest hole to the longest: this par 5 is a three-shotter for even the biggest of hitters, although its limited defences mean that there is little risk in taking on the challenge. Trees line the right side from the tee, but attacking this line will put you in the best position. The fairway is relatively generous from here, so there's plenty of room to factor in a lay-up.

503yds

430yds

240yds

4

Hole 4 – *Par 4* – **503 yards**

This is a very long two-shot hole that will be played as a par 5 by most amateurs. With the tees set back in the trees, it can look a daunting challenge to reach the green in two. The fairway sweeps gently round to the right before straightening up for the second shot. If you can draw the ball from the right side the hole will become much shorter, making par an easier target. Although there is sand on both sides of the green, as well as at the back, you can run a 3-wood in because the entrance is open. But two crisp blows are an absolute necessity if you are to find the green in regulation. Thankfully, those stunning views of the Alps will make the challenge more worthwhile.

Course Guide 10–18

The back nine starts with a testing par 4, and finishes with an epic one as water comes into play. Expect a thorough examination of your short game if the target of the green is missed, as the subtle breaks of the putting surfaces can make them difficult to hold.

Opposite: The 18th is one of the most thrilling finishing holes on the European Tour, where the rare threat of water comes into play to the right of the green.

Hole 10
Par 4
404 yards

The back nine begins with another tricky par 4. Although the wide fairway invites you to open up from the tee, the drive needs to be dead centre. A large sand trap comes into play on the left side, with another, smaller one shortly after. The green is testing with its humps and hollows, and sand narrows the entrance on both sides.

Hole 11
Par 3
204 yards

The 11th is another great par 3 that serves up more stunning views with the Alps dominating the backdrop. Although the approach is open, pine trees frame the green beautifully, with two bunkers to the right side, and one to the left. Again, players have the benefit of running tee shots into the green, although it is perched up slightly.

Hole 12
Par 4
410 yards

A sharp dogleg right, which drops down as the hole turns, then sweeps back up towards the green. Players may take on the right side of the fairway in the hope of shortening the approach, although the first cut of rough ensures there isn't much room. Anything too straight, or left, may find the sand that lurks on the corner. Trees and penal rough surround the green.

Hole 13
Par 3
199 yards

The last of the one-shot holes, the 13th is rated as the course's stroke index-16. That said, it is no pushover and it can be deceiving as the approach sweeps down then gently up towards the putting surface. There is sand on both sides, with a posse of trees waiting at the back to catch out those who overclub. Running a long iron into the green is an obvious benefit here.

Hole 14
Par 5
597 yards

Another long three-shot hole, which tips the scales at just shy of 600 yards; a trap lies on the right side of the fairway at 260 yards, so left of centre is ideal. Water runs alongside the green to the right, and the entrance is pinched even tighter with greenside traps on both sides of the putting surface, so most will play this with a lay-up.

Hole 15
Par 5
516 yards

The 15th is another par 5, with six bunkers strategically placed to test players from tee to green. The first two traps come into play at 270 yards, so those who plan to attack must factor these in. The fairway sweeps gently up, with another bunker to the left side of the lay-up area 80 yards short of the green. The putting surface is small, with some subtle contours.

Hole 16
Par 4
317 yards

A short par 4 where players would be well advised to take less club from the tee to leave room to negotiate a huge fir tree that blocks the path to the green. Right of centre is perhaps the better line to take, as there is more room this side; from here, it's a pitch to find the middle of a putting surface that's flanked right and left by greenside traps.

Hole 17
Par 4
386 yards

The fairway doglegs to the left, but there is little point in taking the corner on as trees and thick rough could leave you scrambling to make your score. Instead, keep it right of centre. The landing zone is relatively wide, just shy of the bunkers positioned on both sides, and then it's a wedge to a green guarded by another two bunkers.

Hole 18 – *Par 4* – **402 yards**

The final hole plays back towards the clubhouse, a magnificent spectacle and finish when the course plays host to the Omega European Masters. Trees dominate the left side, although aiming just right of this line and playing a gentle fade will set you up for the second shot. Beware, though: anything too far right runs the risk of finding one of the two fairway bunkers at 260 yards. Although it is only a short iron or even a wedge to the green, it is a testing shot because the water lying to the right of the entrance most definitely comes into play. There is no sand, but the green drops off, so for those playing it safe, the left side is the best spot. This is a wonderful finish to one of the most scenic courses in the world.

402yds

300yds

18

Described as a heavenly place to play golf, this is the idyllic view from behind the green on the 9th hole at Crans-sur-Sierre Golf Club.

FALKENSTEIN

Falkenstein's Hamburger Golf Club is something of a throwback, maintaining the qualities of a layout that first opened for play in 1930. Despite many changes, this Harry Colt classic is a timely reminder of how great golf courses were in the early part of the 20th century.

Below: Hamburger Golf Club at Falkenstein is a classic heathland test that is one of Germany's most beautiful layouts.

Opposite: Harry Colt's routing forces players to shape the ball both ways from the tee as overhanging trees congest the fairways at Falkenstein.

© 2009 GeoBasis-DE/BKG
© 2013 Google
Image © 2013 AeroWest

At Hamburger Golf Club, Falkenstein, you will find one of Germany's oldest courses. The original layout, a quirky and testing nine-holer, dates back as far as 1906. Set in the district of Flottbek in Hamburg, the course lived off its impressive reputation, hosting a series of top-level tournaments before the First World War. By the 1920s, Hamburger's membership had swelled to well over 300, and so the decision was taken in 1926 to close the course. The search for a new site began, and by 1928, Falkenstein, ten miles further west of the city, was chosen as the club's new home.

To design a truly great golf course, there is a tendency to think that you must have a truly great designer. In fact, a great course can be dependent on the landscape and its surroundings, and if the terrain is uninspiring even the very best in the business will struggle to sculpt a masterpiece. However, in the 1920s, the best golf course architect was the venerable Harry Shapland Colt, and when the Englishman was called in to help mastermind this development at Falkenstein, his commissioners knew exactly what they would be getting in return for their money.

Prior to commencing work here in 1929, Colt had revolutionized a number of Europe's early designs. But it was also a period of new development, and some of the Englishman's finest work could be found around the Surrey and Berkshire sand belts to the south west of London. Here, Colt's reputation as the era's premier course designer had been enhanced with the delivery of such classics as Sunningdale New, Swinley Forest, St George's Hill and the East and West courses at Wentworth. Each one was unique in character, but each one was also consistent in quality.

And it's the same at Falkenstein, where Colt, assisted by co-designers Hugh Alison and John Morrison, has left an indelible mark on German golf; a course that has lived through the ages, maintaining the ambience and overall look that it had when the gates swung open for business a year after work had commenced. It is, quite simply, a glorious layout that meanders back and forth in direction through towering trees and up and over the naturally undulating terrain. Striking heather lines the fairways, and with many bunkers positioned cleverly on the elbow of doglegs, this is not a golf course you can overpower, although some might be

> "A stunning layout that is a thinking man's golf course first and foremost." *Golf Monthly Magazine*

tempted by its modest yardage of under 6,300 yards from the men's tees.

The course is playable to all standards, but in typical Colt style, the routing ensures those who can move the ball both ways through the air will have the opportunity to score well.

The front nine shapes predominantly from left to right, while the back nine shapes right to left. There are also a number of blind shots, requiring drives over sweeping crests and accurate approaches to elevated greens.

Shortly after opening, and due in part to

its growing reputation, tournament golf came calling and from 1935 the course was a regular host to the German Open. It last staged the event in 1981, when a young Bernhard Langer won his first national title at the age of 22. Today, Falkenstein is not long enough to host

top-level professional events, but that in itself may be seen as a compliment, because the twists and turns of the layout are proof that a golf course can still be great without the gargantuan feel of those that continue to go under the knife to meet the standards of an evolving game.

COURSE GUIDE 1–9

A gentle opener is followed by a series of tight driving holes that set the tone for the rest of the course. In classic Harry Colt style, the ability to shape the ball both ways is the key to plotting your way around the course.

Opposite: The par-4 6th is a classic, as the fairway rises for the approach with the green tucked away to the right side.

Hole 1
Par 4
320 yards

Heading away from the clubhouse, this short par 4 offers little space to recover on the right side, with more room if you miss the fairway left. Sand traps squeeze the landing zone from 240 yards, so the safe option is to lay up short of these. From there, because of the shortness of the hole, it is still only a flick with a wedge to a green that has one trap front-right.

Hole 2
Par 5
535 yards

It may be reachable in two, but there is no margin for error from the tee as the fairway is lined on both sides by trees. However, there are no bunkers en route to the green while the hole turns subtly to the left. The putting surface does have a bunker at its left entrance, with another at the back waiting to swallow any approaches fired long.

Hole 3
Par 3
214 yards

The longest par 3 on the course is made harder by the lurking presence of a bunker at the front of the green, so players can't run a long iron in. Trees on both sides channel the hole so the tee shot must be hit straight. The putting surface slopes down to the right side, and if you miss the target here, bogey or worse is the likely result.

Hole 4
Par 5
472 yards

This short par 5 is stroke-index 17. From the tee, players can attempt to shave the corner off the dogleg as the fairway sweeps gently to the right, but there are dangerous bunkers lying here from 230 yards, while a crest makes the second shot semi-blind. Two greenside traps lie to the left of the putting surface, with another short-right.

Hole 5
Par 4
390 yards

Another dogleg right where cutting the corner is fraught with danger, and where trees will force you to play down the line of the fairway – or even left of centre – to a wide-open landing area. From here, the approach tightens up, and if you play safe off the tee it will still be a long iron in. With sand either side of the green, it's a big test of your ball-striking.

Hole 7
Par 4
354 yards

The 7th serves up another tight drive from an elevated tee, which is made even more difficult by a solitary fairway bunker pinching the right side of the fairway at 250 yards. The second shot is tricky too, as a cluster of sand traps protect the right side of the perched green. The smart play is a lay-up short of the fairway trap, which will leave a wedge in for the approach.

Hole 8
Par 3
177 yards

It may only be a mid-iron, but this hole really asks questions, with a sea of heather in front of the tee. Trees are a factor too, especially on the left-hand side. The green is tucked back in the woodland, and two bunkers sit to the right with another left. You really don't want to overclub here, but thankfully there is a bail-out area short of the target.

Hole 9
Par 4
411 yards

The front nine finishes with this tough two-shot hole where left-centre is the ideal line from the tee to open up the second shot. Again, trees hug both sides of the fairway all the way to the green. Sand lies on the green's boundary both right and left, and, as on the 8th, you don't want to go long as there is dense woodland that can lead to a high number.

Hole 6 – *Par 4* – **410 yards**

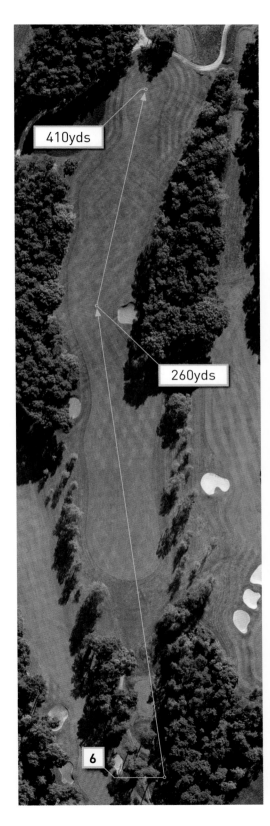

This is a fine par 4 that sweeps majestically up a steep incline. Though the tee is set back in a tunnel of trees, the fairway opens up for an inviting drive. Left of centre is the ideal line from which to attack the green, with the hole turning slightly to the right. However, anything too far left may find the bunker that sits on the fairway's fringe, so you need to be committed and pick your spot. Another smaller trap further up on the right side lies in wait to catch out those longer hitters attempting to shave some yardage off their second shots. The green has no bunkers on its boundary, but there are subtle undulations to contend with, as well as a number of run-off areas.

Course Guide 10–18

In many ways, the inward nine is the more beautiful, and the finish is as grand as anywhere. There are some dramatic changes in elevation, with tabletop greens that put a premium on the accuracy of your approach shots.

Opposite: The par-5 17th, a sharp swinging dogleg left, offers a birdie opportunity at only 471 yards – but the humps and hollows of the land put added pressure on your distance control.

Hole 10
Par 3
170 yards

The inward stretch starts with a great little par 3 featuring another tee set back in the trees. Deep heather catches your eye to the left of the green's approach; however, the right side of the putting surface is relatively open, so if you are going to miss, then miss here. Three bunkers encircle the putting surface, with two left and a single one right.

Hole 11
Par 4
427 yards

This par 4 is rated as the second hardest hole on the course, with trees tightening the drive on the left-hand side. At 250 yards, there is a fairway bunker on the right, after which the hole opens up. Again the approach is narrow, and holding the green is crucial as a posse of trees lie at the back. A solitary trap sits to the front-right of the putting surface.

Hole 12
Par 4
401 yards

Like the 11th, there is no room on the left, with a mass of trees waiting to punish anything that strays. Set in the heather to the right, a fairway bunker lurks at 230 yards. Firing on this line will leave you fighting to save par, so it pays to be straight. A tunnel of trees adds more pressure, and a single bunker sits at the left of the green. A classic hole that asks a number of questions.

Hole 13
Par 4
343 yards

The fairway's landing zone is relatively generous once you have fired safely over a sea of heather from the tee. The first obstacle comes in the form of a bunker that is right-centre at 240 yards. The second shot is tricky, as trees and rough jut in from the right side and the green is raised. If you are in position on the fairway, a gentle fade is the ideal shot to play here.

Hole 14
Par 4
347 yards

Again, heather lurks in front of the tee, and the fairway is very narrow at 220 yards due to a large bunker sitting on the left-hand side. This poses the question: do you take it on and shorten the hole for the second shot, or do you lay up, even though a longer club is required to reach the green? Trees, again, are a constant menace from tee to green.

Hole 15
Par 3
155 yards

The 15th is the shortest hole on the course and is rated the easiest; but trees make the tee shot look imposing as they frame the approach through to the green. There is heather again directly in front of the tee, but with a short iron in hand, hitting the centre of the putting surface should not be a problem. Two greenside traps sit to the left, with a run-off area right.

Hole 16
Par 4
330 yards

A short par 4 that sweeps to the left, where taking on the corner is an option for the longer hitters – although two trees pinch the fairway at around 200 yards, so you'll need to avoid these. Equally, anything that goes too straight and too long can run into a fairway trap at 250 yards on the right. Once in position, it's just a wedge into the green.

Hole 18
Par 4
367 yards

This is another dogleg left that features no fairway bunkers. Dense trees pinch the hole tightly from tee to green, and the drive is semi-blind, played over the crest of a hill. Aim right of centre to open up the hole, because a high, soft-landing approach is needed to carry two bunkers that guard the front of the putting surface, which slopes from the left side.

471yds

260yds

17

Hole 17 – *Par 5* – **471 yards**

A reachable par 5, but be warned, there is little forgiveness on the left side for players looking to take on the dogleg. Fairway bunkers come into play at 200 yards, but the landing zone opens up after this. As the fairway sweeps up and down, heather runs across to test those looking to lay up. Bunkers to the left of the green mean the ideal approach is from the right.

FONTAINEBLEAU

One of France's oldest courses, and one of its most treasured; set in the historical district of Fontainebleau to the south east of Paris, this rugged and character-filled layout is certainly one that deserves to be on everyone's must-play list.

One of Tom Simpson's early designs, Fontainebleau celebrated its Centenary in 2009, and it remains perhaps France's most sacred golf course. Cut through the heart of the Fontainebleau Forest, its peaceful and serene surroundings complement the rugged beauty of Simpson's layout that can be rewarding to patient play, while punishing to those of a more belligerent nature.

The district of Fontainebleau lies 35 miles south east of Paris, and is an area steeped in rich history. Parisians often flock to the Fontainebleau Palace, one of the largest French royal châteaux, and the surrounding forest was a former royal hunting ground that is today recognized as a National Park. Its wildlife and notable boulders make it a popular spot for walkers and hikers.

Blessed with such a natural setting, it is hardly surprising that Simpson left such an indelible design in place when he completed the layout in 1909. Much like his more famous work at Morfontaine to the north of the capital, the course enjoys a wonderful, heathland feel, snaking its way through undulating terrain as banks of heather patrol fairways that are pinched tightly by oak, pines and silver birch. The sandy soil ensures the fairways play hard and fast and the drainage maintains the course's glorious condition, making it playable all year round. During a round, you will often catch sight of deer and other wildlife, the former usually fleeing to escape those errant strikes that clatter among the woodland.

The course's routing is superb, every hole offering its own individual test with the trees hiding you from any outside influences. First you head out east in an anti-clockwise direction before cutting back and forth from the 5th hole. The pace of the course varies; there are sweeping par 5s that are reachable in two, but which are sprinkled with cleverly positioned defences; there are doglegging par 4s that tempt you to fire at the elbow, but with intimidating, deep bunkers that lie in wait to stop you in your tracks; and there are four par 3s that are inviting in length, but impudent in nature with greens that feature a series of run-off areas to challenge your distance control.

Fortunately, there is some respite with the course's modest length of 6,566 yards from the

Below left: There is a wonderful ambience at Fontainebleau, with the attractive clubhouse at home in the beautiful surroundings of the forest.

Opposite: A Tom Simpson classic, while it is not a test of length, Fontainebleau offers no mercy to wayward play with tight fairways and well-positioned sand traps.

back pegs making it playable to most standards and ages. And the rough is limited. But, while there are attacking opportunities, the focus has to be on control, while paying extra attention to the humps and hollows of the greens.

There are many standout holes, but the 12th is more than deserving of its signatory status, a short par 5 where an army of rocks and boulders lurk short of the green to catch out those attempting to reach it in two. Those rocks and boulders of the forest are cleverly integrated into the course's landscape, notable also for the bank that hovers behind the 1st green. It all adds to the character that makes Fontainebleau such a special golf course.

The layout has undergone some changes over the years. Fred Hawtree modified the course in the mid-1960s, bringing it up to date slightly. But thankfully, Simpson's original work hasn't lost any of its personality. Though Fontainebleau is essentially a private members' club, visitors are welcome during the week. And, while there are many reasons to pay a visit to France's capital city, you could do a lot worse than join the Parisians who seek some sanctuary down here. Take your clubs too, because a single round here may not be enough to satisfy you. It's a track that will have you wanting to come back for more.

> "Fontainebleau has all the usual [Tom] Simpson trademarks."
>
> *James Dodson*

COURSE GUIDE 1–9

Course yardage – Championship 6,566 yards
Course GPS – 48º23'36.72" N 2º40'51.53" E

The course eases you in with a gentle opener, but Fontainebleau begins to find its teeth as early as the second hole. It is a layout where finding position on the fairway is crucial to finding the green. After all, you can't attack from the trees.

Opposite: The 7th green is surrounded by sand, with a large, c-shaped bunker that lurks at the front the most menacing defence.

Hole 1
Par 4
335 yards

Fontainebleau's opening par 4, though surrounded by dense pines and oak trees, offers a gentle start to your round. From the tee, three large bunkers cut across the fairway. The hole's length will have some licking their lips as they eye up the green in one blow, but greed can be costly. Instead, a long iron will leave a wedge to the putting surface, which is framed at the back by a steep, rocky bank.

Hole 2
Par 3
177 yards

This is a tough par 3 where errant ball-striking will be suitably punished. The tee is set back, with a sea of heather in front. Tightened by trees, it is a difficult tee shot that favours a gentle fade. The entrance to the green is open, although it is raised with a steep bank on the left side running down into a bunker. Another two traps lie to the right.

Hole 3
Par 5
527 yards

With the tee right back in the trees, this par 5 is an imposing sight as you stare down the fairway towards the huge bunker that dominates the fairway at 250 yards. If you lay up short of the trap, the hole is best played as a standard three-shotter, with the second shot aimed down the left side to open up the green for a pitched approach.

Hole 4
Par 4
411 yards

The 4th is rated as Fontainebleau's toughest hole; a gentle dogleg right with a drive that has to be threaded through a narrow lane of trees. The fairway opens up as it approaches the corner, and left of centre will leave an approach that still has to be struck accurately to avoid a number of sand traps, which line the path to the green.

Hole 5
Par 4
358 yards

Heather and waste rough lie between the teeing area and the fairway, with the back tee tucked up against the right side. Laying up short of the cross-bunker at 220 yards is the smart play, before a high floated pitch to avoid the other five sand traps that lurk around the green. This is not a difficult hole, but it's certainly one you shouldn't underestimate.

Hole 6
Par 4
428 yards

This is another testing hole that has a subtle turn to the left, with a fairway bunker lying in wait on the corner of the dogleg. The hole is crying out for a power draw to shave some distance off the second shot, and the less club you are coming in with, the better, as the neck of the approach is narrowed by sand on both sides.

Hole 8
Par 5
567 yards

The 8th is a straight up-and-down three-shot hole, but for the longer hitters it's one that is there to be taken on. The first obstacle is the cross-bunker that juts in from the left side of the fairway at 260 yards. The entrance to the putting surface is open, tempting you to run in a long iron or hybrid. This is a great hole where good blows can be rewarded with a birdie.

Hole 9
Par 4
331 yards

Playing back towards the clubhouse, the hole doglegs to the right, but there is little point in taking on the corner as two deep bunkers sit here. A straight drive will find the best line as well as the most open area of the fairway. The green is protected at the front by two sand traps, so you'll need to play a lofted shot to find the heart of the green.

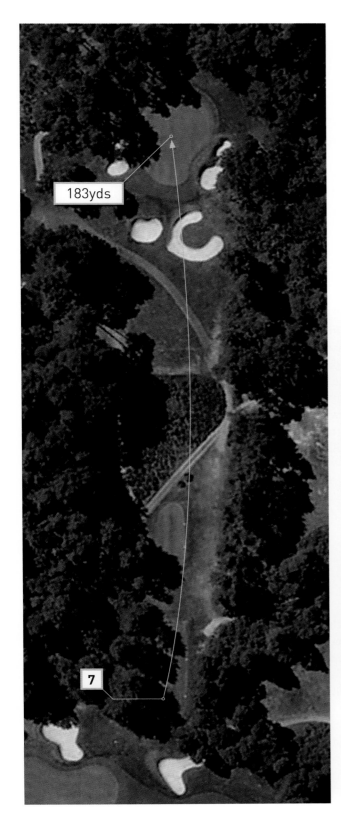

183yds

7

Hole 7 – *Par 3* – **183 yards**

The course's second par 3 is a tight, tree-lined challenge that demands a pinpoint strike to carry a ring of sand in front of the putting surface. At this distance the top pros will probably be playing little more than a 7-iron, which is just as well because the hole is highly demanding of ball control. For amateurs who lack such ball-striking qualities, more club will be needed to find a green that is slightly raised, and so the test becomes even tougher. To add to the trees and the contours of the land, a large, c-shaped bunker is the standout feature that lurks at the front of the green. Be warned, if you find this trap, making an up-and-down could prove very tough.

COURSE GUIDE 10–18

The greens at Fontainebleau can be very testing, with the undulating terrain always a challenge, so pay attention to the pin positions. Also, beware of the short par-5 12th, which can frustrate and delight in equal measure.

Opposite: A little devil – the par-5 12th may not be long but there are a number of challenges to overcome from tee to green with bunkers and rocky wasteland dominating the approach.

Hole 10
Par 3
191 yards

An open and inviting hole, but one that can easily punish anything off line; the bunkers form its ultimate defence, with two traps encircling the green, and another one short on the approach. While the teeing area is relatively open, trees hug the putting surface, which has a number of run-offs around its boundary.

Hole 11
Par 5
554 yards

The first of back-to-back par 5s, where a bunker to the right at 230 yards is a good line to attack from the tee, drawing the ball back into the heart of the landing zone. Going for the green in two is dangerous as the fairway snakes round two sand traps 80 yards short of the green. For those who play a lay-up, bunkers also pepper the right side from 200 yards.

Hole 13
Par 4
383 yards

A good drive down the left side is the shot from the tee on this mid-length par 4, avoiding the large sand trap that lies here. The right side of the fairway is very tight on the approach, but once you're in position it is only a short iron to the green, which has sand protecting its entrance. A number of undulations will test your putting skills.

Hole 14
Par 3
158 yards

The 14th is the shortest hole on the course, and it's only a short iron for good ball-strikers, played over a bank of heather and rough. The green is perched on top of an incline, with three cavernous bunkers acting as a wall protecting its entrance. There is more sand either side of the putting surface. This is one where par can quickly become bogey.

Hole 15
Par 4
430 yards

The drive has to be played over dense heather and rough. The fairway is relatively inviting, with plenty of room on the right-hand side. The blind approach should be aimed over two bunkers that form a guard 80 yards short of the green. The bunkerless green is large and undulating, with dense rough swarming around its boundary to test your short-game skills.

Hole 16
Par 4
378 yards

Another par 4 that sweeps to the left, with plenty of room out to the right side for an inviting drive, which will also open up the hole for the second shot. This is Fontainebleau's stroke-index-two hole, and while it is a test of your ball-striking, the green's open entrance allows players to run in their approaches. Just watch out for the sand either side.

Hole 17
Par 4
285 yards

A short par 4 that has attack written all over it, and at well under 300 yards, many will be tempted to try to reach the green in one blow. A mass of heather and rough stands in front of you on the tee, but the big challenge is getting past the bunkers that sit in front of the green. If you have played a lay-up, then it's a simple pitch over the sand.

Hole 18
Par 4
419 yards

This is a great finishing hole that plays relatively straight, with its kidney-shaped green tucked slightly to the right. The fairway is very narrow, but there are no bunkers to fight against until you get within 100 yards of the putting surface. The key is to keep it straight with your drive, because if you run into the rough, controlling your approach will be very difficult.

Hole 12 – *Par 5* – **454 yards**

This short par 5 is full of character; and it is ranked as the third easiest on the course, but don't be fooled by the numbers. While it is reachable for a lot of players – playing slightly downhill – there is plenty that can go wrong from tee to green. First, the drive is very tight, and there is little forgiveness for errant strikes. Bunkers then come into play from 200 yards on the right, with two pinching the fairway tight on this side. Three more traps feature at 320 yards, and if you are hoping to reach the green in two, you will have to clear a rocky stretch of wasteland from 100 yards short of the putting surface. This is a stunning hole and a classic example of a risk-reward par 5.

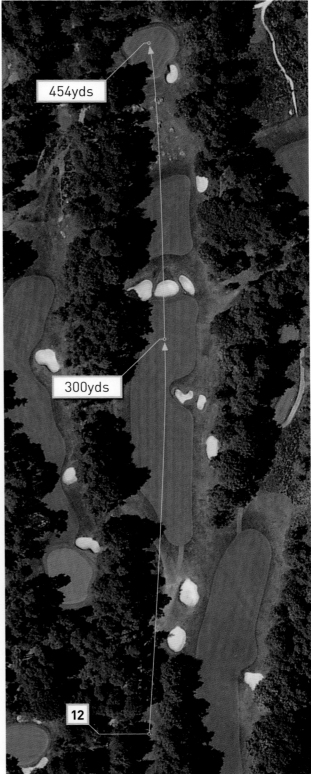

454yds

300yds

12

GUT LÄRCHENHOF

Gut Lärchenhof has quickly established a reputation as Germany's top tournament venue, which is hardly surprising when you see the layout and the test it presents for the professional game. One thing you will quickly notice is that a number of water hazards lie in wait to punish weak approach play.

Below left: Gut Lärchenhof has become a key venue on the European Tour, hosting the game's best players during the BMW International Open.

Opposite: Jack Nicklaus crafted the layout on flat farmland, with sprawling sand traps peppered around man-made lakes.

A modern course for the modern game; Gut Lärchenhof, to the north east of Cologne, is Jack Nicklaus' one and only design in Germany. Built specifically for tournament golf, the course opened for play in 1997 and within a year it would welcome the German Masters. Later renamed as the Mercedes-Benz Championship, the tournament ran for another 11 years, consistently pulling in many of the biggest names on the European Tour. From 2012, Gut Lärchenhof became the new home of the BMW International Open.

When it comes to tournament-style courses, there are few in the business to rival Nicklaus. The Golden Bear and 18-time Major winner has a mightily impressive portfolio of works around the world, with the company building a reputation for turning flat and unpromising land into grand designs that can test the game's very best players. From his earliest work at Harbour Town Links in 1969 – which hosts the annual Heritage on the PGA Tour – to his grand 1974 creation, Muirfield Village in Ohio – that welcomed the 1987 Ryder Cup – Nicklaus knows exactly what both fans and players want from a layout. The test for one complements the thrill for the other.

Critics will claim this design is too artificial, that its man-made influence plays a far too powerful role in its appearance. But it's a stigma that should be ignored, because while some courses live off their revered status and old-school traditions, others feed the adrenaline of those looking for a spectacular challenge. At Gut Lärchenhof, they will find exactly that.

The course's conditioning is first-class. Impressive to look at with not a blade of grass

out of place, there is a touch of Florida at Gut Lärchenhof, with imposing water hazards that thrill at every turn. Essentially, it is a target-style course, but there is also an inland-links feel about it with rolling fairways and fiendish, penal rough.

That said, a design philosophy of Nicklaus has always been to reward good shots, and there is certainly an element of fairness to the course.

Unlike a rugged links that can punish even the purest of strikes, what you see is pretty much what you get at Gut Lärchenhof; the hazards can be easily identified from the tee, and if you can drive the ball well, pick your spots on the fairway and, at all costs, avoid the water that comes into play on six of its holes, then scoring opportunities are there to be taken.

During the BMW International Open, the

"I have been playing golf in Germany for more than 30 years and we've never had such a good course."

Bernhard Langer

course stretches to well over 7,000 yards, but from the men's back tees the test is friendlier at 6,945. Though some muscle is needed to chase down a score, it pays to play with a good deal of patience. While one player may choose to attack, another may opt for a positional strategy. Both can be highly rewarding.

With the momentum swings of tournament golf in mind, Nicklaus added a twist to the course with the toughest challenge coming towards the end of each nine. The 8th – a mighty par 3 weighing in at over 240 yards for the professionals – is one of the most notorious one-shot holes on the European Tour. Meanwhile, the 17th is the last-chance saloon for those making a closing run: a hole that is short in length at just 349 yards, but with water all down the right side.

Despite its age, Gut Lärchenhof has matured well, and modifications will continue to keep it up to date. And, while its modern nature may not suit everyone's eye, there can be little argument that this Nicklaus design is now firmly established as one of its country's finest layouts.

COURSE GUIDE 1–9

Course yardage – Championship 6,945 yards
Course GPS – 51° 2'8.44" N 6°47'8.41" E

If your approach play is in good shape, then scoring opportunities can be found. Just make sure your ball-striking isn't off colour when you get to the long par-3 8th – Gut Lärchenhof's signature hole.

Opposite: Going right from the tee could land you in trouble on the par-4 9th, where two huge bunkers lie in wait.

Hole 1
Easy Going
Par 4 – 356 yards

As its name suggests, this is a hole to ease players into their rounds. A large fairway bunker features on the right side, so left-centre is the best line. From here, there is an open view of the green as the fairway sweeps up and down. If you are in position, it's a simple short iron to find the putting surface. Quick tip: it's best not to get too greedy; par is a solid start here.

Hole 2
Bridges
Par 4 – 386 yards

The drive is over a small water hazard as the fairway starts to climb gently towards the ideal landing zone. There are two sand traps to the left to catch anything that strays off line, while deep rough can come into play on the right side. The green is narrow, and there are two deep bunkers positioned here – one to the left and one guarding the entrance.

Hole 3
Downwind
Par 5 – 547 yards

This is a great par 5 that is framed all the way on the left side by trees and rough as it sweeps to the right. The fairway's landing zone is relatively generous, but anything too far right could find either of the two bunkers that lie here. For those who choose to attack in two, bunkers pinch the entrance to the green tightly, making it difficult to run a ball in.

Hole 4
Toads
Par 3 – 190 yards

The water to the left comes into play because the green is partly behind it, so that much will depend on the pin position. The obvious bail-out option is to the right side, where the first of the greenside traps lies. There's another one at the back of the putting surface, and if your ball goes there you risk playing back towards the water!

Hole 5
Wild Boar Run
Par 4 – 412 yards

There may be no fairway bunkers to deal with, but the drive is tight with a mass of rough on both sides. The second shot can be tricky because the fairway features a number of undulations, making downhill lies a factor. Water then hugs the left side of the putting surface, and three sand traps sit to the right on a greenside bank.

Hole 6
East End
Par 4 – 435 yards

A long, tough par 4 that plays straight up and down; long hitters will need to consider the fairway bunker that sits to the right side at 270 yards. The green is raised slightly, and anything short will run back down the slope. Deep, mounded bunkers protect the putting surface's boundary to add to the challenge of ball control. Par here is always a good return.

Hole 7
Up and Down
Par 5 – 577 yards

The 7th is Gut Lärchenhof's stroke-index one, and from the championship tees it is an imposing challenge. As the hole turns gently to the right, players will be tempted to shave the corner off, but four huge bunkers lie in wait, and any distant hopes of reaching the green in two will end here. Again, the slightly raised putting surface features a number of testing undulations.

Hole 8
Apple Trees
Par 3 – 215 yards

The narrow creek aside, the big test is avoiding the large, sprawling sand trap that lies to the front-left of the green. There is a temptation to err long to be sure of clearing the bunker, but anything that runs through the back of the green could end up nestled in the rough that lines the banks behind it. Pick your club and commit to the strike.

Hole 9 – *Happy-Hour* – **Par 4 – 414 yards**

This is a very clever par 4, which looks tougher on paper than its rating as the course's seventh hardest – so don't be fooled. Firstly, the tee shot needs to avoid the bunkers to the right, otherwise only the best will be able to take on the green with their second shot. If you have found the fairway to the left side, the approach can be played to an open and inviting putting surface, but beware: a lake positioned to the right waits to sink anything off line. The green features a number of undulations, and there are sand traps back right and left, so it's best to leave yourself short and under the hole if you have to miss the target.

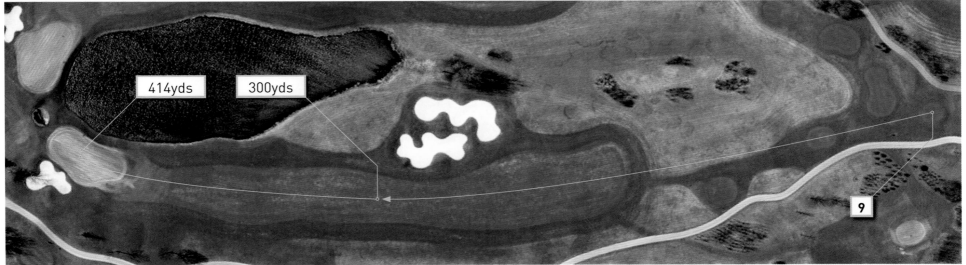

414yds   300yds

9

Course Guide 10–18

The back nine starts off gently, and then finishes with a nasty bite. The short par-4 17th can be a real knee-trembler, as well as a card-wrecker for those who attempt to attack the green over the water.

Hole 10
Second Chance
Par 4 – 416 yards

Another straight-up-and-down par 4 where the ideal line is to the left side of the rolling fairway. This is the best angle from which to attack the green, where no bunkers feature, so it is possible to run an approach shot in. Rough and steep banks envelop the putting surface. A fine hole where two good strikes will take you to the green in regulation.

Hole 11
Signature Hole
Par 3 – 157 yards

The 11th is a fantastic short hole where players are never safe until they have holed out. The green is angled slightly to the right, so it is shallow in depth, making it difficult to hold. The undulations on approach are very noticeable, but not as noticeable from the tee as the huge bunker that lies to the front of the green, with another at the back.

Hole 12
Hidden Green
Par 4 – 387 yards

A dogleg left that entices players to eye up cutting the corner; however, a solitary fairway trap lurks here with rough all around it. The hole is short enough to attack from the right side of the fairway, although anything too straight or too far right could run into a bank of rough here. The green has a small, deep trap to its left, with a steep bank to the right.

Hole 13
The Oaks
Par 5 – 520 yards

A relatively short three-shot hole that snakes to the left; a good strategy is to take the corner on as there is no sand to contend with. Those who fade the ball should certainly attack on this line. There is a lot of sand protecting the putting surface, but encouraged by the hole's moderate length, longer hitters may well be eyeing up a birdie chance.

Hole 14
Sun Valley
Par 4 – 454 yards

The length of this par 4 is the primary reason why it stands as the course's stroke index-two. Bunkers sit far left of the fairway, but they shouldn't really come into play. There is, however, a menacing sand trap to the right as the landing zone sweeps up and down. Right of centre is the best position to come in from, as the green is open on this side.

Hole 15
The Peak
Par 5 – 519 yards

Another par 5 that sweeps round to the left, with an undulating fairway asking questions of the second shot. A bunker sits on the dogleg, so this is the first obstacle, and for those who choose to lay up, another deep pot bunker sits in the middle of the fairway within pitching distance of the green. A good birdie opportunity, but choose your game plan and stick to it.

Hole 16
Lake View
Par 3 – 193 yards

A classic par 3 that needs a crisp strike to find the green; the lake dominates the right side all the way from the tee, so a draw is ideal as there isn't much to worry about left. Two bunkers are positioned short-right of the putting surface, which is raised and very undulating with a lower portion to the left side. Banks and dense rough add to the hole's defences.

Hole 18
Home Run
Par 4 – 418 yards

The course finishes with this testing par 4, where the green is tucked away to the left with water beside it. To shorten the hole, players may look to aim down the left side of the fairway, but then it's a longer carry over water for the second. Playing it safe to the right will open up the entrance to the green, although a greenside trap does lurk here.

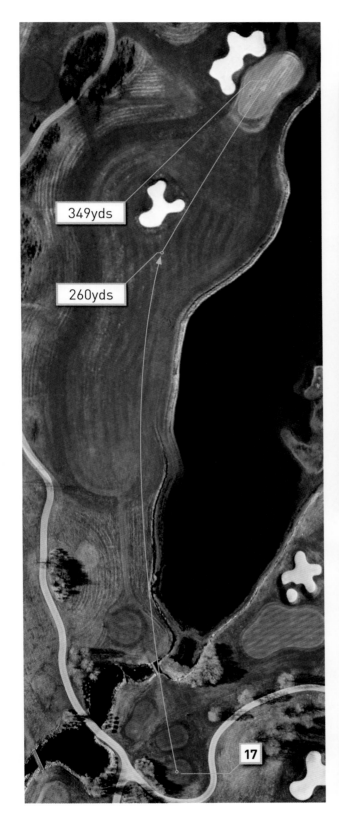

349yds

260yds

17

Hole 17 – *Waterfall* – **Par 4 – 349 yards**

The shortest par 4 on the course, but it has a number of defences, making its length a secondary factor. For the boldest and longest, there is the option to drive the green in one, something big-hitting American John Daly attempted on a regular basis in the German Masters. Naturally, a long carry over water is needed to do this, and even then, the green has a steep bank that runs down towards the lake – so accuracy is also required. The smart play is to aim left of centre with a long iron, and then play a short iron to the heart of the green. A large bunker is positioned left, and if you find this, a delicate splash shot back towards the water is needed to hold the green.

LE GOLF NATIONAL – L'ALBATROS

The host venue of the 2018 Ryder Cup serves up a procession of thrilling holes where players can be rewarded for a brand of bold and attacking golf. But with danger seemingly everywhere, Hubert Chesneau and Robert von Hagge's L'Albatros course demands a solid game plan to counter its unforgiving defences.

With sweeping dunes, elevated tees, fast-running fairways and a myriad of artificial water hazards, Le Golf National's L'Albatros course, just 20 miles from the centre of Paris, is regarded as one of continental Europe's toughest layouts. Opened in 1990 and fashioned over the flatland region of Guyancourt that surrounds the historic Château of Versailles – which was once home to Louis XIV – L'Albatros course serves up something of an inland-links feel despite the tooting car horns and thick city air only a short car drive away.

L'Albatros is the work of Hubert Chesneau and Robert von Hagge, who crafted the layout from scratch on land that had once been a rubbish tip. Unlike at so many courses that are built on undulating terrain, Chesneau and von Hagge worked from a totally blank canvas. Here the land was flattened, which allowed the designers to create every corner just the way they wanted it. As a result, the routing is one of the best in Europe, displaying all the hallmarks of a mature layout that has been specifically built for the modern game.

The thinking behind the design was simple, as the French Golf Federation was seeking a natural home for the country's top tournaments with the growth of the game on the rise throughout the 1980s. They wanted

to enhance the experience for spectators. Big events. Big atmospheres. After opening, it was formally announced as the host venue for

the French Open, and since 1991 – with the exception of 1999 and 2001 – L'Albatros has welcomed many of the world's greatest players to one of the European Tour's most celebrated tournaments. Year after year, the French Open delivers with a roll call of A-list names who thrill the crowds on a course that is ideal for attacking golf.

If hosting big events was the objective of the FGF when they set out their vision, their dream

was realized in 2011 when Golf National's L'Albatros course was named as the host venue for the 2018 Ryder Cup. This came after huge investments in Le Golf National from the State and local authorities, who poured in over €9 million to the development of the site to ensure it beat off opposition from Spain, Germany, Holland and Portugal.

As well as catering for the spectators, the course is made for matchplay golf, demanding from tee to green. Players are faced with sharp, doglegging fairways where they must pick their landing zones and strike with conviction. Water lurks on almost every corner, the greens are slick and contoured, while rugged sand traps add to the old-school ambience.

The course enjoys a wonderful mixture of holes, from those twisting two-shotters to monstrous par 3s that demand long carries over water. However, with the layout open to the elements, wind direction plays a huge part and club selection can vary from day to day. When the wind is up, patience is essential for good scoring, and knowing where to miss is as important as knowing where to hit.

Arguably, few courses have a finishing quartet of holes that can deliver to the level of L'Albatros, with the par-4 15th, par-3 16th and par-4 18th in particular all deserving of signature status. However, that distinction has been awarded to the last, where dunes envelop the right side of the fairway, giving patrons prime viewing as players drive from another elevated tee. This is all about risk-and-reward, with the second shot played over another stretch of water to a grandstand green with a mass of spectators on its banks. Thrilling doesn't do it justice.

> ## "There is a lot of drama on this golf course. That's why the crowd love it."
>
> *Thomas Levet*

COURSE GUIDE 1–9

Course yardage – Championship 7,300 yards
Course GPS – 48°45'16.81" N 2° 4'32.79" E

L'Albatros' outward stretch is riddled with water hazards and sprawling sand traps, so there is no mercy for wayward hitters and a player's ball-striking qualities are tested from the opening tee shot.

Opposite: A crisp, solid blow is needed to find the green on the long, water-lined 2nd hole, where par is a fine return.

Hole 1
Par 4
416 yards

An opening hole that demands a pinpoint drive to a fairway that opens up, despite water lining the left side all the way up to the green. Anything right will end up in dense rough, so left-centre is the best line to take from the tee. The putting surface has two bunkers on the bank to its right. Play to the heart of the green and take your par.

Hole 3
Par 5
563 yards

The course has a real inland links feel, though trees also dominate the hole from tee to green. It turns round to the right, and three well-struck shots are needed – the hole's shape makes it difficult to reach in two. Left-centre is the best landing area for the drive, and will open up the second shot, as trees block off the right side of the green.

Hole 4
Par 4
487 yards

A relatively straight hole where going left off the tee is a no-no because of a mass of sand dominating this side of the fairway. Banks and penal rough hug the right side, and the approach narrows to a green that is raised with run-off areas short-left. Three bunkers also protect a putting surface that is big enough for three-putts to be a constant threat.

Hole 5
Par 4
405 yards

Again, a huge bunker lines the left side, but going too far right, or even too straight off the tee, could leave you blocked out by a cluster of trees. The fairway is quite narrow, but if you have an open shot to the green it is a good birdie chance. However, three bunkers lie on the left side, and the putting surface features some subtle breaks.

Hole 6
Par 4
383 yards

There are no bunkers on this hole, and the fairway is quite generous. For longer hitters, it's best to play for position from the tee with a 3-wood. From the middle of the fairway it is then a short-iron to a contoured green. While the hole may look innocuous, there is unforgiving rough, particularly around the green, that can leave you scrambling just to make par.

Hole 7
Par 4
450 yards

The 7th is a very difficult par 4, rated as the second hardest on the course, which requires two good shots to find the green in regulation. Players must drive over dense rough to reach the undulating fairway, and then the approach must be threaded through a narrow channel with trees right and duneland left. Sand also protects the left side of the green.

Hole 8
Par 3
208 yards

The second short hole, but an altogether different test from the water-lined second; the green is raised with run-off areas on all sides. Wind can dictate club selection from a long iron to a sweetly struck hybrid. The surface slopes from the back with a series of borrows; one solitary bunker sits at the front waiting to gobble up those rusty strikes.

Hole 9
Par 5
596 yards

The tee shot can look intimidating, as it needs to be struck over dense bushes and lush vegetation on this dogleg right par 5. The perfect position is left-centre to open up the hole for the second shot. If attacking in two, the entrance to the green is narrow, with bunkers short-right and thick rough left. This is a great three-shot hole where course management plays a crucial part.

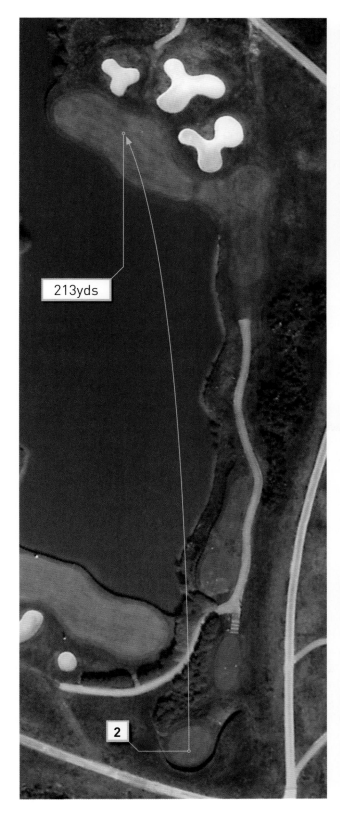

213yds

2

Hole 2 – *Par 3* – **213 yards**

This is a great early par 3, where water dominates and players need to back themselves from the tee. Depending on the wind, it can be anything from a mid-iron to a hybrid for the professionals, because if you are short your ball will end up wet. The green is at a slight angle from the tee, making it shallow in depth. With three huge bunkers positioned at the back on a steep bank, going long leaves the threat of playing from the sand back towards the water. The green is undulating with many subtle breaks, so putt-reading can be tricky. Making a par here is a great return because it is a potential card-wrecker so early in the round.

COURSE GUIDE 10–18

Arguably tougher and more imposing, the back nine can still offer huge momentum swings for those chasing a score with a number of superb risk-reward holes. Then it's a grandstand finale with a quartet of finishing holes that thrill and torment in equal measure.

Opposite: The 18th, with its amphitheatre setting, has played host to some fine finishes in the French Open as players are forced to attack the green over the lake.

Hole 10
Par 4
383 yards

Water comes back into play here, with a lake positioned left of the fairway. Players will aim right to clear the route for a better approach. The green is raised, and you'll need to hit a high ball in, as its entrance is pinched tight with lush rough and a bunker to the left. There are a number of run-off areas, notably back-left, so club selection is crucial.

Hole 11
Par 3
191 yards

This is another great one-shot hole that demands a solid carry over thick rough, as the approach drops down and then sweeps back up to the green. Anything short will not hold the bank at the front. Although there are no bunkers, hitting the green is essential if you want to make par, as the surface is fast and undulating, and is difficult to hold.

Hole 12
Par 4
443 yards

The 12th is a great-looking par 4 that doglegs sharply to the right for the second shot. Long bunkers snake either side of the fairway, but if players can thread a drive between them, they will have a clear shot to another raised green that is bunkerless. However, hitting the target is important as run-off areas and deep rough will make an up-and-down tough to make.

Hole 13
Par 4
427 yards

This stroke-index three is a sharp dogleg right with the second shot over water and through a channel of trees – two good blows are needed to reach the green here. Going right with the drive will block you out for the approach, so left is the best spot to play in from. The green has water both at the front and back-left. However, it is better to be long than short.

Hole 14
Par 5
607 yards

A great par 5, where you will find some of the best viewing spots on the course, with towering dunes enveloping the fairway. The hole doglegs right to left, and the fairway has two levels. It's not reachable in two, so players will look to find position to the right of a sprawling sand trap before pitching in to the green. Expect the 14th to create much excitement at the 2018 Ryder Cup.

Hole 15
Par 4
399 yards

From one great hole to another, and this requires a straight drive to hit the fairway. Going left will find the lush rough on the dunes, going right will find the water. The approach is then a test of nerve, playing to an island-style green that has something of TPC Sawgrass' iconic 17th to it. Only the best ball-strikers will survive on this nerve-shredding hole.

Hole 16
Par 3
175 yards

With the tee elevated, it is a long carry with water to the right, and players can be forced into taking more club than required as the front of the green slopes down to the lake. Three large bunkers are positioned left of the green, with steep grassy banks making an up-and-down tough should you miss the target. For the spectators this offers a great amphitheatre setting.

Hole 17
Par 4
484 yards

The 17th is an imposing challenge from the tee with a narrow-looking fairway that is pinched by imposing dunes on both sides. The rough here is brutal and if you stray off line it may have to be a wedge back into play. The fairway then rises up towards a green that is bunkerless, but has many subtle undulations, and there is more lush rough surrounding its boundary.

Hole 18 – *Par 4* – **470 yards**

This hole plays as a par 4 in the French Open, but it's a par 5 for the members. The pros will generally aim left-centre of the fairway in order to shorten the second shot to the green, though the landing zone drops down to the left, with water becoming an early threat. Those who are protecting a score may opt to play it as a three-shotter, baling out right with their second before playing an easier pitch over the water to the green. However, for those chasing a closing birdie, it's a long or mid-iron to carry the lake. A bunker lurks left of the green, and it's not the worst place to be because going long brings more water into play – a superb end to a great golf course.

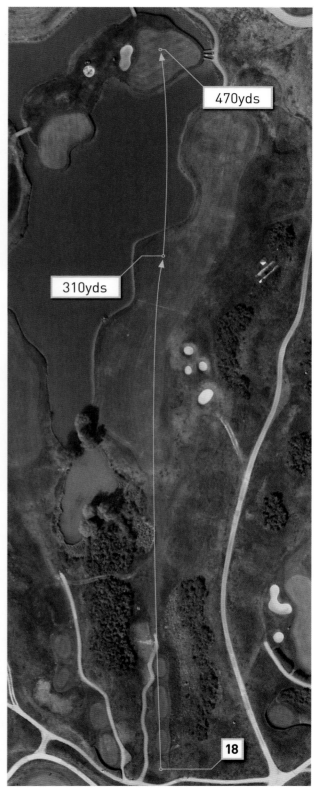

470yds

310yds

18

LES BORDES

Les Bordes brings a touch of Florida to France, and one of the grandest designs of the modern game. An exclusive members' club, it is one of the toughest tests in golf with water and huge, cavernous bunkers playing havoc from start to finish.

Just 90 minutes south west of Paris in the Loire Valley region, Les Bordes is France's most exclusive golf course. Set in the Sologne Forest and threading its way through oaks and silver birch, it is the design work of Texan Robert von Hagge, who was commissioned by Baron Marcel Bich – the co-founder of ballpoint Bic pens – and his business associate Yoshiaki Sakurai. von Hagge went to work on land that was formerly the Baron's private hunting estate, shifting over 500,000 cubic metres of soil, and shaping the layout above flowing streams and lakes. The course opened to critical acclaim in 1986, and today is perpetually rated as one of the finest in the world.

There are many contenders, a number of which are covered in this book, but for its imposing and intimidating nature, there are few who would argue against Les Bordes being Europe's toughest golf course. It's tough because so many holes demand shots that must be executed under the most intense pressure. Quite simply, the course has no time for the rash or bold. Its tight, tree-lined fairways snake around sharp doglegs; huge sprawling sand traps congest the landing zones; and there is trial by water on 11 of its 18 holes. As a result, Les Bordes commands respect, courage and intelligence, and a strategy built on simplicity will often see the better players prevail.

Some claim Les Bordes is the epitome of risk-reward golf. For the purest of ball-strikers, that might be the case. But for the mere mortals, it is more a case of survival, because disaster can strike on any hole, from its fiendishly tight par 5s to those water-ridden par 4s. Meanwhile, there is little mercy offered at the par 3s, with all but one requiring full carries over the lakes of the Sologne. There is, unquestionably, an

American feel to the layout with its water hazards putting a premium on your target game. However, this is complemented wonderfully by the tranquil feel of the forest through which the course wends its way.

Like Spain's Valderrama, there is an alluring elegance about Les Bordes. It was designed to be a masterpiece, but the intention was always to make it a challenge. For many years, Frenchman Jean van de Velde held the course record of 71, which is confirmation of the test in front of you. Meanwhile, those who break 80 get their name on the honours board – a statement of one's playing capabilities if ever there was one.

It was the Baron's original vision that Les Bordes be recognized as "The Augusta National of Europe". There are similarities, but the main one is down to the exclusivity the two courses

share. After the Baron passed away in 1994, Sakurai took over ownership. He too passed away in 2004, and four years later, his company sold up. Keen to get more visitors through the door before the sale, the course opened on a pay-and-play basis. As the numbers swelled, however, it began to suffer overcrowding issues; the conditioning went downhill, and some of its aura was lost.

Now, thanks to the excellent and continued hard work of its green staff and further

investments by new owners, happily the course has been returned to its once brilliant best. And, for those who want to sample Les Bordes, a second 18-hole layout, again designed by von Hagge, will open for play in 2014 to the paying public along with an onsite hotel. A championship venue in its own right, the new will undoubtedly complement the old, making Les Bordes one of the most charming golf resorts anywhere in the world.

> "Les Bordes raises expectations dangerously for the rest of your golfing life."
>
> *Tom Cox*

Course Guide 1–9

Course yardage – Black tees 7,000 yards
Course GPS – 47°44'3.07" N 1°40'51.66" E

Your ball-striking qualities are tested early at the narrow par-5 2nd. If you are not fully committed to the shot, the threat of water throughout the front nine will get the better of your game, so strike with conviction, or revert to a safety-first policy.

Opposite: One of the great three-shot holes, where only the best ball-strikers need worry about tackling the green in two with a 200-yard carry needed over water.

Hole 1
Par 4
438 yards

A challenging opener; from the black tees, the drive must be played over a small stretch of water. The left side of the fairway is peppered with grass bunkers from 230 yards, which could thwart your attempts to reach the green in two. Sand dominates the boundary of the putting surface, which is essentially an island green with a single bunker running around it.

Hole 2
Par 5
521 yards

The hole doglegs sharply left, then turns gently back to the right. The drive is very tight through a channel of trees, and it doesn't open up much more after that. To reach the corner it's 240 yards, and it's a bold play to attack in two, with no margin for error owing to the fairway's claustrophobic nature. Laying up with a mid-iron will leave a pitch to the green.

Hole 3
Par 4
388 yards

Trees are a menace all the way up to the fairway bunkers that come into play on the left at 210 yards. Aiming at these with a soft fade will put you in prime position on the fairway; while long hitters will have to take note of the small water hazard to the far right side. It's all carry for the second shot, with bunkers in front of the green.

Hole 4
Par 3
165 yards

Forget the trees around you on the tee; and forget the bank of dense rough at the back of the green – just focus on the water and the full carry needed to get over it. With the putting surface set slightly to the left of the tee, the preferred shot shape would be a soft draw, or else just go direct with a solid mid-iron.

Hole 5
Par 4
435 yards

There is a slight threat of water in front of the tee, but even from the back tees it's only a carry of 170 yards. A large bunker lurks on the left at 260 yards, but if you have found good position, a short iron is all that is needed to reach the green. The putting surface is two-tiered, with two bunkers, one at the back and the other guarding the front-right entrance.

Hole 6
Par 4
384 yards

It is very tempting to open the shoulders from the tee, as there is no water to fight with, but players must avoid the huge trap, which snakes up the right side from 225 yards. The fairway is tight with rough and trees on both sides. The approach is tough, because the green is narrow, with a hollow on the right side. A loose shot here could prove very costly.

Hole 8
Par 3
156 yards

Another par 3 needing a full carry over the lake; this is the shortest hole on the course, where players must block the mental challenge of the water out of their minds. Once you get over the water, the only issue is avoiding the two bunkers that sit to the green's left side. The putting surface is kidney-shaped, and there's more room to the back as it opens up.

Hole 9
Par 4
390 yards

There is a lot of sand to contend with around the green, but to get there, a drive must first be threaded through a tunnel of dense woodland. Meanwhile you also need to avoid a large bunker that sits to the right of the fairway. The longer you can go, the better, although water lurks at 285 yards, so don't go that long. A cluster of sand traps protects the green.

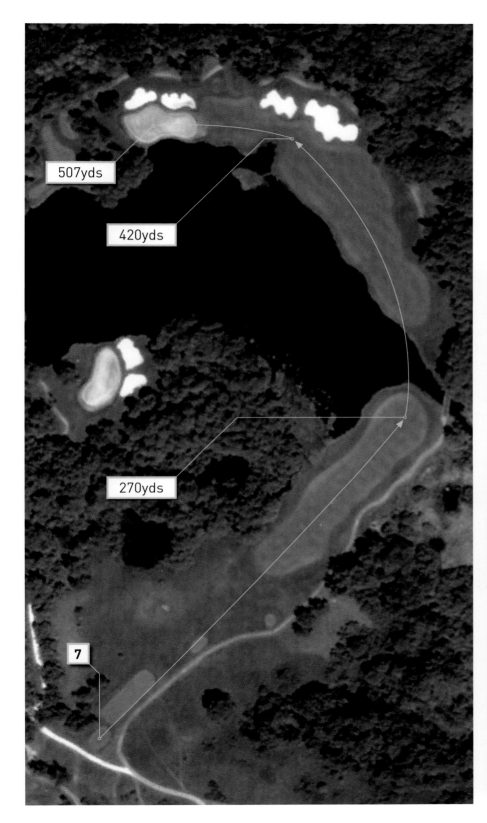

507yds

420yds

270yds

7

Hole 7 – *Par 5* – 507 yards

A stunning hole that asks questions on every shot; firstly, the drive must be threaded down a narrow neck of the fairway, which itself is very demanding. Then comes the dilemma: do you attack, or play it safe? Taking the green on in two requires a monstrous carry of well over 200 yards over water as the hole sweeps round to the left at an almost 90-degree angle. But even playing the hole in three is tough, as a mid-iron has to be played over a small corner of the lake to find the widest part of the fairway. From here, the approach will be a wedge that cannot go right as there are two greenside traps, and certainly not left, as there is water. Good luck!

COURSE GUIDE 10–18

Get ready for a fantastic inward stretch of holes, among which the 14th and 18th are the standout tests. Mercifully, there is a run of holes from the 15th to the 17th that feature no water – so it's best to make the most of them.

Opposite: Another classic par 5 comes at the 14th. The fairway snakes gently to the right, before players face the daunting prospect of playing their approach to an island green.

Hole 10
Par 5
511 yards

Although it looks like one of the more straightforward holes at Les Bordes, shot placement is crucial and once you run into trouble it's a tough test to get back on track. An accurate drive is needed to avoid the two traps on the left side of the fairway. Attacking in two is fraught with danger, with five bunkers guarding the approach from 100 yards in.

Hole 11
Par 4
399 yards

The hole turns sharply to the left; the corner of the dogleg is at 240 yards so a driver is not always the best option to find position. There is no sand protecting the green, and it's nothing more than a short iron or wedge to get you home. Water, once again, is the only obstacle as it hugs the left side of the approach all the way to the putting surface.

Hole 12
Par 4
412 yards

A short carry is needed to get over the water. The fairway begins to narrow at the 240-yard mark, with a series of clever undulations also coming into play, and grass bunkers peppering both sides. There is a huge, sprawling bunker hugging the left side of the approach, and a well-directed mid-iron is needed to clear the three traps that protect the front of the green.

Hole 13
Par 3
184 yards

It's water again on the course's third par 3, and it's a long carry as well with 170 yards needed to reach the front of the green. The putting surface features a number of undulations and there is deep rough at the back. One large bunker dominates the right. If in doubt, take an extra club and play to the back of the green because anything short will prove very costly.

Hole 15
Par 4
437 yards

A large sand trap will catch the eye on the right-hand side of the fairway; however, there are many more perils to overcome from tee to green. Grass bunkers pinch both sides of the fairway, and the landing zone is very narrow from 200 to 260 yards. The approach to the green is wide open, but pay attention to the large hump in the middle of the putting surface.

Hole 16
Par 3
215 yards

Players may be licking their lips at the sight of a par 3 that features no water, but this hole plays long and up a slope to a green that drops viciously from the left side. A large bunker lying close to the right entrance means a full-blooded long iron has to carry the hazard all the way to the green. This is a really testing one-shotter.

Hole 17
Par 4
454 yards

The penultimate hole sweeps round to the right, and a good drive will take you to the corner of the dogleg at 260 yards. But the longer the drive, the better, as the ideal way to approach the green is from the left side of the fairway. A large bunker hugs the right-hand side of a narrow green. Two very good strikes are needed to find the green in regulation.

Hole 18
Par 4
447 yards

The 18th is a fantastic final hole with water coming into play on both the drive and approach. A soft draw will shave off some yardage for the second shot as the fairway opens up slightly from 250 yards. The approach is a long carry over water, but the green is tough to hold, with a series of testing breaks and run-off areas. Two bunkers also lurk at the back. What a finish!

Hole 14 – *Par 5* – 557 yards

Some will question what Robert von Hagge was doing when he designed the 14th, because for many players it is simply too tough. Water lies everywhere: in front of you on the tee; to the right of you on the fairway; to the left of you on the approach; and all around you on the island green. Thoughts of attacking must be instantly dispelled, as there is just too much risk in taking this green on in two. Instead, the strategy needs to be broken down, shot by shot. Firstly, aim the drive at the sand trap on the right and play for a soft draw. Secondly, lay up to the left of the bunkers 100 yards short of the green. Thirdly, pitch over the water to the green, and hope for the best.

557yds

480yds

250yds

14

Les Bordes has been described by its Texan
architect Robert von Hagge as a course
representing "authentic and uncompromised golf".

MORFONTAINE

One of the most beautiful and natural courses in Europe, Morfontaine has changed little since Tom Simpson's work in 1927. An exclusive members' club, its old-school charms take you away from the stresses and strains of everyday life.

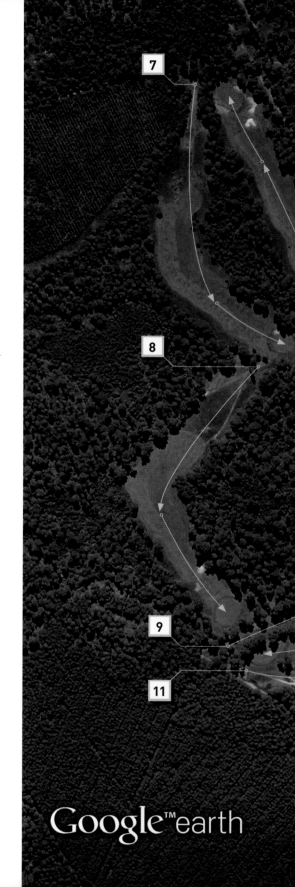

Left: Scotch pines are a feature at Morfontaine, congesting the fairways of Tom Simpson's beautiful layout in the Ermenonville Forest.

Opposite: Morfontaine demands pinpoint accuracy from the tee, and while the greens are not overly populated by sand, many subtle run-offs challenge a player's approach skills.

They do things by tradition at Morfontaine; from the moment you enter through the gates and take the one-mile drive up to the clubhouse, you will know it is a very special place, with a very special golf course. This is one of the most tranquil layouts to play, cut through the Ermenonville Forest – one of the Three Great Forests, along with Chantilly and Halatte – just 25 miles north of Paris.

The club's story began in 1913, when the Duc de Guiche, Armand de Gramont, transformed an old polo playing field into a golfing playground for himself and his friends. British architect Tom Simpson designed what is today known as the Vallière course – a nine-holer that, with its rustic setting, found immediate success and acclaim. But, after the First World War, with the game growing in popularity across the continent, action was taken to build another 18-hole layout, and Simpson's magic was called on again to create Morfontaine's championship masterpiece. He accepted, and the "Grand Parcours" opened for play in 1927.

Simpson, along with the great Harry Colt,

would play a major role throughout what would become a great era for golf course design in the 1920s and '30s. He would go on to have many notable works in the UK and Ireland, but arguably, his most impressive came during the early part of his career in France, at both Fontainebleau and Chantilly.

An eccentric man, who was educated at Cambridge, Simpson had worked briefly as a lawyer before turning his attentions to golf course design. He was a scratch player who many claimed carried something of an attitude. But whatever he did and said, he was always one to deliver on a promise, and his work at Morfontaine has stood the test of time to remain one of European golf's classic designs.

Naturally, there is something of a British feel to the course, with its sand-based soil and heathland setting. As you would expect, given its surrounding, dense woodland, the layout is tight and tree-lined with scotch pines framing the route as you swing back and forth in direction. It is not long at 6,535 yards, and there is little to be gained from attempting to bludgeon your

way around. Nor is it overly claustrophobic, having a distinct lack of fairway bunkers, but it does demand a strategic game plan from the tee because the real test will be your approach play to Morfontaine's many well-guarded and contoured putting surfaces.

There is a wonderful, eclectic mix of holes, and right from the start, where you fire out of the blocks on the dogleg right opener, the course flows beautifully. Throughout the front nine, the predominant shot shape is right to left. Some of the turns are subtle, others more acute, as at holes seven and eight. The back nine plays straighter, before the grand 18th sweeps right, back towards the clubhouse.

You'll also notice there are five par 3s, each and every one a classic in its own right. Ranging in length from 146 yards to 195, they are tempting for the very best ball-strikers, while at the same time menacing for the lesser due to the ring of defences that encircle the greens.

Despite its heritage, Morfontaine cares little for grand proclamations. They do things their own way here, and there has never been any ambition to host top-level tournament golf. With a somewhat understated and minimalist feel, the layout has remained relatively unchanged since Simpson's original work, although American Kyle Phillips was called on to make some minor modifications in 2005.

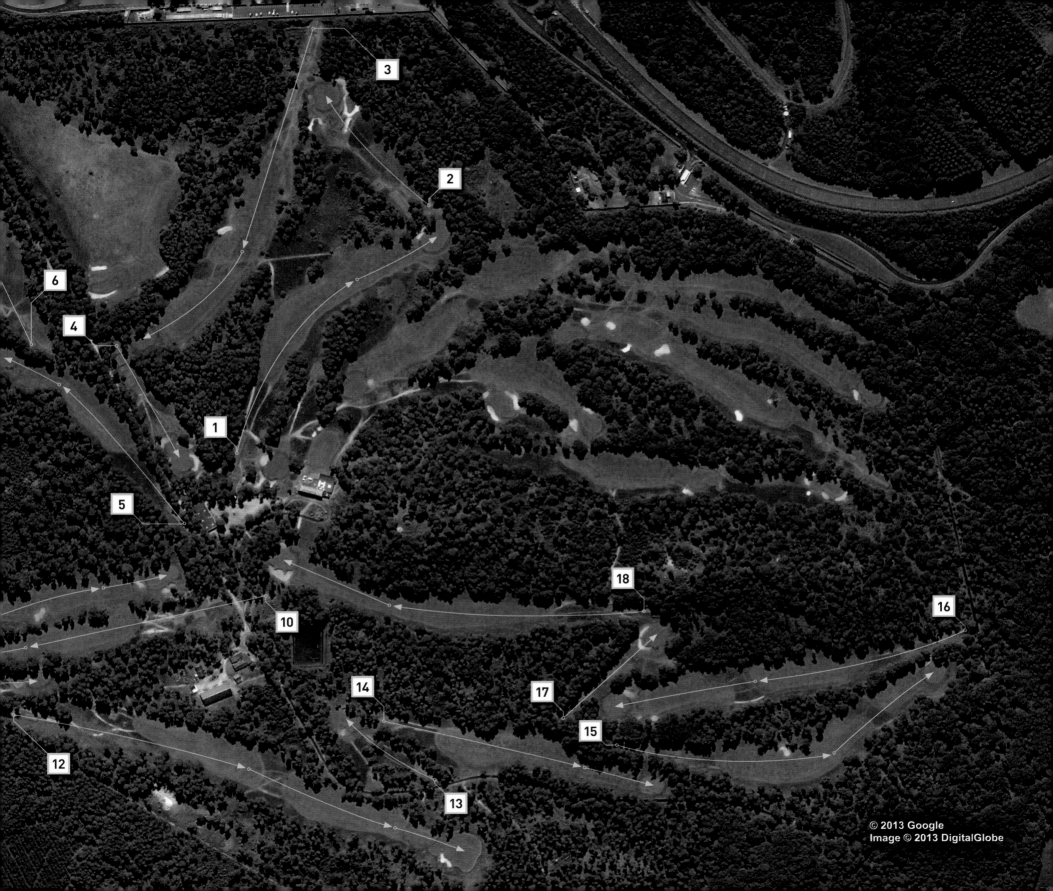

Course Guide 1–9

A tricky start, but a birdie chance awaits at the 3rd – the course quickly finds its rhythm with a premium placed on accurate approach play. If chasing an early score, playing for position is better than playing for distance.

Course yardage – Championship 6,535 yards
Course GPS – 49° 8'50.96" N 2°36'4.83" E

Opposite: The par-4 7th favours those who can attack with a soft draw aimed down the left side of the fairway, which will open up the green for the second shot.

Hole 1
Par 4
450 yards

The course opens with a tough dogleg right, where a fade from the left side will set you up to attack with your second shot. If the tee shot is too straight, it will run into the rough and heather that hug the left side of the fairway. The green has a bunker to the left, and this side of the approach is more tightly pinched with trees.

Hole 2
Par 3
195 yards

A solid mid-iron is needed on this par 3, with the green angled to the right. A mass of heather lurks in front of the tee, and again a fade is the required shot shape, as the left side of the putting surface is more open. The greenside traps are deep, and anything right will find the long strip of sand that snakes up the side of the putting surface.

Hole 3
Par 5
497 yards

This short par 5 doglegs gently to the right, and there is nothing to be gained by taking the corner on, with sand and trees blocking the path. Instead, a straight drive, short of the cross heather at 320 yards, will leave an open route to the green. If attacking, it needs to be arrow-straight; on the right is tree trouble, and then it's a scramble to make par.

Hole 4
Par 3
178 yards

The second of the par 3s, and a real test of the short game as its green is very unforgiving, with run-off areas channelling your ball away into the traps – especially the large one to the left side. Again, it's only a mid-iron, but such are the defences around the putting surface that missing the target can quickly ruin any hopes of making par.

Hole 5
Par 4
348 yards

Not a long par 4, but with the tee set back in a narrow corridor of trees, it is one that fully tests a player's accuracy. For the second shot, the fairway sweeps round to the left, and the green is tucked away on this side. Owing to the hole's length, it's best to play a hybrid from the tee, which will leave you with little more than a wedge to find the putting surface.

Hole 6
Par 4
390 yards

This hole plays straight up and down, and the drive is tight with little forgiveness on either side – although there are no fairway bunkers to contend with. Left of centre is the ideal line from the tee, as going right could block you out for the approach. The green is peppered with sand on both sides; however, there is more danger to the right.

Hole 8
Par 4
426 yards

An even sharper dogleg right than the preceding 7th, and it calls for an altogether different strategy. Here, the hole sweeps dramatically at 200 yards, so a much longer approach awaits and it's best to play for position from the tee. Two cross-bunkers lie short of the green, and the fairway drops down from the right side. This is a tough hole, but one of the most eye-catching.

Hole 9
Par 4
369 yards

The back tee is elevated, and the drive is tight through the trees. A fairway bunker lies on the right side at 180 yards, and for those taking a driver, it should be easily cleared. A straight blow should leave a floated pitch to a green that features a number of subtle breaks. Sand lies up the right side of the putting surface, and another trap lurks back-right.

427yds

260yds

7

Hole 7 – *Par 4* – 427 **yards**

A long, sharp dogleg par 4 that demands two solid blows to find the green in regulation; the line from the tee should be right of centre, with a draw bringing the ball back into the heart of the fairway as the hole turns at 280 yards. Anyone who takes on the corner of the dogleg runs the risk of finding a mass of dense woodland and towering pine trees. Even if they are avoided, chances are you will be blocked out for the second. The right side of the green is open, though it features a gentle ridge, with a number of other run-off areas and undulations. A deep bunker sits to the left side of the putting surface.

Course Guide 10–18

The back nine is straighter from tee to green, with a great mix of holes to test your shot-making skills. To score well it's all down to making the most of your approach play, as the greens are not receptive to imprecise ball-striking.

Opposite: The unusual sight of a large tree stands before you on the tee of the par-3 13th, but firing a short iron over it is the ideal line to attack the heart of the green.

Hole 10
Par 4
415 yards

Playing back in the opposite direction to the 9th, the outward nine begins with another straight hole that features a generous landing zone. However, the approach is pinched tight as the green is framed beautifully by dense woodland. There are no greenside traps, but the putting surface drops off and, if the target is missed, an up-and-down can be tough to make.

Hole 11
Par 3
150 yards

The 11th may only require a short iron, and in fact it is rated as the course's easiest hole, but this little par 3 can easily catch players out. The key is to avoid the deep bunker to the right of the green's entrance. Left is therefore the best line to take, as there is more room to miss without penalty on this side of the putting surface.

Hole 12
Par 5
616 yards

This is the longest hole on the course, and a daunting challenge that will punish over-ambitious attacking play. A mass of heather crosses the fairway at just over 300 yards, so big hitters will need to hold back. A lay-up played down the left side will then leave a wedge to an open green, which is guarded by a solitary, large bunker to its right side.

Hole 14
Par 4
370 yards

At well under 400 yards in length, and with no bunkers from tee to green, this par 4 will obviously tempt some players to pull out the driver and swing at will. But no hole at Morfontaine should be underestimated, and the smart play is a well-directed 3-wood up the left centre, then a short iron to the green. The undulating fairway drops down from the left side.

Hole 15
Par 4
447 yards

This long par 4 snakes to the left, and a well-positioned drive should be aimed down the right side, ideally drawing back round the corner to shave some distance off the second shot. Attacking the elbow of the dogleg is fraught with danger, as a single sand trap lies in wait. With the entrance to the green open, a long or mid-iron can be run in, avoiding the greenside traps on the left side.

Hole 16
Par 4
453 yards

A long two-shotter that plays back towards the clubhouse from the course's most western point. The fairway is very tight, in fact one of the narrowest on the course, with a swathe of heather and rough running across at 300 yards. Left of centre is the best line to approach from, as a large bunker protects the boundary of the green on the right side.

Hole 17
Par 3
168 yards

The last of the short holes, and another that requires you to hit the heart of the green. A steep bank of heather lies at the back, but the test is to avoid the narrow bunker that swings from the front of the putting surface round to the left side. Anything that drifts right will not hold the green, as many subtle breaks wait to channel your ball away.

Hole 18
Par 5
490 yards

The 18th is a grand finishing hole, and one that opens up a birdie opportunity for those who can find the left portion of the fairway. From here, a long iron can be targeted to the right of the green – just not too far right, or you'll find the trap. The bunker to the left is huge, and the green has a number of breaks to prey on those final-hole nerves.

Hole 13 – *Par 3* – **146 yards**

From the longest hole on the course to the shortest, but one that is full of character with a number of challenges to overcome en route to the green. On the tee, the imposing bulk of a large pine tree dominates the view, and can have you reaching for a club with much more loft in the hope of clearing it. The best ball-strikers will feel confident striking a sweet 8-iron directly over the top of it, taking them to the heart of a putting surface that has one deep trap to the right, and another two on the left. If the target is missed, an up-and-down will be very tricky because the subtle undulations can channel your ball off in all directions. Take a par and move on!

146yds

13

159

OCEANICO OLD

Around the fishing port of Vilamoura just 20 minutes from Faro international airport, the Oceanico Group has built up a portfolio of great tracks to sate the appetite of Europe's travelling golfers. Despite new developments, none has the history and charms of the Old Course with its pine-lined fairways and rolling terrain.

They just keep coming, day after day, week after week, month after month, year after year. From Palmares in the west to Quinta Da Ria in the east, the Algarve has become the golfing Mecca of Europe, and lovers of the game flock endlessly to Portugal's southern coastline in search of fine wine, a warm welcome, an almost constant supply of sunshine, and some of the best courses the public can pay to play.

Of those, Vilamoura's Oceanico Old, more commonly referred to simply as Vilamoura Old – or the Grande Dame – is one of the region's most understated layouts. Classic in every way, it has remained almost unchanged from the design that was beautifully manufactured by Frank Pennink in 1969, despite Martin Hawtree's respectful upgrade in 1996 when a state-of-the-art irrigation system was introduced.

Playing through a channel of umbrella pines, there is a touch of the inland England about the Old. Indeed, some would argue that it remains almost too English, guilty of meandering along in the same tone, its dense pines protecting and hiding you from the elements, meaning the test never changes from day to day.

This may be true; the Old doesn't have the jaw-dropping coastline of San Lorenzo, nor does it have the man-made lakes that make for such a thrilling round at the nearby Oceanico Victoria, host of the annual Portugal Masters. However, there is an almost sacred feel to Pennink's design. Its secluded fairways leave you unsure of what is to come next and there is most definitely a touch of Spain's Valderrama in the layout.

While it may look daunting at times, the Old is actually very playable for amateurs, and the front stretch allows you to find your range with a number of short par 4s and reachable par 5s at the 2nd and 5th holes. There are times when the course begins to bare its teeth, as at the par-3 6th that plays from up high in the clouds, measuring a cool 231 yards from the back pegs, and at the 8th, a monster of a par 4 that weighs in at 458 yards, seemingly playing all uphill to a tiny green that appears unreachable for all but the longest of hitters.

But overall, if you can keep it straight off the tee, scoring opportunities abound. And, while the putting surfaces are slick, they are not overly protected by sand, thus ensuring there is ease on your approach play. Just beware: the pines, and their overhanging branches, remain the course's ultimate defence, so your long game needs to be in top shape. On the back nine, three par 5s open up more scoring opportunities, with the predominant shape of the holes sweeping gently from left to right.

Despite its pedigree and wonderful conditioning, the Old doesn't carry much top-level tournament heritage. Those tight, tree-lined fairways and its almost claustrophobic atmosphere make it uninviting for spectators. Charismatic Englishman Brian Barnes did win the Portugal Masters here in 1979, but the course's reputation is enhanced more by the huge numbers who swarm to play it, and the huge numbers who continue to swarm back.

Golfers really are spoilt for choice in the Algarve, but nowhere more than in the purpose-built town of Vilamoura, which itself has a myriad of fine layouts suiting the needs of every level of player. That said, the charms of the Old have helped it stand the test of time despite a cluster of developments threatening to overhaul its status as a, if not the, must-play track in the Algarve. Play it once, and you'll always want to return for more.

> "I honestly don't think there is a more complete golf offering anywhere else in Europe."
>
> *Ricardo Santos*

COURSE GUIDE 1–9

Course yardage – White tees 6,832 yards
Course GPS – 37º 6'7.33" N 8º 6'58.05"W

Players can find their feet with a short par 4 and a reachable par 5 – but beware, there are a number of tricks and treats waiting as the front nine begins to find its teeth. Pay attention to the fairways' landing zones as overhanging trees can block your route to the green.

Opposite: It may be short in length, but the par-3 4th asks a number of questions, with a large oak tree blocking your path to the green.

Hole 1
Par 4
339 yards

The tee is elevated, and players can be lured into firing away with their driver down a fairway that narrows near to the green and has overhanging trees. Anything right, and you'll be playing back through the umbrella pines, so many will opt to play short with a 3-wood or long iron. The green is relatively flat with shallow traps guarding its entrance on either side.

Hole 2
Par 5
475 yards

This is the first of the par 5s and it's a good chance to get a score going. The fairway widens up to invite players to open their shoulders, and once you have a good tee shot away, the green can be attacked in two. The fairway does rise slightly, but there are not many defences waiting to catch you out. Two solid blows will set up an inviting birdie opportunity.

Hole 3
Par 4
354 yards

Overhanging umbrella pines make the hole appear tight from the tee, so players should take advantage of its modest length and play for position on the fairway with a long iron. The ideal line is right-centre, as a large pine pinches the left side of the approach. Sand lurks either side of the green, but with a wedge in hand there is no excuse for missing your target.

Hole 5
Par 5
530 yards

A long three-shot hole that wends gently to the left, making the ideal spot right-centre of the fairway for a clear route to the green. Far right is out-of-bounds – you will be on the course's driving range – and two bunkers also hug this side of the fairway at the 250-yard mark. The green is heavily contoured, sloping from back to front.

Hole 6
Par 3
231 yards

The long 6th is a fantastic par 3 that can strike fear into the hearts of even the crispest of ball-strikers. The green, seemingly miles away with the tee perched high in the clouds, has two deep traps guarding its entrance. Use these hazards as a marker for where to aim your tee shot, as trees make the approach very narrow. Shorter hitters may even take a driver here.

Hole 7
Par 4
429 yards

A dogleg par 4 that turns to the left, and with two fairway bunkers on the right-hand side, this is one hole where it pays to cut the corner. As the fairway turns, there is a steady incline and you will have to play semi-blind to the green. A great hole that is one of the tightest on the course, with umbrella pines overhanging the fairway.

Hole 8
Par 4
458 yards

This is the course's stroke-index one, and rightly so. It's a long par 4 that plays gradually uphill, so you need to fire your best out of the blocks, avoiding a fairway bunker on the left-hand side at 250 yards. From here, it's another long iron to a small green that has sand to its right. Two hefty blows are needed, and many amateurs will play this as a three-shot hole.

Hole 9
Par 4
289 yards

After the course's longest par 4 comes the shortest, which leads many players to get carried away and try to bludgeon their way to the putting surface. Instead, the smart play is to take nothing more than a mid-iron to the left side of the fairway. From here, pitch on to the green and try to make birdie with the putter. If you get greedy, a bogey may result.

Hole 4 – *Par 3* – **178 yards**

Instantly recognizable by the towering oak tree that sits directly in front of the green on the other side of a pond, this par 3 can have you switching clubs several times before you pluck up the courage, step on to the tee and give it a go. Ideally, flushing a high-flying 7-iron over the tree is the ideal line to take, but you need to strike with conviction as a large trap lurks just beyond it. Another two greenside bunkers lie to the left of the putting surface while there is little room to bail-out right – a steep bank and thick trees will leave you scrambling to make even bogey. A great hole which, depending on wind direction, can play very differently from one day to the next.

178yds

4

Course Guide 10–18

With three par 5s on the inward stretch, there are birdie opportunities. But shot placement is key here with some great dogleg holes and two tricky par 3s. Look out for the 17th, where players have to drive semi-blind up and over a hill.

Opposite: The par-5 12th sweeps to the right, where only the longest and bravest dare take on the corner in an attempt to shorten the hole.

Hole 10
Par 3
167 yards

It may look innocuous, but this little par 3 tests a player's ability to hit the target like no other as the green is set on a steep bank. Anything short and the ball will roll back down; anything long and it's a nervy chip from penal rough to a sloping green that can take you back to where you just came from. It's a hole that demands the utmost respect.

Hole 11
Par 4
426 yards

This is another stunning hole where players can see it all from the tee, despite the fairway turning gently to the left just shy of the green. In terms of driving, the landing zone opens up so you have more freedom with the driver. That said, you don't want to go left, as your approach could be blocked out. The green is subtly contoured, so pin position is crucial.

Hole 13
Par 4
380 yards

It's similar in shape to the 12th, but it pays to cut the corner on this par 4 if you are looking to make up a score on the back nine. That said, caution must be shown as the fairway drops from left to right. Again, ideally you want to be in position on the left side. The approach is downhill to a small green. Left is the safer option; right is dead man's land.

Hole 14
Par 5
481 yards

Another par 5, and an ideal scoring opportunity; bunkers lie either side of the fairway – the first at 240 yards, the second at 270. The hole doglegs slightly to the left, and three bunkers protect the green, which has some subtle undulations. Some players can be caught out when attacking in two, as the fairway lifts up slightly, so more club may be needed.

Hole 15
Par 3
164 yards

This is another short hole that players underestimate at their peril. A sweetly struck mid-iron will take you to the heart of the green, but again the putting surface sits on top of a steep slope, so anything short will drift away, forcing you to scramble just to make par. Bunkers lie either side, but if you do miss the green, they aren't the worse place to be.

Hole 16
Par 5
562 yards

The 16th is the longest hole on the course, and perhaps one of the most open from the tee. Again, the hole sweeps round to the right, so left-centre is the perfect position. From here, a bold 3-wood fade will give you a chance of reaching the green in two; otherwise it's a lay-up to the widest part of the fairway. Bunkers protect the green on both sides.

Hole 17
Par 4
386 yards

From the tee, players can see little of the hole – just two bunkers that sit on top of the hill on the left-hand side of the fairway. Long hitters can take on the line of the bunkers, leaving a shorter approach. The landing zone is relatively inviting to the right, but the hole then rises again towards the green, which has two deep traps to its right.

Hole 18
Par 4
451 yards

The home hole is a long and straight par 4 with trees lining the fairway on both sides. A bunker lies some 120 yards short of the green on the left, and a towering pine can block out the approach from the right. Two sprawling bunkers lie either side of the green, which features some subtle contours. This is a fine finish to a fine golf course.

532yds

460yds

270yds

12

Hole 12 – *Par 5* – **532 yards**

From the tee, few holes can look as fearsome as this dogleg right
par 5, as your drive needs to be threaded through a channel of umbrella
pines. Long hitters, or risk-takers, will try and cut the corner, but
out-of-bounds hugs this side. The ideal position is left-centre of the
fairway, which will open up the hole; anything too straight will leave
you fighting to navigate your way past the trees. From the left you can
attack in two, or lay up and attempt to get up and down for birdie. Two
bunkers guard the entrance to the green, one on the right, one on the
left. A beautiful par 5 that commands respect every time it is played.

Famed for its meandering layout over gently undulating terrain, Oceanico Old is renowned all over the golfing world.

TERRE BLANCHE – LE CHÂTEAU

Just 45 minutes inland from the Côte d'Azur in the south east of France, you will find the luxurious resort of Terre Blanche, and the impressive Le Château course that has been turning heads ever since its completion in 2000.

It is an intriguing place with an intriguing story. On land that was once owned by the actor and James Bond star Sean Connery, British designer Dave Thomas has created two of Europe's prettiest layouts that meander through the forest in the foothills of Tourrettes, a medieval village some 25 miles west of Cannes. Terre Blanche features 36 holes, Le Château and Le Riou, with the former its signature track, which is the host of the European Senior Tour's French Riviera Masters. There are numerous other leisure facilities onsite that are complemented by the Four Seasons hotel, but it is unquestionably the golf courses, and Le Château in particular, that led to the complex being named as Europe's 2012 Golf Resort of the Year by the International Association of Golf Tour Operators.

When the land was owned by Connery, the Scot believed it was the perfect plot for the development of a top-class golf resort. He eventually sold up, some 265 hectares, to German software entrepreneur Dietmar Hopp in 1999. Shortly after, work began on the construction of the site. Today, Connery's vision has been realized with a venue that is ready and waiting to host the very best players on the continent. Everything about Terre Blanche is grand in stature; everything about it oozes class.

Some golf courses, particularly those with such modern designs, would struggle to fit in with their surrounding area. But Thomas is

the master of blending a layout seamlessly into the landscape; his philosophy being that there should always be "an appreciation of the wider natural setting and to understand how to adapt the golf course into the existing features and terrain". At Terre Blanche, he has done exactly that. Few courses can challenge Le Château for its beauty, or for the way it fits like a glove into the backdrop of limestone peaks and oak forests. The château itself, set high in the hills – which Connery also owned – overlooks the landscape like a guardian angel.

The course's fairways are naturally tree-lined, with sprawling sand traps placed cleverly on both sides. In terms of strategy, it's set up for risk-reward golf, with a series of doglegs asking questions from the tee, and a number of water features testing the second shot. Thomas is no stranger to creating such challenges, one of his most notable works being the Belfry's Brabazon in England – a four-time host venue of the Ryder Cup – that prides itself on those make-or-break holes that are designed to deliver the thrills and spills of tournament golf.

You don't need to be bullish to overpower this course, because those who play with patience – plotting their way and positioning themselves on the fairways – will undoubtedly score well. As a result, the course is playable to all levels of player, and one who possesses good course management is always likely to do better than one who simply huffs and puffs while attacking constantly.

That said, it pays to show a bit of muscle from time to time as a series of sweeping par 5s tempt you to attack in two. But one thing you cannot do is lose your focus, and it's best to formulate a game plan and stick to it. The course also features some tricky little par 3s that

may look welcoming, but are anything but in terms of the challenge they present.

To add to the course, golfers can enjoy the wonderful climate in this south east corner of France, with sunshine baking the fairways for an average of 300 days a year.

"An exceptional golf course."

David Russell

"The best golf resort in Europe."

Raphael Jacquelin

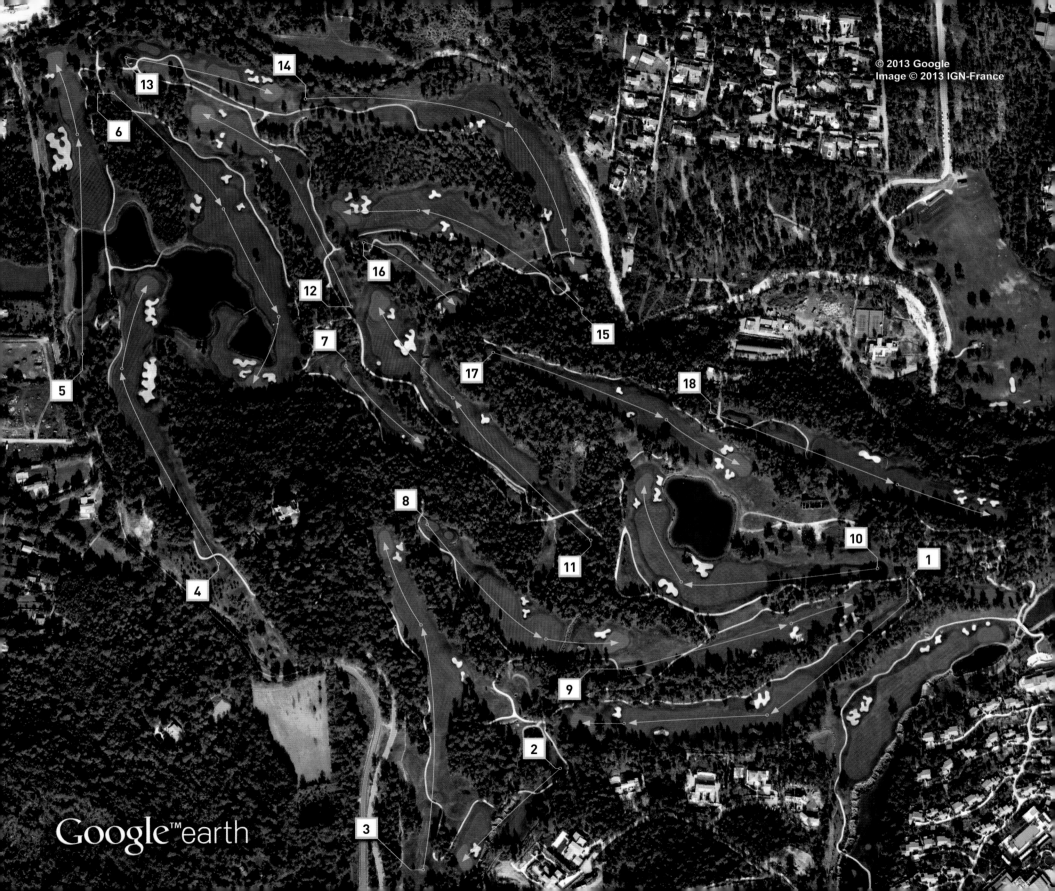

COURSE GUIDE 1–9

Course yardage – White tees 7,079 yards
Course GPS – 43°35'52.81" N 6°43'56.23" E

Players are challenged early on by a series of intimidating doglegs, while the front nine is complemented by a number of beautiful features, from waterfalls and rocky creeks to the towering pines that stand guard along the fairways.

Opposite: Whether you choose to attack in two or play it with a lay-up, the par-5 6th remains one of Terre Blanche's toughest tests.

Hole 1
Par 5
533 yards

This is a picturesque three-shot hole that sweeps dramatically to the right, but taking on the dogleg brings much danger as players can easily run out of fairway. The best option is to play left-centre and look for a fade to open up the second shot. A bunker pinches the left side of the approach, and there is another sprawling sand trap short-right of the green.

Hole 2
Par 3
182 yards

A visually stunning hole with waterfalls and a creek cutting across the entrance to the green; the surface is slightly raised and there are a number of testing contours to challenge your putt-reading skills. A deep bunker lurks at the front, so a solid, crisp strike is needed to clear it. Towering trees on the left side narrow the approach.

Hole 3
Par 4
466 yards

A sharp dogleg left, this hole is lined from tee to green by dense trees, and anything wayward will likely lead to a high number on the scorecard. Two bunkers sit to the right side of the fairway, but this is the ideal line for the tee shot to set up an easier approach. Another three bunkers protect the green, and the real test is the second shot.

Hole 4
Par 4
461 yards

Avoid going right from the tee or it may be hard to reach the green, with a huge sand trap that side. Keeping your ball left is crucial to making a score here, but there is more danger up by the green, with another, equally punishing bunker to the right. The putting surface is undulating, and three-putts are a constant threat.

Hole 5
Par 4
444 yards

Following a tee shot over water, the fairway opens up, but there is a mass of sand to left side at 250 yards, so the ideal line is right-centre. The approach is once again narrowed with overhanging trees, and there is another sand trap short-left of the green. The entrance is relatively open, so you have the option to run a long iron in.

Hole 7
Par 3
160 yards

It may only be a mid-iron, but miss your spot on this par 3 and a bogey surely awaits. The best line is to the right of the green, as a bank runs down helpfully on this side, but two small bunkers lurk here, and these will need to be carried. Anything sent left from the tee runs the risk of finding the trees, as the hole drops down dramatically.

Hole 8
Par 4
390 yards

A creek runs across the fairway some 80 yards short of the green, so longer hitters may want to play something less than a driver from the tee. That said, two bunkers are positioned left, so aim at them and look to fade the ball right to find the best spot. In position, it's a birdie opportunity although there is sand to the left of the green.

Hole 9
Par 4
401 yards

This is one of the more direct holes at Le Château, as there is no dogleg to contend with. However, it can still catch many players out as the fairway features a number of rolling contours and there is sand peppering the right side. Aim left-centre for the ideal position from which to attack the green; just don't go too far left because tree trouble looms here.

Hole 6 – *Par 5* – **559 yards**

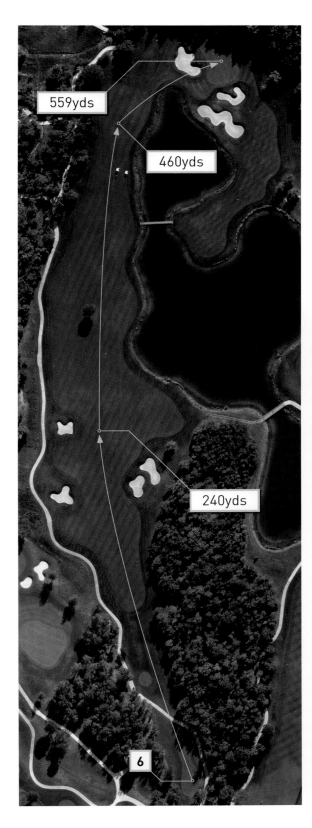

Few holes offer such a dramatic backdrop as this par 5, with 'Le Château' – the course's namesake – looking down high in the hills from behind the green. It is a beautiful hole, but it is also an examination in ball-striking because even if you play it with a lay-up, the fairway narrows as it sweeps round to the right. If you want to attack in two, it's a crisp blow with a wood over a water hazard – pure risk-reward. The green is also protected at the front by two bunkers. Back on the tee, sand pinches the fairway on either side, while for those attempting to play the hole in three, a large tree positioned in the centre of the fairway could block you out for your second shot.

COURSE GUIDE 10–18

The inward nine takes no prisoners, but if you can play with patience, pick your spots and master the subtle breaks of Le Château's lightning-fast greens, there are scoring possibilities. Good course management will prevail over all-out attack.

Opposite: Another hole that sweeps round to the right, the 10th sets the tone for what is to follow on the course's back nine.

Hole 11
Par 5
506 yards

A short par 5 where players will look to attack in two, although the tee shot demands accuracy, as the fairway is narrowed with a bunker to the right and a rocky creek that cuts in from the left side. That creek runs right across the fairway as the hole drops downhill. The lay-up area is protected by sand, as is the green, with a large trap protecting its entrance.

Hole 12
Par 4
375 yards

Another dogleg, this time sweeping to the left, where the second shot is especially difficult as the green is raised and has sand either side of its entrance. Players may look for the 'safety first' route from the tee by playing a long iron to find the wide part of the fairway. Taking the left corner on is too big a risk as there are dense trees here.

Hole 13
Par 3
220 yards

The 13th is the longest of the par 3s, where a solid, crisp strike is needed. But while it is testing in length, the strategy is straightforward as the right side of the green is open, which allows players to attack with a hybrid or long iron. Keep it this side, though, as anything directed left may find a cluster of bunkers dotted around a mass of lush, punishing rough.

Hole 14
Par 5
545 yards

Another par 5 with a dogleg, this hole swings to the right, and with a rocky creek guarding the front of the green, it is very tough to reach in two blows. Two fairway bunkers lurk on the dogleg, so players who try to cut the corner run the risk of finding sand. Another testing trap sits at the back of the green, so there is danger there too if you overclub.

Hole 15
Par 4
392 yards

This is one of the more open holes on the course, and a very tempting one from the tee. Players may well opt to take the left corner on, as the fairway doglegs in this direction. Bunkers pinch the fairway at 230 yards, with another posse lurking short-right of the green. If you have poor position there is plenty of room left of the putting surface as a bail-out option.

Hole 16
Par 4
156 yards

The 16th is another short par 3, this one is elevated from the tee with a backdrop of trees dominating the view. Another rocky creek runs in front of the putting surface – which is contoured with a ridge at the back – and a sand trap sits to the right. This is a stunning little hole that demands the utmost respect as well as the right choice of club.

Hole 17
Par 4
415 yards

The penultimate hole may look straightforward, but it is one that features a very undulating fairway, so sidehill and downhill lies can add to the perils of a second shot. Tight and tree-lined, there is little forgiveness for wayward hitters, and the approach is also fraught with danger as three traps guard the green, with two at its entrance and another to the right.

Hole 18
Par 4
439 yards

Visually stunning with trees enveloping the fairway from tee to green, the home hole is the final test in ball-striking, where right-centre is the ideal line for your drive. The fairway drops down on the left towards woodland, and with bunkers lining the left side of the approach to the green it pays to keep the ball right. This is a wonderful finish.

435yds

290yds

10

Hole 10 – *Par 4* – **435 yards**

In shape, this is something of a little brother to the par-5 6th. The dogleg-right 10th is a tester because from the tee players must pick a strategy and stick to it for the best results, and anything wild will be suitably punished. A large bunker lies to the right of the fairway, with another 40 yards up on the left side as the hole begins to turn at an almost 90-degree angle. If you lay up short of the first one, it means a carry over water to a green with two sand traps right and one left. If you attempt to shorten your second shot by taking on the corner, trouble awaits in the form of a large oak tree that could be blocking your path. This is a very clever hole, where being conservative with you driver could be the best play – it just means a solid blow will be needed to find the green, as the lake becomes an obvious threat.

VALDERRAMA

Consistently rated as the best in Europe, there are few courses that can rival the golfing test of Valderrama. Designed by the legendary Robert Trent Jones, the host venue of the 1997 Ryder Cup has witnessed some of the game's most emotional golfing adventures.

With its heritage, its aura, and its beautiful conditioning, Valderrama is undoubtedly continental Europe's premier golf course. Right up in the Andalucian hills in the town of San Roque, this Robert Trent Jones classic was first designed and opened in 1974. Originally known as Sotogrande New, it was the younger sibling to Sotogrande, Jones' 1964 creation, and in many respects, during its early years, the New was considered the weaker of the two courses. Good in many ways, but lacking greatness in so many others.

Then after Trent Jones came Jaime Ortiz-Patino, a Bolivian tin magnate who had come to live on the Sotogrande estate during the late seventies. By 1981, the New had been renamed as Las Aves. Ortiz-Patino, a visionary who saw nothing but its potential, formed a five-man consortium to buy the course in 1984. Other patches of land that formed the Sotogrande estate were also purchased, and to finish off what he had begun, Trent Jones was brought

> "Valderrama was Ortiz-Patino's masterpiece. He wanted to make it a very special place, and he did."
>
> *José-Maria Olazabal*

back to start redesigning the course. Once work was complete, the layout was renamed again, and Valderrama's star was born.

Following Trent Jones' rejig, Valderrama continued to grow in stature. It became a thriving members' club. But its exclusivity needed to be supplemented, and so when the lure of top-level tournament golf appeared, Ortiz-Patino welcomed the opportunity with open arms. In 1988 Valderrama hosted the European Tour's season-ending Volvo Masters for the first time, and barring a five-year period from 1997 to 2001, it was its regular home for the next 20 years.

With so much riding on the event as the Tour's Order of Merit was set to be decided, the Volvo Masters always delivered, with European golf's front-runners on show. As well as the Volvo Masters, Valderrama hosted two World Golf Championships in 1999 and 2000, and since 2010 has been the home of the Andalucia Masters. However, it was in 1997 that the course achieved its crowning moment, when it hosted the Ryder Cup, the first time the biennial contest had been played outside of the US or British Isles.

Despite horrendous weather as the rain teemed down for three days, Europe, captained by an inspired Seve Ballesteros – Spain's greatest golfing son – held firm to win by 14½ points to 13½. It was, and still is, one of the most emotional events European golf has witnessed.

Ballesteros himself played a major part in Valderrama. Trent Jones enlisted him to help with his redesign work in the mid-eighties. Of those changes, it was the reconstruction of the par-5 8th – now the 17th since the two nines

have been switched – that attracted the most attention. Originally, the hole was deemed to lack character, and so Jones and Ballesteros shortened it, and positioned a lake at the front of the green to create the ultimate test in risk-and-reward where players could fire for glory or lay up to play safe. Valderrama's 17th is now one of the most iconic holes in world golf.

Some call Valderrama Europe's answer to Augusta, but in truth, the courses have little in common in terms of their design. Valderrama

is fiendishly tight, with overhanging cork trees narrowing the fairways, and its greens are small and raised. Augusta has wide fairways, its pines towering high above the land with large, undulating greens below. That said, both courses share a bond when it comes to their revered status.

Ortiz-Patino sadly passed away in early 2013, but his legacy, and his passion for turning a good golf course into one of the world's true greats, lives on with every round played at Valderrama.

Left: Spain's Sergio Garcia tastes victory at the 2011 Andalucia Masters, played at Valderrama.

Above: Valderrama has become one of the most revered golfing landscapes in the world, respected for its heritage and aura.

"Nobody had ever seen a golf course presented in the way that Valderrama was."

George O'Grady

COURSE GUIDE 1–9

Course yardage – Professional 6,988 yards
Course GPS – 36º16'58.11" N 5º19'38.50" W

Players will need to be on fine ball-striking form to counter the tight, tree-lined fairways at Valderrama, with little forgiveness offered from the tee. A series of raised greens, surrounded by sand, can make approach shots seem daunting.

Opposite: Miguel Angel Jimenez fights to get back into position on the par-4 8th during the 2010 Andalucia Masters – a hole that many underestimate due to its modest yardage.

Hole 1
Sol y Sombre
Par 4 – 399 yards

The left side of the fairway is the ideal line, with the hole opening up slightly to tempt you from the tee. Take care with this, as it is position from the tee that plays a big part in determining your score. The slightly raised green, which is very quick, is well guarded with four bunkers encircling its boundary; so take aim and fire at its centre.

Hole 2
El Arbol
Par 4 – 421 yards

The hole is named after a large cork tree that sits in the middle of the fairway, and you need to avoid this as it lurks around the landing zone at 240 yards. The best route is again down the left side, which will leave an easier approach to avoid more overhanging trees that pinch in on the right-hand side. Large bunkers protect the green.

Hole 3
El Tunel
Par 3 – 195 yards

This is a very tricky par 3 where you really need good position on the green, which is set up on the hill. Anything that goes left is in danger of running into tree trouble as the hole feeds down, while bunkers guard the entrance of the putting surface on both sides – it's a real test in mid-iron ball-striking where par is tough to make.

Hole 4
La Cascada
Par 5 – 563 yards

La Cascada – meaning the waterfall – comes into play by the side of the green. If attempting to get there in two, you will need a couple of solid blows, to which a huge amount of risk is attached. The green is two-tiered, and as well as the water to the right, there is sand to the left. The green is long and narrow, so approaches need to be spot on.

Hole 5
Los Altos
Par 4 – 380 yards

The 5th is a testing hole that runs adjacent to the 4th. The fairway drops as it sweeps round to the left, and the ideal position for the drive is right-centre. Fairway traps lie in wait far right, pinching in the landing zone on this side. The approach is very tough, with a tree crowding the right entrance to the putting surface, and four large bunkers lurking nearby.

Hole 6
El Vallejo
Par 3 – 162 yards

The green is very tricky, as it slopes from the back, and with bunkers all around it, your ball-striking needs to be in top shape. The approach to the green is very tight, adding to the challenge from the tee. Although this is the shortest par 3 on the course, you underestimate it at your peril and a committed strike is needed for success.

Hole 7
El Mirador
Par 4 – 496 yards

Two crisp blows are needed for you to have any hopes of reaching this green in two, and there is no margin for error from the tee. Two big fairway traps lurk around 250 yards, and the green features subtle undulations to make putt-reading difficult, while five bunkers protect it, so your short-game skills will be tested should you find any of the sand.

Hole 9
El Muro
Par 4 – 440 yards

This is another long par 4 that looks imposing from the tee as there are trees hugging both sides of the fairway and you have to play through a narrow channel. Like so many greens at Valderrama, the 9th is slightly raised with a number of breaks. Sand lies on both sides, and at the back, and a surgeon-like touch is needed to stop the ball on the putting surface.

Hole 8 – *El Bunker* – **Par 4 – 349 yards**

A hole that is just waiting to catch out those who fail to give it the respect it deserves. A driver is not required from the tee for the longer hitters, and it's all about finding the right spot on the fairway so you are in the best position to float a wedge into the green. The entrance to the putting surface is extremely tight, with trees giving it an almost claustrophobic feel. As the hole's name suggests, a bunker features prominently, with sand guarding the front and side of the green in a large horseshoe shape. Effectively, you are almost playing into an island green as it is totally surrounded by hazards, so the less club you are hitting in, the better. That said, get into position with your drive, as pitching from the fairway offers more control.

Course Guide 10–18

Valderrama's back nine has built a reputation as one of the toughest inward stretches in Europe. Again, driving is made difficult by overhanging trees and those greens seem to get slicker and slicker. Dare you go for glory at the 17th?

Hole 10
El Lago
Par 4 – 389 yards

Although water features on both sides of the fairway as the hole sweeps dramatically to the right, it shouldn't really come into play. Again, it's all about position to open up an easier shot in. The green is raised, and those who don't carry the front portion of the putting surface could find their ball drifting back down the fairway, as the bank is steep and fast-running.

Hole 11
Un Sueno
Par 5 – 546 yards

A short par 5 but with ten bunkers featuring along it, and with the green perched up on a plateau, two great strikes are needed. If the wind is against, it's best to lay up and play it as a three-shot hole. The right side of the fairway is dominated by sand traps, and you need to draw your ball away from them as the land slopes from the left side.

Hole 12
Las Camelias
Par 3 – 212 yards

The target on this long par 3 can look very small, being framed by dense sand and overhanging trees. The putting surface has a number of undulations and it slopes predominantly from the back; so good putt-reading skills are essential. If you do miss the green, the front-right bunker isn't the worst place to be, as you are then playing below the hole and back up the slope.

Hole 13
Sin Bunker
Par 4 – 411 yards

There is no sand on this hole, but that doesn't make the task an easy one because trees are a problem here, especially on the right-hand side as they pinch in on the approach. Left-centre is the ideal target from the tee. If in position, it's nothing more than a short iron to another green that is tough to hold, with various run-off areas posing a threat.

Hole 14
La Piedra
Par 4 – 369 yards

Not a long par 4 but, like so many holes at Valderrama, it's all about hitting your spot, both with the drive and the approach. The fairway's landing zone is relatively generous, and the hole then turns to the right; the green is perched up high on a hill with sand dominating its boundary. Anything long could nestle in a steep bank, making a chip back very awkward.

Hole 15
El Puerto
Par 3 – 225 yards

A short hole that is a little different from the others at Valderrama. The tee is elevated, and there is a big drop with a mass of cork trees in front, meaning you are playing over the top of them. The real test comes with the green, which slopes from back-left to front-right on a hill. Three bunkers protect it, and you must avoid the two on left side.

Hole 16
Muy Dificil
Par 4 – 433 yards

The drive is crucial because anything right, or too straight, leaves you with a slog just to get to the green, as trees will be constantly blocking your path. As the name suggests, this dogleg right can play as the hardest hole on the course when the wind is against. Aim left of the fairway to open up the approach to another raised green with four sand traps protecting it.

Hole 18
Casa Club
Par 4 – 453 yards

This is a beast of a finishing hole, where players hope to be rewarded for hitting a big drive over the trees on the left-hand side. That said, it's fraught with danger because as the hole turns to the left you can easily run out of fairway and leave yourself blocked out. The green – encircled by three large bunkers – is perched on top of a hill.

535yds

460yds

260yds

17

Hole 17 – *Los Gabilones* – **Par 5 – 535 yards**

The hole that Trent Jones and Ballesteros tricked up in order to guarantee excitement, and boy there is always plenty of that at Valderrama's 17th. Most of the professionals will have a go in two, but finding position off the tee isn't easy as the fairway has a number of areas where the rough cuts in and there are two sand traps; one at around the 230-yard mark on the right; another further up on the left. Past this, it's all about that risk-reward approach into the green, just beyond the pond. The surface has a steep bank, so anything that doesn't quite have the legs will roll back down to a watery grave. The hole has witnessed some great moments, none more so than Graeme McDowell's albatross in the 2007 Volvo Masters.

Graeme McDowell, a winner of the Andalucia Masters in 2010, escapes from the deep greenside trap at the 8th hole during the 2011 tournament.

The 7th hole of the stunning Royal Melbourne West course features a contoured and demanding putting surface.

KINGSTON HEATH

The modern way of course design is all about length, as designers extend old layouts to keep pace with the game's progression. But at Kingston Heath on the Melbourne Sandbelt, you will find a layout that is set up for the world's best players despite being less than 7,000 yards.

The "Melbourne Sandbelt", some would say, is as revered a stretch of golfing land as the links at St Andrews and those in the north west of England. Australia's spiritual golfing home, the Sandbelt lies 15 miles to the south of one of the world's most cosmopolitan cities. Originally, in the early part of the 20th century, many of Victoria's best courses lay in and around the towns and the city of Melbourne itself.

One of those was Royal Melbourne Golf Club, which, with its membership growing, moved further south to its Sandringham site in 1901, seeking to take advantage of the area's sandy soil that was ideal for the development, and maintenance, of golf courses. It wasn't long before

many other clubs followed, and so it was that the Sandbelt region became the most celebrated plot of golfing land in the Southern Hemisphere.

The Sandbelt is made up of the "Magnificent Eight" – a cluster of courses within a few miles of each other. As well as Royal Melbourne, it includes Huntingdale, Yarra Yarra, Victoria, Comonwealth, Peninsula, Metropolitan and, finally, Kingston Heath Golf Club. It was Kingston Heath that was first designed by Dan Souter in 1925. And, while there seems to be little argument that the original trendsetter, Royal Melbourne, remains the king of the Sandbelt pack, there is a general consensus that Kingston Heath stands proudly as its second in command.

Indeed, Victorians like to argue that Royal Melbourne is the best course in the world, but Kingston Heath is the best course in Melbourne.

The club has a grand history. It was formed in 1909 as Elsternwick Golf Club, but relocated to its current site of Heatherton – on the Sandbelt – in 1925. Soutar would begin work on the development of the new layout immediately. A year later, renowned British architect Dr Alister MacKenzie was busy drawing out his own design plans for Royal Melbourne's West course during a 12-week visit to the country. Keen to tap into his knowledge, many of the Sandbelt clubs came calling, and MacKenzie gladly offered his services.

Though he is not responsible for the routing,

his influence is clearly visible in the layout's bunkering. As Kingston Heath's reputation grew, the course, which was long for that era at over 6,300 yards, began to attract international players and tournaments. It became a host venue for the Australian Open, and today is on the rota of courses that welcome the annual Australian Masters.

Though it is not particularly long now by modern standards at 6,940 yards, it is a fine test with its variety of holes favouring a more creative approach. The course asks questions from the very start and every club in the bag is needed to navigate the numerous twists and turns of the layout; plotting tee shots on the right lines to attack the green; negotiating escape routes under overhanging trees that congest its fairways; surveying pin positions to avoid the fatal traps should your distance control let you down; and those round-changing decisions – like whether or not to attack the short par-4 3rd – that leave nothing but a heavy dose of punishment if your bold ventures fail to come off.

Perhaps the greatest compliment to Kingston Heath comes from the players themselves. In contrast to the common trend of bringing a course up to standard simply by adding yardage, this layout allows players to work their craft. Just ask Ian Poulter, the course record holder after a 64 in the 2012 Masters, who said: "Kingston Heath is totally awesome. Someone please tell modern-day architects that we don't need 8,000-yards tracks. Best yet."

"One of my top five courses in the world."

Jason Dufner

Course Guide 1–9

Course yardage – Blue tees 6,940 yards
Course GPS – 37°57'19.00" S 145° 5'4.90" E

There is a wonderful, eclectic mixture of holes on the front nine, starting with a long par 4 where both position and power are needed. Look out for the short par-4 3rd – its yardage makes it look easy but it always bares its teeth.

Opposite: Playing back towards the clubhouse, the 6th hole presents a fierce test with large, sprawling bunkers from tee to green.

Hole 1
Par 4
457 yards

The opening hole plays straight; there is a cluster of sand traps sitting to the right of the fairway, but good ball-strikers should be able to clear them. A soft draw will take you to the ideal area from where to play an approach, and then it's a mid-iron to the green, which slopes towards the front-left side. Three bunkers sit short-right of the putting surface.

Hole 2
Par 4
383 yards

A testing dogleg left; the corner is made tight by a number of bunkers, dense rough and trees, and the fairway is also very undulating. To score well, it's all about the tee shot. Ideally, players will fire centre, or just right of centre, to open up the approach. Once in position, it's a short iron into a green that has a lot more sand protecting its boundary.

Hole 3
Par 4
295 yards

A very short par 4, but one that players underestimate at their peril, because once out of position, it's very tough to get back to where you should be. If attempting to drive the green, take note: it is very small and its boundary is peppered with treacherous sand traps. Best to lay up with a long iron and then pitch on, in the hope of a one-putt birdie.

Hole 4
Par 4
390 yards

Players must formulate a game plan on the tee; do you lay up short of the fairway bunker on the left side, or power away with a driver in the hope of playing a wedge for your second? The ideal line is left-centre, as the green's entrance is more open on this side. That said, there is a mass of sand both right and left, so hitting your target is crucial.

Hole 5
Par 3
190 yards

A par 3 that looks daunting from the tee with sand seemingly everywhere, as well as dense rough. The length is awkward because it's tough to hold a long iron through the narrow entrance of the green. Sand is more prevalent on the right side of the approach, but the trap to the left is more punishing. The green is very undulating, so putt-reading is tough.

Hole 7
Par 5
505 yards

The 7th is a superb par 5 that is certainly reachable in two for those who take it on. Players are faced with a tricky tee shot as a large cross-bunker comes into play at 260 yards, but if you can avoid it there is plenty of room to run in a long iron or wood. There is a slight depression before the green, and leaving your ball short could ruin hopes of a birdie.

Hole 8
Par 4
435 yards

The drive is blind, and with fairway bunkers tightening the landing zone at 260 yards, it's easy to feel as if you are in the lap of the gods. The best strategy is to play short of the sand, which will leave a mid-iron approach to a putting surface that is relatively open. The large green is shared with the 16th, so make sure you pay attention and don't run out of position.

Hole 9
Par 4
360 yards

Although modest in length, the 9th is no pushover. The drive is very tight, and blind. The hole turns to the left, but taking the corner on is too big a risk as trees line this side and three deep bunkers also lie in wait for any errant shots. Driver from the tee isn't the best option. Instead, take an iron and you can still play to the green with an element of control.

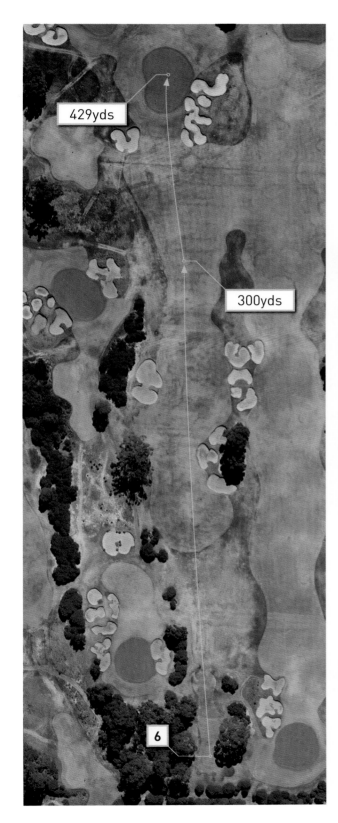

429yds

300yds

6

Hole 6 – *Par 4* – **429 yards**

The 6th hole plays alongside the 1st, but in the opposite direction back to the clubhouse. Course management will play a huge part in getting a score here, because bunkers pinch the landing zone on both sides at 250 yards, making the drive very tough. The fairway also sweeps up a hill and down again, but it pays to commit to the club you choose, and then fire confidently over it. Once in position, a mid-iron will take you to the heart of the putting surface, which is well protected to the right side with a number of greenside traps and dense rough. This is a great hole, enhanced by the visual appeal of the iconic clubhouse.

COURSE GUIDE 10–18

The back nine continues to ask questions of your positional play, and hitting driver is not the only option from the tee. Look out for the par-4 16th, which starts a very tough finish where coming home in par is a great result.

Hole 10
Par 3
138 yards

A short par 3 by anyone's standards, but one that is mightily imposing from the tee as players have to fire over a mass of dense wasteland and bunkers to find a green that has a very narrow entrance. As well as the sand, the green is two-tiered, with a ridge and run-off area at the back, forcing you to pick wisely when it comes to club selection.

Hole 11
Par 4
415 yards

Rated as Kingston Heath's third toughest hole, this par 4 sweeps gently to the right, with bunkers guarding the corner. Not only that, a set of traps lie in the middle of the fairway at 240 yards, making positional play crucial. If you choose to lay up short of these, it is still a strong mid-iron to the green, with a procession of sand traps lining the right side of the approach.

Hole 12
Par 5
556 yards

This is a great par 5, which asks a number of questions, even when played with a lay-up. Sand dominates the middle of the fairway, with bunkers lurking at 250 yards. Left of these provides the better line in, with a 3-wood needed to take you over the sand that lies on the left side of the approach 100 yards short of the green.

Hole 13
Par 4
354 yards

This is another of Kingston Heath's short par 4s where the difficulty lies not in yardage but in its defences. There are fairway traps on the left side, but this is the best angle from which to approach the green. The putting surface drops off at the back, and there is sand on both sides. Getting a good drive away is imperative for making a score.

Hole 14
Par 5
564 yards

The last of the par 5s, where those who are chasing a score will fancy their chances of reaching the green in two. However, sand peppers the right side of the approach, so if you are coming in with a 3-wood or long iron, control is the key. From the tee, it's a drive down the left side. If playing with a lay-up, stay on this line before pitching to the green.

Hole 15
Par 3
155 yards

Like so many great par 3s, this hole is modest in length, but it induces in players a false sense of security. From the tee it is little more than a 7-iron, but you need to factor in the hole's elevation, as well as a swathe of sand and dense wasteland. The green is narrow at the front, opening up towards the back. Take aim and hope for your best!

Hole 17
Par 4
460 yards

The penultimate hole is a monstrous par 4 where a drive to the right-hand side short of the uphill slope will put you in prime position from where to attack the green. There is no sand protecting the putting surface, but players are faced with a number of subtle undulations, so distance control coming in is critical. Making par here is never easy.

Hole 18
Par 4
427 yards

A fantastic finishing hole, shorter than the preceding 17th but just as testing. The best line from the tee is to the left side of the fairway, despite a huge sand trap lurking here. Then it's a mid-iron to the home green. Sand protects the putting surface on both sides, so keep it straight if you want to walk away with a closing par.

Hole 16 – *Par 4* – **427 yards**

The course's toughest hole sweeps round to the right-hand side, and is made even tougher by a blind drive over a hill. A cluster of fairway bunkers pinch in from the right, so left of centre is the line to take from the tee. How much club you pull from the bag is your choice, but driver is not necessarily the best option. For the second, you need to factor in the slopes of the green, which is shared with the 8th, because if you stray out of position here you could be left fighting against the dreaded three-putt. Run-off areas to the left and back of the putting surface make the challenge even tougher. This is a classic example of a hole that doesn't need yardage to make it difficult.

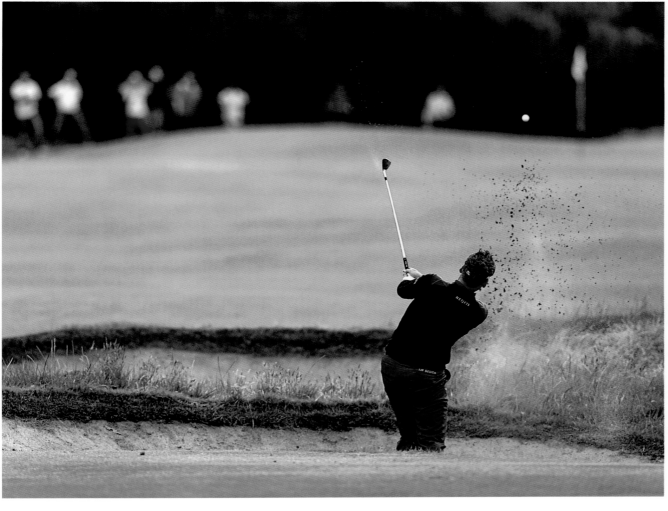

427yds

270yds

16

VICTORIA

The Victoria Golf Club – another Melbourne Sandbelt classic – may live somewhat in the shadows of Kingston Heath and Royal Melbourne, but it is a fantastic course in its own right, with championship pedigree as the host of the Australian Masters.

Below: The unmistakable Ian Poulter in full flow during his victorious run at the 2011 Australian Masters at Victoria.

Opposite: Another Sandbelt classic – Victoria plays short at less than 7,000 yards but remains a fine test for even the very best players.

While it may not have the majestic and imposing nature of Royal Melbourne, or the creative test of Kingston Heath, the course at The Victoria Golf Club is rightly regarded as one of the Melbourne Sandbelt's heavyweight designs. A true classic, it is a track that always delights. Though it has hosted the Australian Masters in recent years, this beautifully proportioned layout is more than playable to all standards, with a wonderful mix of holes from start to finish.

The club's roots can be traced back to as early as 1903, although the current course, set in the Melbourne suburb of Cheltenham, was opened for play in 1927. There is nothing but a single strip of road separating the course from its near-neighbour, Royal Melbourne. And it was at Royal Melbourne in late 1926 that Dr Alister MacKenzie was crafting the West course along with the esteemed duo of Alex Russell and Mick Morcom. As at other courses on the Sandbelt, there seems little doubt the great man played a part with some subtle course recommendations at Victoria, as well as the positioning of its many bunkers that give the course its most demonic feature. But exactly how big a part he played remains debatable.

Founder William Meader – along with club captain Oscar Damman and curator Frank Lennox – is widely credited with the design work as well as the superb routing that delivers the course's ultimate thrill. And there can be no debate about the quality of the legacy these men have left at Victoria.

There is a sense of something quite different here from the very first hole; a par 4 of little more than 250 yards. Even those with the most modest of golfing talents will be eager to take on the challenge, but it is no pushover, with sand scattering the approach and to the right side of the green.

The routing heads along the course's north perimeter, then cuts down its most western side before zigzagging back and forth, and eventually heading back east towards the grand clubhouse. Because of this, no two holes are the same and the challenge comes with the placement of your ball. Like nearby Kingston Heath, a fellow host of the Australian Masters, Victoria is not a long test for the professionals at 6,863 yards. But the wind can be chaotic and your scores have to be manufactured.

You'll be challenged with some impressive holes; the par-5 9th is the course's longest at 611 yards and demands three well-positioned blows to find the sanctuary of the putting surface; the 15th is one of the finest short par 4s anywhere; while the par 3s are little devils, with MacKenzie's bunkering proving an unrelenting obstacle.

There have been some impressive players to come out of The Victoria Golf Club. Most famously, the great Peter Thomson, a winner of five Open Championships, was a member here.

Former Australian player turned course designer, Mike Clayton, was brought in to work on some subtle course renovations. Clayton, who is a design associate of 2006 US Open champion Geoff Ogilvy, worked on the restoration of some of the bunkers, as well as the regeneration of trees. But, generally, what you play today is not far removed from Meader's original work. Everything about The Victoria Golf Club is graceful, and its conditioning makes it playable all year round. A fine layout that is a tribute to the old-school philosophies of course design.

"It's probably in my top 10 courses, architecturally and from a design standpoint."

Luke Donald

COURSE GUIDE 1–9

It gets tougher after the short opener as the course sweeps anti-clockwise with two testing par 4s at the 2nd and 3rd. It is crucial to pick a safe spot on the par 3s, as the cavernous greenside traps can leave you scrambling just to make bogey.

Opposite: The outward nine comes to a close with a monster of a par 5 that stretches to over 600 yards, so it's a three-shotter for most!

Hole 1
Par 4
257 yards

A very short par 4 where players will be eager to take aim and fire direct at the green with a driver; but beware, bunkers to the left side are an obvious danger, and the smart play is to lay up short of these. Even with a mid-iron off the tee, you'll still need only a wedge to hit the heart of the green, which has sand protecting the right side.

Hole 2
Par 4
428 yards

After being eased in on the 1st, matters become somewhat tougher on this long par 4 that has sand on both sides of the fairway. Left of centre is the best line, although anything too far left will run into trouble as there are trees and dense rough here. Three bunkers lurk around the green, although the entrance is open, so it is possible to run in your approach.

Hole 3
Par 4
438 yards

This is another long, straight par 4, although the fairway winds subtly round a huge sand trap that juts in from the right-hand side. There is space to the left, and approaching from here makes the trees that line the right side all the way to the green less of an issue. The putting surface is angled slightly and is shallow in depth. Precision is needed with the approach.

Hole 4
Par 3
180 yards

Here club selection can change dramatically, and with the wind in your favour the green will be reachable with a short iron. The first challenge is to fire over a mass of sand that dominates the approach. The entrance to the putting surface is very narrow, with bunkers on both sides; the one to the left features a steep bank that makes the escape particularly tough.

Hole 5
Par 4
435 yards

A good drive is needed to put you in prime position from which to attack the green, and a drive to the left opens up the hole for the second shot. There is a fairway bunker to consider, but it's just shy of 300 yards away, so only the longest will reach it. Two large traps protect the front of the green, so the safe play is to go longer rather than short.

Hole 6
Par 4
435 yards

The 6th is one of the toughest par 4s at Victoria. First, the drive is very demanding because bunkers jut in on both sides of the fairway from 240 yards. The right side is the best line, but if laying up in front of those fairway traps, you'll still need a solid long-iron shot to reach the green. Be warned: the putting surface slopes quite dramatically from the back.

Hole 7
Par 3
180 yards

The green is slightly raised, with a deep, steep-walled bunker to the right being the obvious threat from back on the tee. The putting surface slopes from the left, so those who play to the right do so at considerable risk with that cavernous trap ready and waiting. Trees tighten up the hole slightly, but it's all about avoiding the sand on this classic par 3.

Hole 8
Par 5
490 yards

This is a reachable par 5 if you can find the narrow fairway with your drive. The back tees are set back in a tunnel of trees, and the fairway snakes gently to the left, with a bunker lurking here at 240 yards. If attacking in two, a soft fade from the right side will run up the entrance to the green. Bunkers lurk right and left, but it's most definitely a birdie opportunity.

Hole 9 – *Par 5* – **611 yards**

From one par 5 to another, although the outward nine's closing hole poses an altogether different challenge from the preceding 8th. Firstly, it is the longest on the course, and at a little over 600 yards it needs to be played with a lay-up and a lot of common sense. The first fairway trap, on the left-hand side, forces you to aim right of centre from the tee. The landing zone does open up more here, although there is more sand at 300 yards, of which long hitters must be aware. For the lay-up, a 7-iron will take you to within pitching distance of the green, which has two large bunkers at the front, and two smaller ones at the back.

611yds

520yds

290yds

9

COURSE GUIDE 10–18

It all sets up for a grand finish at Victoria, with the menacing par 3 at 16, followed by back-to-back three-shotters to end your round. Again, stay away from the sand at all costs – it pays to plot your way home.

Hole 10
Par 4
380 yards

The fairway sweeps to the left early, so there is the temptation to take on the corner. However, dense trees protect the dogleg's apex and a bunker waits too should you not clear the danger. The fairway is quite undulating, and the approach needs to be threaded through a cluster of traps. Holding the perched green is tough with run-off areas all around its boundary.

Hole 11
Par 4
405 yards

The 11th is a very pretty hole, but one that requires two well-executed shots. Trees hug the right side from the tee, with a posse of sand traps dominating the left. It's better to be left of centre with your drive, and from here it's a mid-iron for the approach. If you have to miss the green, left is best, as deep, cavernous traps lie to the right.

Hole 12
Par 4
426 yards

The 12th plays down to the south-west corner of the course. With the tee set to the right side, it's best to play for a soft draw, taking you away from the large bunker that guards the corner. Be careful, though, because going too far left could leave you blocked out for the second. A single bunker sits to the back-left of the green.

Hole 13
Par 4
428 yards

Playing along the course's south border, you have no room right off the tee as thick rough, and then a line of trees, envelop the fairway. There is also a huge bunker on this side at 200 yards. Once you are in position on the fairway, a mid-iron can be run into the undulating green, which has bunkers defending its boundary on both the right and left side.

Hole 14
Par 3
155 yards

Victoria's shortest hole, but that doesn't make the test any easier. As it climbs uphill, a sea of heather and thick rough sweeps in front of the tee and up the left side of the hole, with a cluster of rugged sand traps adding to its visual appeal. Anything short-right will find a greenside bunker, while anything long could find either of the two traps lurking at the back of the green.

Hole 16
Par 3
194 yards

As with all the short holes at Victoria, sand is a constant menace, with deep, cavernous traps dotted all the way up the left-hand side as the terrain rises. Here, however, there is room on the right to run your approach in – not that this is the advised play. Rather, a high, soft-drawing long iron to the front of the green is best to leave yourself below the hole.

Hole 17
Par 5
601 yards

In something of a role reversal to the 8th and 9th, the 17th is a long par 5, while the 18th is a shorter, reachable one. On this penultimate hole, with a reservoir to the right, it's best to forget about finding the green in two blows. Instead, play down the left side, staying clear of a fairway bunker here. The approach will then be open for a lay-up and a pitch to the green.

Hole 18
Par 5
504 yards

Victoria's final hole serves up a closing birdie chance, but players are reliant on getting a good drive away. If you can split the fairway bunkers you'll be in position to attack the green in two. Taking aim over the first bunker on the right side of the approach is the best line. If you've chosen to lay up, you may want to play a bump-and-run on to the putting surface.

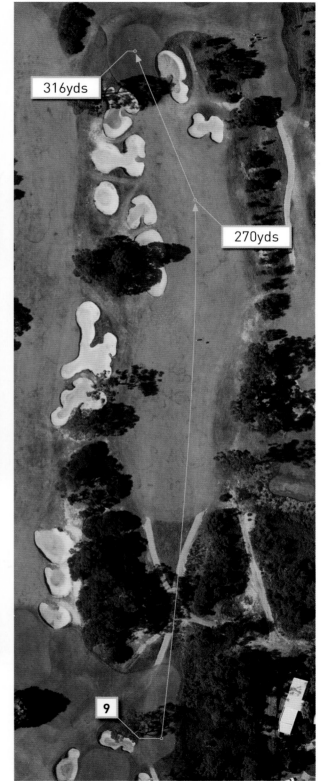

Hole 15 – *Par 4* – **316 yards**

Many players will look at this hole's yardage and assume an easy birdie chance looms. But the 15th challenges your positional play and those who underestimate its defences will usually walk off with a high number on their scorecard. Short it may be, but the drive is tightened with trees on both sides of the teeing area. The fairway is also narrow, with a sea of sand pinching the left-hand side from 200 yards. The bold and brave will aim right with their driver to take the bunkers out of play – with a touch of draw – but more sand lurks short-right of the green. To play it conservatively, it's a 5-iron and then a wedge. Anything that lacks control will not hold the green.

316yds

270yds

9

A grand finish to your round. A good drive to the 18th green can give players an excellent birdie opportunity.

ROYAL MELBOURNE

One of the world's best courses by one of the great pioneers of golf course design, Royal Melbourne's West remains a very special place to play. Rugged in nature, the course is a strategic test where your positional skills are firmly challenged.

Mention the name Dr Alister MacKenzie and the pristine fairways and beautifully manicured greens of Augusta National instantly spring to mind. But for those who knew the great man, and for the many who respect and appreciate his philosophy on golf course design, his finest work has arguably been in the Southern Hemisphere on the Melbourne Sandbelt, most notably at Royal Melbourne Golf Club.

There are two courses at Royal Melbourne, the East and the West. Both are of championship pedigree, with the West the more senior of the two by a single year after MacKenzie completed the design in 1931. Although MacKenzie continues to receive most of the plaudits for creating the West, it was certainly no solo effort with much of the work done in collaboration with renowned Australian player Alex Russell, while the equally legendary Mick Morcom, the club's greenkeeper, also played a hand. But whoever gets the credit, there is one, single statement that remains consistently true: Royal Melbourne's West course is not only one of the finest designs in Australia, but one of the finest and grandest in the world.

Shortly after opening, the West's reputation grew quickly, and membership at Royal Melbourne began to thrive. A year later, once Russell had completed work on the East, the club had two championship layouts, making it Australia's premier golfing venue. It would take a while, but eventually top-class international golf came calling. In 1959 Royal Melbourne hosted the Canada Cup, now known as the World Cup, and in recognition of the quality of both the East and West, a composite course was crafted from both layouts: six holes from the East, 12 from the West. The Canada Cup came back again in 1970, and Royal Melbourne remains the only venue outside the United States to have hosted the prestigious Presidents Cup twice, in 1998 and, most recently, in 2011.

Despite the West outranking the East in terms of status, it lacks the length necessary to challenge the game's best players at just 6,622 yards from the championship tees, which is why the mixing of both courses is necessary to satisfy international events. However, the West remains a thorough examination of one's course management skills, with the legacy of MacKenzie's design work, his bunkering, playing a prominent role throughout with traps deftly located to catch out all standards of player.

Apart from the sand and its positioning, perhaps the most impressive aspect of the layout at Royal Melbourne's West comes down to its hidden defences, and it is a credit to the work of MacKenzie and the way he is able to adapt to varying landscapes and challenges. At Augusta, players are offered the comfort of seeing all the trouble in front of them. At Royal Melbourne, it is a very different test, with the danger hidden from your prying eyes.

The par-4 6th is a prime example of MacKenzie's camouflage techniques, where a number of hidden bunkers add to the thrill of this risk-reward two-shotter that swings 90 degrees right. There are many other classic holes, like the driveable par-4 10th, the reachable par-5 12th, and the long par-3 16th with a green featuring a number of testing breaks.

Despite its difficulty in terms of your positional play, the West's fairways can look inviting from the tee, allowing the higher handicapper more freedom to enjoy the course. But, as ever, the better player will be lured into attacking the more dangerous areas in order to set up an easier approach, bringing those MacKenzie sand traps back into play. This is a very clever, and very beautiful, golf course.

"It's such a special place, just perfect for golf. There is space to play the game and the player must decide where to play."

Geoff Ogilvy

Course Guide 1–9

Course yardage – Championship 6,622 yards
Course GPS – 37º58'6.58" S 145º 1'49.41" E

Right from the word go, you need to take particular care on your approach shots; missing on the wrong side of the green can leave you in three-putt territory or, worse, facing a devilishly difficult chip to make an up-and-down.

Opposite: The par-4 6th demands two good blows to find the heart of the green, but those who take the corner of the dogleg on could be rewarded with an easier approach.

Hole 1
Par 4
428 yards

The opener looks inviting, as the hole sweeps gently round to the left with the green tucked to this side. But the fairway narrows dramatically after 300 yards, and anything left could find trees and thick rough if you get too greedy from the tee. There are a number of testing undulations to contend with on the putting surface, while a deep bunker lies to the right.

Hole 2
Par 5
480 yards

An early birdie opportunity on this short par 5 that plays back alongside the 1st. It's relatively straight, but the fairway gives the impression of a dogleg right as it sweeps around rough and trees on the left side. Playing a soft draw over the fairway trap means you can attack in two with a long iron, avoiding the large bunkers on either side of the green.

Hole 3
Par 4
354 yards

A good drive to an open fairway leaves a straightforward pitch, but the green runs off at the back, so the approach demands great control. One bunker lies to the right side of the putting surface, with another two to the left. A final point: the ground in front of the green is very undulating, so a bump-and-run is not the most advisable shot to play.

Hole 4
Par 5
507 yards

On this, the second of the par 5s, the drive is played up and over a hill with a cluster of cross-bunkers. Long hitters will feel bullish about taking the green on, as the entrance is open. However, anything right will run into the first of three sand traps on the approach. Again, the putting surface features a number of breaks to challenge your putt-reading skills.

Hole 5
Par 3
176 yards

The green slopes from the back on this testing par 3, while the approach drops and then sweeps back up to the front of the putting surface. A solid mid-iron is required, and there is little forgiveness around the green, with three bunkers lining the right side, and another two left. This is one of the most attractive holes on the course, framed beautifully by trees.

Hole 7
Par 3
148 yards

This is a short par 3, but one that plays uphill – so you may need to take an extra club. The contours of the green are probably the biggest defence here; you can't simply play to the heart of it because the pin position may call for greater accuracy. Four deep bunkers surround the putting surface's boundary – a real test in shot-making and short-game control.

Hole 8
Par 4
379 yards

Sand is the dominating factor on this hole, with the tees set back in a tunnel of trees with heather in front. The fairway is wide, which invites players to thread a drive through the bunkers at 200 yards to set up an approach with a short iron. The terrain sweeps up and down as you approach the green, which itself slopes away towards the back.

Hole 9
Par 4
416 yards

Running back in the opposite direction to the 8th hole, this tough par 4 rounds off the outward nine. The fairway bunkers on the right should be easily avoided at 200 yards, and the fairway opens up past the hazards. Undulating, the approach sweeps up towards the green, which is tucked away at a slight angle. The putting surface is dominated by sand.

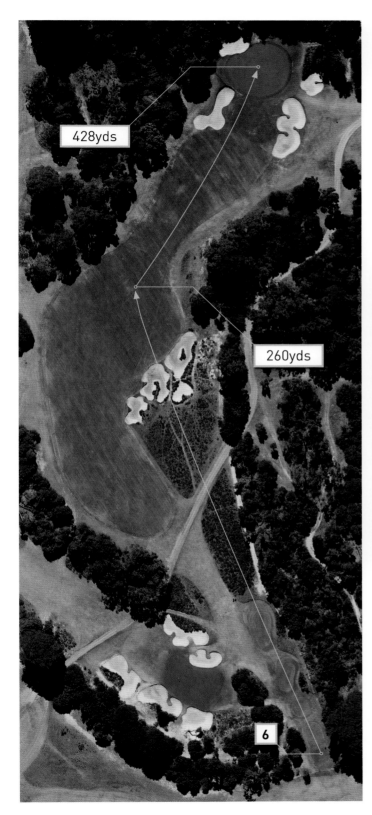

428yds

260yds

6

Hole 6 – *Par 4* – **428 yards**

A fantastic dogleg right, the 6th is a fine test in risk-reward golf, because if you can shave the corner off with a carry over dense rough and the unsighted bunkers on the right-hand side, a much shorter route to the green allows you to attack with greater control. However, anything that doesn't make the 220-yard carry will leave you with little option but to play back to the fairway. Two large bunkers sit either side of the approach to the green, which is elevated. Once you are on that green, its many undulations add to the hole's challenges and three-putting is always a threat. Another two bunkers sit at the back, and a number of run-off areas ensure the putting surface is tough to hold.

Course Guide 10–18

There are some tempting holes on the back nine, like the driveable par-4 10th, and the short par-5 12th. However, it is very easy to lose your way at Royal Melbourne, and once you are out of position, it's tough to get back into play.

Hole 10
Par 4
312 yards

As the hole sweeps round to the left, its modest yardage tempts players to cut the corner in an effort to reach the ultimate target of the green in one blow. But the Sahara fairway bunker lies in wait to catch anything weak. Subtle undulations define the make-up of the green. The conservative approach is to play right of centre, before floating a wedge on to the putting surface.

Hole 11
Par 4
455 yards

This is a tough test of ball-striking as two solid hits are the bare minimum required to reach the green. To shorten the approach, players may again be tempted to shave off the corner of the dogleg as the hole turns left. But two bunkers are positioned here, and a good carry is needed to clear them. Even with a good drive, the second will be a long iron for most.

Hole 13
Par 3
147 yards

The green can be reached easily with a short iron, but there are myriad defences to take into account. Five greenside traps pinch the approach tightly, and the surface drops in elevation to test even the best of putters. From tee to green, trees frame the hole, especially on the right-hand side. Proof that a par 3 doesn't have to be long to pose a stern challenge.

Hole 14
Par 4
366 yards

Eleven bunkers protect this hole, and the approach is dominated by sand – so the less club players are coming in with, the better. Once in position with the drive, a wedge or short iron should be enough for your approach; but take note of the pin position, as the green slopes dramatically from the right side. Good course management is essential to scoring well here.

Hole 15
Par 5
477 yards

Another three-shot hole that can be a two-shotter for the longer hitters; the fairway is open, although traps on both sides challenge you to split a drive through the middle. The green is tempting as its entrance is open on the right; but, if attacking in two, watch out for a bed of heavy rough running across the fairway some 130 yards short of the putting surface.

Hole 16
Par 3
221 yards

Owing to its length, and the mass of sand that surrounds the green, it's not uncommon for players to lay up short of the green to leave themselves below the hole. That said, the orthodox strategy suggests a hybrid or 5-wood from the tee. The green features a subtle ridge, with other breaks coming into play. Making a par here is always a great result.

Hole 17
Par 4
439 yards

The drive is best fired down the left-hand side over two bunkers on the fairway's boundary; but beware, because dense rough and trees tighten this line. Trees also become a factor for the second shot, as they dominate the backdrop of the green, so there is no mercy if you overclub and go long. To add to the test, the putting surface is also raised.

Hole 18
Par 4
451 yards

The finale is a dogleg right, which favours an attacking line from the tee to carry the bunkers, trees and rough. This will significantly shorten the hole; it will only be a short iron to a green with sand at the front, back and sides. But don't get carried away; those testing undulations on the putting surface can leave you fighting a frustrating finish.

456yds

250yds

12

Hole 12 – *Par 5* – **456 yards**

This par 5 is reachable in two, but it's a clever hole as the fairway is angled away from the green, and a narrow strip of rough splits the two. If you have cleared the cluster of sand traps on the left side of the fairway, you will be in prime position to attack in two. However, with the wind against, there is too much danger in going for the putting surface because the rough that surrounds it, and the deep trap to its front, can leave you scrambling just to make par. The lay-up is best played up the left side, and then it's a short pitch over the trouble. The margins between success and failure are slim here, and a birdie opportunity can quickly become a bogey.

Defined by its island-style green, the iconic 9th is the signature hole of the Sun City course.

SUN CITY – GARY PLAYER

South Africa's premier golf course that was designed by the country's greatest ever player – the Gary Player Country Club at Sun City continues to challenge the world's best, while a number of teeing options make the layout playable for all standards of golfer.

Below left: Well-protected, sloping greens are a key feature at Sun City, as well as water featuring predominantly on the closing holes.

Opposite: The Gary Player Country Club lies in the depths of an extinct volcano, but the course comes alive with a number of daunting holes with the Rustenburg bushveld all around you.

It was 1978 when Gary Player won the last of his nine major championships with victory at the US Masters. That same year, work would begin on arguably the most defining golf course in his native homeland of South Africa. That Player was enlisted to carry out the design was a no-brainer. Entrepreneur and hotel magnate Sol Kerzner was seeking a big name to help bring the glitz and glamour of the golfing world to Sun City, a sprawling hotel and casino complex in the country's North West Province some two and a half hours from Johannesburg.

Player has never been a man to do things by halves – he is a perfectionist who hates to settle for second best. "The Black Knight" was challenged with crafting a course that would be bedded into the rugged Rustenburg bushveld.

"It's always a fantastic course to play and I've always loved it."

Charl Schwartzel

But at first, even he was sceptical; the plot of land was dense and dry, set in the depths of an extinct volcano. Meeting Kerzner's demands would not be easy. Eventually, Player did take it on, and by 1979, the Gary Player Country Club – the first of Sun City's two championship courses – was ready for play.

The course's conditioning and reputation, not to mention the mighty challenge it was to pose, proved enough to tempt the game's best players to come and see it for themselves. It hosted The Million Dollar Challenge – today known as the Nedbank Challenge – for the first time in 1981. One of golf's richest tournaments, it was open only to the game's grandest heavyweights. American Johnny Miller won the inaugural event, with many other illustrious names, including Seve Ballesteros, Bernhard Langer and Nick Faldo, adding to the roll call of winners over the next decade. It's been back every year since, and the big names continue to flock, always entertaining the galleries on a golf course that has a beastly bite, weighing in at a little under 8,000 yards from the championship tips.

Though it is a slog in length for the pros, there are a number of teeing options to allow recreational players greater enjoyment. Refreshingly, the intermediate or forward tees take nothing away from the design; with a remit on ball control for both driving and approach play, where if you stray, you pay. The fairways are beautifully manicured with Kikuyu grass, while the bent grass greens are fast and undulating.

Every hole presents its own challenge, but the 9th and 18th stand out for special attention, with man-made water hazards dividing the greens from the fairway. Another of the course's chief defences comes with its bunkering, hardly surprising when you consider Player was one of the finest sand players the game has seen. Well positioned, the fairway traps will punish anything loose from the tee, while the greenside bunkers can be hellish. The key to scoring is to simply grit it out, something for which the course's designer was himself renowned.

Today, Sun City – in the foothills of the surrounding mountains of Pilanesburg National Park – has developed into one of the world's leading leisure developments. The area is home to South Africa's Big Five of Elephant, Rhino, Leopard, Lion and Buffalo, and there are four hotels onsite, as well as a water park. In 1993, a second 18-hole layout was added, the Lost City Country Club, also designed by Player. However, for golfing aficionados, it is his original piece of work that has, and always will be, the star attraction, bringing in huge numbers who leave with a sense of fulfilment knowing they have played one of the world's most iconic courses.

COURSE GUIDE 1–9

Course yardage – Championship 7,814 yards
Course GPS – 25°20'46.17" S 27° 5'56.12" E

Your driving game needs to be in top shape straight from the off, with a solid game plan to avoid the cavernous bunkers on the fairway. Judging the pace of the greens could save your score later in the round.

Opposite: There are few par 5s that can play as tough as Sun City's 9th, with a small green surrounded by water – so control is needed with your approach.

Hole 1
Par 4
440 yards

Sun City's opener is a tough driving hole, with the tee nestled in a tunnel of trees. At 440 yards, it also demands two solid blows to reach the green in regulation. Fairway traps come into play at 250 yards, with the landing zone very narrow here. The green's neck is also pinched tight, with bunkers on both sides of the entrance. Par is a very solid start.

Hole 2
Par 5
568 yards

A classic three-shot hole that is reachable for the long hitters, but only if a drive can be threaded to the left of the two bunkers at 260 yards. The fairway also narrows here as it snakes its way past more sand. If you are laying up, the water to the right demands your attention; if attacking, it's a 3-wood to a green with large bunkers on both sides.

Hole 3
Par 4
449 yards

This is another difficult driving hole, which is rated as the third toughest on the course. Trees dominate the right side from the tee, and a solid blow is needed to find the first strip of fairway at around 200 yards. A bunker needs to be avoided on the right side. The green is very narrow, and the bunker to its right entrance is the biggest peril for the approach.

Hole 4
Par 3
213 yards

The first of Sun City's short holes; a daunting test because a long iron or hybrid is needed to clear the water that threatens on the right side. Aiming left and playing for a soft fade is not the worst strategy, but anything that cuts too much is likely to end up wet. If the water is cleared, the large, sprawling trap that lies beyond will also come into play.

Hole 5
Par 4
491 yards

For many this long par 4 may be out of reach, and with the green well defended by sand, its stroke-index-11 rating is somewhat puzzling. The drive is again tough, although the fairway opens up slightly after 250 yards. The more distance you can get from the tee, the better, as a shorter iron with more loft is needed to clear the ring of sand around the putting surface.

Hole 6
Par 4
424 yards

Straight and narrow, the 6th is far from being among the longest par 4s at Sun City, but it is still a daunting challenge, and it says much about the difficulty of the course that it is only its stroke-index-15 hole. Big hitters should take note of the fairway trap to the right. Approaching the green from this side is the best line, with a large bunker front-left.

Hole 7
Par 3
225 yards

From the back pegs the pros will take only a 4- or 5-iron, but amateurs will need something longer to find the green on this difficult par 3. The putting surface has something of a z-shape to it, with two bunkers to the left and another right. Be careful not to overclub here, because a mass of sand waits at the back to catch those errant strikes.

Hole 8
Par 4
481 yards

This daunting par 4 is ranked the hardest hole at Sun City, and from the back tees a monster carry is needed to find the first cut of fairway. The hole has a notable shape to it, first turning slightly to the left, and then bending back to the right. Hitting the green in regulation is made even more of a challenge by the sand dominating its entrance.

596yds

490yds

300yds

9

Hole 9 – *Par 5* – **596 yards**

The 9th is Sun City's signature hole, and one that is fully deserving of such status. Over the years, this superb risk-reward three-shotter has witnessed some great moments in the Sun City Challenge, and more recently the Nedbank. It is defined by its island-style green, and anything that lacks the necessary control coming in will end up wet. From the tee, the only defence in sight is the large bunker to the right of the fairway. Only the longest can consider attacking in two, and even when the hole is played with a lay-up, the challenge of holding the putting surface, which is tucked slightly to the left, is not easy. This is one of the great holes in world golf.

COURSE GUIDE 10–18

The back nine builds steadily towards a grand finish with water waiting to drown any hopes of a late flourish at 17 and 18. Again, a good driving game is essential, and so is staying clear of those punishing traps that protect the greens.

Opposite: The 18th is another great finishing hole, which always serves up a thrilling climax in the Nedbank Challenge.

Hole 10
Par 5
546 yards

After the long 9th comes another par 5, but a much easier one that could yield a birdie with two solid blows. However, the test lies in finding what is a very narrow strip of fairway, made even tighter by sand traps at around 280 yards. The hole then swings to the right. Cutting the corner is the attacking line for the second shot, or you can play a lay-up to the left side.

Hole 11
Par 4
458 yards

This sharp dogleg left requires a powerful drive over wasteland that is well placed to the left side of the fairway. Taking on the corner of the dogleg is, as always, risky, with trees and dense rough here, while anything that runs too long and straight could find the bunker on the right. The green is peppered with sand around its entrance – another tough hole.

Hole 12
Par 3
218 yards

Sand is the immediate threat on this long one-shotter, with the huge trap that lurks at the back of the 7th coming into play on the left side. The green is narrow and undulating, with a number of run-off areas, and two more, smaller bunkers to the right side. A high, soft-landing hybrid or 5-wood should be the club of choice.

Hole 13
Par 4
444 yards

The layout heads out to its most western point at the 13th – the course's stroke-index two – which is another very tight driving hole with fairway traps scattered on both sides. Trees are also a threat, especially on the right. The safe strategy is to lay up short of the hazards and play a long iron in to the left entrance of the green.

Hole 14
Par 5
601 yards

This par 5 turns gently to the right, and from the back pegs it presents an imposing challenge with trees congesting the corner of the dogleg. At over 600 yards the green isn't really there to be attacked, and it's a brave golfer who takes it on with a huge bunker protecting the front of the putting surface. A lay-up and wedge will leave you a couple of putts for par.

Hole 15
Par 4
471 yards

Again, two huge blows are needed to reach the green on this two-shotter that for most visiting players will likely be played in three. A large bunker juts into the fairway on the left-hand side, but short of this you'll find a generous landing zone. However, the lay-up will leave a long second to a green with bunkers guarding its entrance.

Hole 16
Par 3
211 yards

The last of the par 3s, the 16th is rated as the course's easiest hole. With the lake to your left, a crisp long iron must be threaded through a channel of trees that press in from the right-hand side. The entrance to the green is relatively open, but take note of the pin position as a number of breaks make putting tough. Some would suggest it's a late birdie chance.

Hole 17
Par 4
477 yards

There are a number of teeing options, but from the championship pegs during the Nedbank Challenge what's needed is a long carry that cuts the corner across the water from the left-hand side. This is a fine hole that rewards a good tee shot. But the approach here is also tricky, as the green is tucked away, with more water running around its left side.

Hole 18 – *Par 4* – **501 yards**

The course finishes with its longest par 4, which never disappoints as one of the most thrilling home holes in the game. For those players needing to make a closing par to hold on, this sharp dogleg left is as tough as they come. Firstly, you need to show some muscle out of the blocks with a long, straight drive that stays clear of the fairway bunker on the right side, because going in here will severely dent any hopes of reaching the green in two. Secondly, the approach has to be played over a large water hazard with the entrance to the green narrowed on both sides by deep bunkers. During the Nedbank Challenge, there is always a wonderful amphitheatre setting around the green.

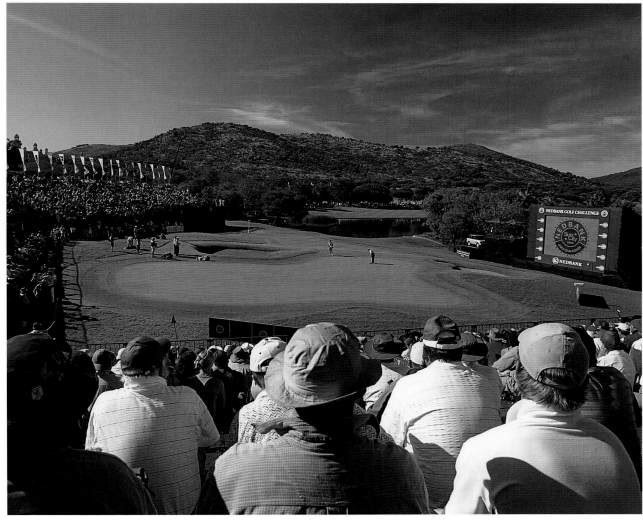

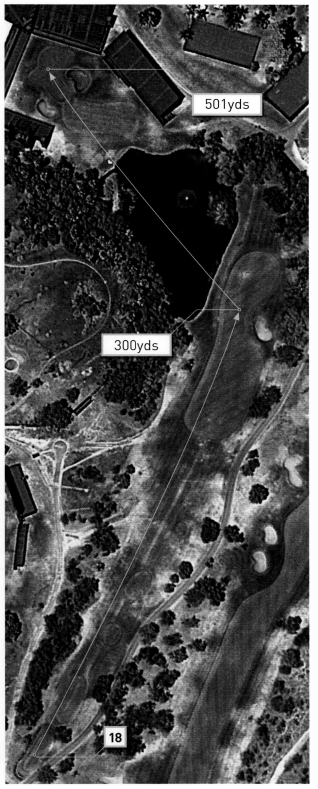

An aerial view of the 18th at Sun City's Gary Player Country Club, where deep bunkers add to the challenge of carrying the large water hazard in front of the green.

Expansive and cunningly positioned bunkers as well
as a number of menacing creeks are just a few of the
challanges that lie in wait at Shanghai's Sheshan course.

SHESHAN

Sheshan International is one of the modern heavyweights of the game, which welcomes the world's best players every year for Asia's richest tournament – the HSBC Champions. As you would expect, the test on this stunning course in Shanghai's south-western hinterland is far from easy.

© 2013 Mapabc.com
Image © 2013 DigitalGlobe

Renowned and respected, Sheshan International lies 20 miles southwest of the hustle and bustle of the city of Shanghai. It has quickly gained a reputation among both players and critics through hosting the HSBC Champions, the fourth and final World Golf Championship event of the year, that pulls in the biggest names from both the PGA and European Tour.

Designed by the prolific Nelson & Hawarth, Sheshan International is located high in the hills and was opened for play in 2004. They moved heaven and earth to create the course, bringing in some 50,000 trees, while shifting over 1.5 million cubic tonnes of earth. The surroundings of the crowded forest deliver an air of tranquillity to the layout – hardly in keeping with its nature when you consider the teeth that it can bare. Sweeping up and down over undulating terrain, its beauty is complemented by its brutality.

For the professionals who are able to fight their way past its fiendish defences, the test is more a passage of navigation than survival. But for its members, who pay a high price for the exclusivity of playing Asia's finest golf course, a round at Sheshan can be punishing in the extreme.

At a little under 7,200 yards, Sheshan has plenty to offer in terms of its length. But you need more than just a bit of muscle to play well here. Expansive bunkering is at first your chief tormentor, positioned cunningly on the angles of doglegs and within firing range for those big hitters who choose to attack the par 5s. Then there's the water, with the course home to several lakes and menacing creeks, as

well as an 80-year-old rock quarry that must be tackled on the signature par-4 16th and par-3 17th.

The bent-grass greens are slick and undulating. But perhaps the biggest challenge a player faces is finding them. Many are elevated and tucked away from the natural line of the fairway, a clever element of the design that favours those who can shape the ball from left to right.

As well as the quarry-ridden 16th and 17th, there are a number of eye-catching holes to take on, most notably the par 5s. The 2nd is an early examination of a player's ball-striking as it wends its way through a tight channel of trees; the 8th stretches to over 600 yards with a creek challenging your eye-line on every shot; the 14th is a dramatic and imposing hole where both power and precision are needed to avoid the water; and the 18th is a final teaser,

reachable for the professionals hunting a late score, but daunting for others with a green that has the ripples of the lake lapping against its banks.

It is because of holes like this that the HSBC Champions has become such a success. Since the inaugural event in 2005, this end-of-season showpiece has delivered with a roll call of winners who, despite the difficulty of the course, always score well.

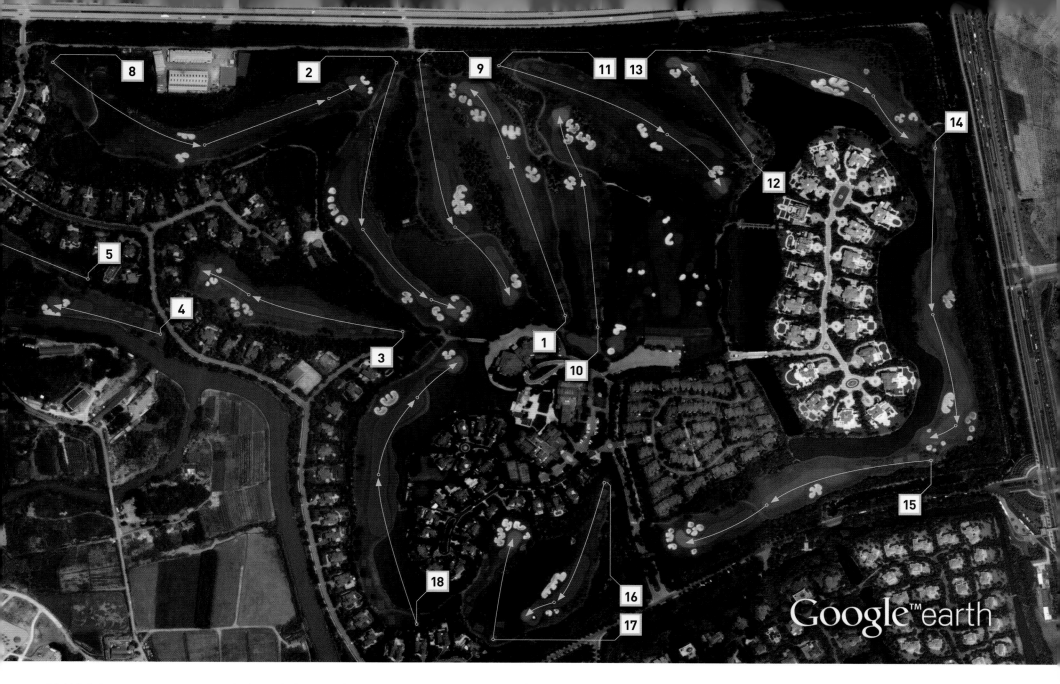

Phil Mickelson is a two-time victor, and other notable winners include Y. E. Yang, Sergio Garcia and Martin Kaymer.

As you would expect of such an exclusive members' club, the course is always in wonderful condition. The club's surrounding villas are some of the most expensive properties in Shanghai, while the Tuscan-style clubhouse adds to the charming ambience.

In 2012, the HSBC Champions found a new home at China's impressive Mission Hills. But it didn't stay there long, and just weeks later it was proudly announced that Asia's premier golfing event would be heading back to Asia's premier golf course, its love affair with Sheshan gratefully rekindled.

Opposite: The HSBC Champions has established itself as one of the game's biggest tournaments, always pulling in the biggest stars as the season draws to its climax late in the year.

Above: With tight, winding fairways, Sheshan is a tough test from the tee, while water plays havoc with wayward approach play.

> ## "Shanghai is a wonderful city, and Sheshan is a world-class golf course."
>
> *Phil Mickelson*

COURSE GUIDE 1–9

A series of long holes test ball-striking qualities to the limit, but shot-shaping and creativity will also be rewarded, as a number of doglegs come into play, and many of the greens are elevated.

Course yardage – Black tees 7,195 yards
Course GPS – 31° 6'33.16" N 121° 12'59.68" E

Opposite: The long, par-5 8th is demanding for even the very longest of hitters. Here, Phil Mickelson attacks the green on his way to winning the 2007 HSBC Champions.

Hole 1
Par 4
459 yards

A tough, long par 4 to get things started. Ideally, the tee shot should be aimed at the first bunker on the right-hand side of the fairway, with a soft draw providing you with the ideal position from which to approach the green. Sand traps are scattered to the left side of the putting surface, which is raised and angled slightly to the left.

Hole 2
Par 5
550 yards

The second hole is a superb par 5 with water all the way up the left side. A row of fairway bunkers lurk on the right at 250 yards, but again, use this line as your target for a soft draw to set up an attacking second to the green. Bunkers continue to complicate matters on the approach. If in doubt, play a lay-up, as anything long will end up wet.

Hole 3
Par 4
362 yards

A short par 4 with a raised green tucked away to the right. The drive is best aimed down the left side, avoiding three bunkers at around 260 yards. The approach will be nothing more than a wedge, but anything short will find the sand that pinches the neck of the green tightly on both sides. A good tee shot here can bring an early birdie opportunity.

Hole 4
Par 3
200 yards

A solid mid-iron is needed on this attractive par 3; water lines the whole of the left side, with trees on the right and framing the hole beautifully. The elevated green, with its entrance to the left side, features a number of undulations and a notable ridge at the front. It may be rated as the course's second easiest hole, but position and power are needed in equal measure.

Hole 5
Par 4
459 yards

This long par 4 is one of the toughest holes on the course, the stroke-index three. Ideally, the tee shot should clear the bunker on the left side at 230 yards as the fairway sweeps upwards; anything right will likely find one of the three traps on this side. Another four sand traps are positioned to the right of the green, so an up-and-down for par is tricky.

Hole 6
Par 3
200 yards

Another mid-length par 3, but with water very much a threat, as you need a full carry over the lake to find the green. While anything short will end up wet, anything long may find the large bunker that waits at the back of the putting surface. If you're not confident of attacking, there is more room out to the right side, so play for an up-and-down for par.

Hole 7
Par 4
346 yards

A short par 4 that seems to be just begging to be attacked; however, sand is a menacing defence from 230 yards, and what may at first look like a birdie chance can quickly become a scrap to save par. The conservative strategy here is a lay-up short of the fairway bunkers. If you want to attack, aim over the bunker on the left and hope for the best.

Hole 9
Par 4
466 yards

It doesn't get any easier on the final hole of the outward nine, with this long par 4 the course's toughest hole. A good drive is needed to put you in position, avoiding the large bunker to the left. From here, a long iron needs to be faded in from the left. There is water on the right, and if you go through the back of the green, there too your ball will find a watery grave.

218

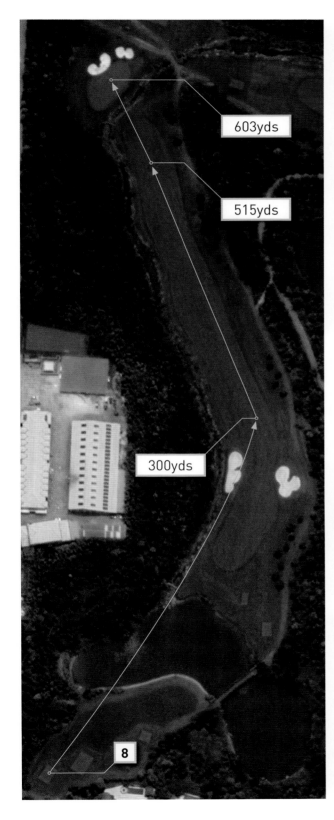

603yds

515yds

300yds

8

Hole 8 – *Par 5* – **603 yards**

Where do you start? Length, sand and water – they all play a part on perhaps the course's most imposing hole, which offers a birdie chance only to the very longest of hitters. The tee is elevated from the fairway, and the first challenge is to tackle the apex of the dogleg as the hole sweeps to the left at 280 yards. The drive is played over a small pond, and there are bunkers either side of the fairway. Going too far left is dangerous because a creek meanders up this side all the way to the front of the green. For the second shot, a lay-up with a mid-iron will take you to within wedge distance of the green, leaving the final challenge of a pitch over that creek. Two traps lie at the back of the putting surface.

COURSE GUIDE 10–18

First-time visitors to Sheshan will no doubt be eyeing up the scorecard and licking their lips at the prospect of playing the short par-4 16th. But don't be fooled; it is one of the most famous two-shot holes in the world – and fraught with danger.

Opposite: Y. E. Yang plays out of position on the water-lined par-5 14th during his HSBC Champions win in 2006, while Tiger Woods battles with the greenside traps in the first round of the 2009 tournament.

Hole 10
Par 4
401 yards

The inward nine begins with this mid-length par 4 that is best played with a solid 3-wood from the tee, and then a short iron for the approach. The green is elevated, and the best line to come in from is the left side. Pay close attention to the pin position, as the green is very undulating, so three-putting is always on the cards.

Hole 11
Par 4
435 yards

Another long and tough two-shot hole that for many could easily play as a par 5. The fairway plays straight up, while the green is perched up on the right-hand side with lush rough around its boundary. Staying left with the tee shot will avoid the two traps at 230 yards. A good carry is then required to hit the sloping putting surface, as a large bunker guards its entrance.

Hole 12
Par 3
217 yards

It says something about the challenge at Sheshan that the course's stroke-index 18 is a par 3 of well over 200 yards. From the back tees, the shot shape is a soft draw as the right entrance is the more open. Four large bunkers dominate the left side of the green on the approach. The green is shaped like a footprint, with subtle breaks towards the back.

Hole 13
Par 4
430 yards

The 12th offers a birdie opportunity for the bold, while playing it conservatively should make for a fairly routine par. The drive can be aimed at the two fairway traps on the right, with a draw putting you in the best position from which to approach. Another two bunkers lie to the front-left of the green, and there are a number of undulations around the putting surface's boundary.

Hole 15
Par 4
487 yards

This is a monster of a par 4, with a number of defences to overcome. First, water hugs the right side up to 280 yards, and sand lies on the left to narrow the landing zone. Longer hitters will aim to get past this, but it's still a real task to find the green in two. The left entrance to the putting surface is open, but that's the only part of this hole where any mercy is shown.

Hole 16
Par 4
288 yards

The 16th and 17th are known as "Terrifying Valley" – and both are signature holes. This is a par 4 where players can fire at the green, but a water-filled quarry right of the fairway brings a considerable degree of risk to anyone attempting to cut the dogleg. Playing to the left of the large sand trap at 200 yards will open up the approach. Take a deep breath!

Hole 17
Par 3
191 yards

The second hole of the "Terrifying Valley" requires a mid-iron from the back pegs. Although there is water in front of you, the entrance to the green is open. The challenge is to not over club, because four bunkers form an arch around the back of the putting surface. The green then challenges players with many breaks, and a notable hump in the middle.

Hole 18
Par 5
538 yards

One of the great finishing holes in world golf, which often serves up a thrilling climax in the annual HSBC Champions. The pros will go for this in two, by firing down the left side off the tee to leave a full-blooded wood over the water that separates the green from the fairway. Sand lies to left of the putting surface, while anything too long will find the lake.

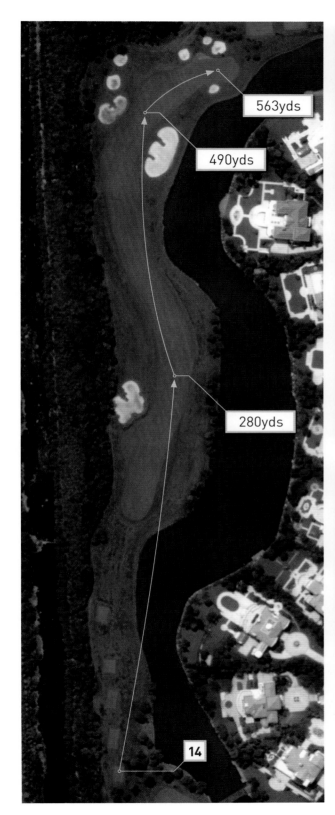

563yds

490yds

280yds

14

Hole 14 – *Par 5* – **563 yards**

A par 5 that, while thrilling in nature and stature, can be torture to play, with water a constant menace on the right side. A solid drive is needed to find the fairway's landing zone at 280 yards – if you're harbouring any hopes of reaching the green in two. Then it's a choice between laying up or attacking, the latter requiring a blow of 250 yards to carry the lake that juts into the fairway. If playing the hole in three, a 7-iron should be placed between the two traps 100 yards short of the green. The putting surface pinches in midway, so there is more room at the front and back. Again, take note of the breaks when lining up your putts.

INDEX

CREDITS

The publishers would like to thank the following sources for their kind permission to reproduce the pictures in this book.

Action Images: /Brandon Malone: 214-215

Andrew Bertram: 128, 131BR, 133BL, 154L, 157BR, 159B

CBKfoto: 193BL, 195TL, 195BC

Getty Images: /David Alexander: 21TR, 77TR; /Scott Barbour: 190; /Robert Beck/Sports Illustrated: 24-25; /David Cannon: 8-9, 15TR, 15B, 31TC, 37R, 38-39, 40C, 45TC, 55R, 57TR, 60, 63TR, 65BC, 71TC, 75TR, 79BR, 80C, 80TR, 80BR, 83BR, 84-85, 89TC, 89BR, 91BL, 94L, 97BR, 99BR, 100-101, 119TC, 120-121, 146, 149BR, 151T, 152-153, 182-183, 187BC, 198, 201TR, 203BR, 204-205; /Robert Cianflone: 189TC, 196-197; /Chris Condon/PGA Tour: 51TC, 51BL, 203TR; /Michael Dodge: 187TR, 189BL; /Tim Dominick: 29B, 31BL; /Stephen Dunn: 6; /Mike Ehrmann: 32; /Stuart Franklin: 21BR, 23TC, 23BR, 83TR, 92-

93, 113BR, 139TR, 139BC, 143TC, 143BR, 145TC, 206, 211BL, 212-213; /Scott Halleran: 219TC; /Martyn Hayhow/AFP: 65TL; /Richard Heathcote: 75BR, 108BL, 174BL, 177BL, 180-181, 209BR; /Boris Horvat/AFP: 140; /Harry How: 45BR; /John Kelly: 18C; /Ross Kinnaird: 27BL, 63BR, 117BR, 119BL, 179TR, 179BR, 211TC, 221TR, 221BC; /Paul Lakatos/Asian Tour: 216C; /Streeter Lecka: 35TL; /Warren Little: 91TL, 117TR, 145BL, 209TR; /Andy Lyons: 77BR; /Richard Mackson/Sports Illustrated: 46L; /Donald Miralle: 43TR; /Brian Morgan: 58-59; /Dean Moutaropoulos: 111TL, 111BC, 113TC; /Stephen Munday: 114; /New York Daily News Archive: 52BL; /Montana Pritchard/The PGA of America: 35BC; /Andrew Redington: 10, 13L, 69TR, 86BL; /Jose Luis Roca/AFP: 177TC; /Paul Severn: 224; /Ezra Shaw: 49B; /Tim Sloan/AFP: 57BC; /Jamie Squire: 16-17; /Rick Stewart: 43BR; /Bob Thomas: 72BC; /William West/

AFP: 184BL; /Andrew Wong: 219BR

Courtesy of Golfclub Beuerberg e.V: 102, 105BR, 107BL

Courtesy of Hamburger Golf-Club e.V: 122L, 125BR, 127TL, 127BC

Kevin Murray Golf Photography: 66BL, 69BR, 71BL

Courtesy of Oceanico Golf: 160, 163BL, 165BR, 166-167

Press Association Images: /Imago Sportfotodienst/Bruno Press: 137T; /Mika Volkmann/DPA: 134

Courtesy of Terre Blanche Hotel Spa Golf Resort: 168, 171TR, 171BR, 173BR

Every effort has been made to acknowledge correctly and contact the source and/or copyright holder of each picture and Carlton Books Limited apologizes for any unintentional errors or omissions that will be corrected in future editions of this book.

Above: A fitting end to a fitting round: the Swilcan Bridge that leads to the 18th fairway on St Andrews' Old Course is one of the most famous and sacred golfing landmarks.